RETIRE SOONER RETIRE RICHER

How to Build and Manage Wealth to Last a Lifetime

FRANK L. NETTI

McGraw

New York   Chicago   San Francisco   Lisbon   London   Madrid   Mexico City
Milan   New Delhi   San Juan   Seoul   Singapore   Sydney   Toronto

*The **McGraw·Hill** Companies*

Library of Congress Cataloging-in-Publication Data

Netti, Frank.
     Retire sooner, retire richer : how to build and manage wealth to last a lifetime /
Frank L. Netti.
          p.   cm.
     Includes bibliographical references and index.
     ISBN 0-07-139699-3
     1. Retirement income—Planning.   I. Title.

HG179.N444   2003b
332.024′01—dc21   2002045216

To my father and mother

This publication is designed to provide accurate and authoritative information in regard to the subject matter covered. It is sold with the understanding that neither the author nor the publisher is engaged in rendering legal, accounting, or other professional service. If legal advice or other expert assistance is required, the services of a competent professional person should be sought.

—From a Declaration of Principles jointly adopted
by a Committee of the American Bar Association and a Committee of Publishers

1 2 3 4 5 6 7 8 9 0   DOC/DOC   2 1 0 9 8 7 6 5 4 3

ISBN 0-07-139699-3

Interior design by Rattray Design

McGraw-Hill books are available at special quantity discounts to use as premiums and sales promotions, or for use in corporate training programs. For more information, please write to the Director of Special Sales, Professional Publishing, McGraw-Hill, Two Penn Plaza, New York, NY 10121-2298. Or contact your local bookstore.

This book is printed on acid-free paper.

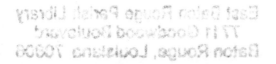

Contents

Acknowledgments

Thanks to my wife, Deborah, for the gifts of love and time. Thanks to retirees Harry and Cynthia Smith for the initial reading of Chapters 1, 3, and 4. Thanks to Gene Parrs, Esq., and Richard Scolaro, Esq., for their suggestions on the legal issues. Thanks to Robert Just, CFP, who made suggestions regarding Chapter 11. Thanks to my agent, Terri Brunsdon, and my editor, Ela Aktay, for their confidence in this book. Thanks to Frank Smith of Syracuse Design Group for the charts and graphs. A humble thanks to the team at McGraw-Hill, especially to Katherine Hinkebein and Kelli Christiansen. And a special thanks goes to Dr. Katharyn Howd-Machan, poet and writer, for her encouragement, and to my friend Bob Calimeri for his critical reading of the text.

Ad Majorem Dei Gloriam. This old saying is contributed by one of my clients, a retired Latin teacher; it means, "Give all glory to God."

Editor's note: A portion of the author's net income from this book will be donated each year toward low-income workers and their families affected by September 11, 2001, and to charities serving the hungry and homeless, such as Greater New York Labor-Religion Coalition, Second Harvest (U.S.), Catholic Relief Services (outside U.S.), and Habitat for Humanity International.

Introduction

"No person loves life like the one who is growing old."

—SOPHOCLES

Fred Hall (age 111) lives nearby. Each morning he reads the local paper and does his routine exercises. Mr. Hall is a retiree of the railway mail service; he worked there forty-six years ago. A coworker of mine visits her 104-year-old grandmother, who has a grandchild with grandchildren. These people are among the seventy thousand centenarians in the United States. Will we live fifty to sixty years longer than we are planning for? Will we survive longer than our income does?

In *Life Extension Planning*, Susan K. Bradley writes, "Not long ago, I had felt I was doing a good job helping my clients prepare for retirement. Then one day, I saw a small article on the inside page of *USA Today*: Scientists had determined that humans can live to be 140—two decades past the previous longevity mark of 120" (*Journal of Financial Planning*, January 2001, p. 38). Because estimating longevity is an essential part of planning for retirement, an underestimation will cause people to save too little, retire too early, and spend too much. If you don't have a realistic estimate of personal longevity, how can you know whether you have the right retirement plan?

To further complicate matters, many people are expecting to retire earlier than the historical norm. In 2001, an *EBRI News* survey found that "one in three workers expected to be retired less than 20 years" (*Journal of Financial Planning*, March 2001, p. 120). But in 1990 the U.S. Census Bureau estimated that when leading-edge baby boomers begin turning 100, more than 834,000 citizens might already be centenarians, adding, "And, if we see even more rapid increases in life expectancy, as assumed in the highest series, the future number of centenarians could be substantially higher." The number the report offers: 4,218,000 souls! This report implies we could live in retirement *decades* longer than we first expected, even if we do not retire early. It notes that 100 is considered "extreme old age," but only because we are not there yet. At one time, 70 was extreme ("Projections of the Resident Population by Age, Sex, Race, and Hispanic Origin: 2000 to 2050," Population Projections Program, Population Division, U.S. Census Bureau, in *Centenarians in the United States*, U.S. Department of Health and Human Services, July 1999, p. 3). The 2000 U.S. Census report found that the number of people over age eighty-five increased 40 percent from 1990 to 2000. Rapid advances in health and medical technology and practice may usher in a new Genesis in aging. Like our biblical ancestors (the first Adam begat his son at 130), we may enjoy a grand portion of life's blessing cup. How financially prepared you are to maintain a consistent standard of living for an extended life, is a question that should give you—and the thoughtful financial advisor of your choice— much to consider. It is only recently that I have come to realize, as clients have presented me with their retirement plans, the complexity of retirement planning for the twenty-first century.

If you have recently retired, or would like to retire within three years, and you hope that your (or your spouse's or ex-spouse's) pension, 401(k), cash balance plan, or TSA plan will support you *for life*, and you urgently need to feel secure about the hard choices that you face, this book is for you. In an objective way it will help you form an investment strategy the way the chief financial officer of a multimillion-dollar endowment fund does. If you need to gain confidence and trust in evaluating professionals who manage money, read this book. According to Employee Benefit Research Institute (EBRI), 1999 was the first year that individual retirement account (IRA) assets, totaling $2.47 trillion, exceeded 401(k) and pension plan assets. Each year now a million people are retiring. Ready or not, each retiree will face tough money-management decisions. If you are one of them and you want your retirement-plan dollars to support you, you must make the right moves now.

I've dedicated this book to my dad, who, like many people, failed to save enough. Oftentimes, through no fault of their own, people fail to realize that they can outlive their income or that investments can sour. Although many are offered contributory retirement plans, such as a 401(k), they do not participate. What these people need is a professional to coach them to invest and to help them take proper risks. For many employees who are making contributions, professional advice can help keep them on the right track, even if they plan to work after retirement from their primary job. It is good that people stay busy. According to Rutgers University, "68 percent of

Americans expect to work after retirement, but not for the money." While some of these people will volunteer their time, I believe others will be forced to do full- or part-time work to supplement their income. Some will have sufficient resources, allowing them the choice not to work again. Will you be one of them?

As people retire, their retirement money needs to be managed. Who will manage it? Contrary to your working years, when you work for money to sustain your lifestyle, during retirement, money must work for you. Those who were unconcerned about fluctuations of their investments while employed become more mindful of the market when their budget demands that withdrawals begin. At withdrawal time many people become uncomfortable with their nest egg. They wonder, "Is it going to last?"

Unlike many retirees of the new millennium, my dad, a master carpenter, had the health, skill, and capability to work part-time until his early seventies. He also had a substantial Social Security check that met the remaining needs of his frugal lifestyle. He had a big family, and he was thankful for that blessing and for having survived World War II in Normandy. He told me once, in a plaintive tone, "You'd better save for retirement." But he dated himself when he added, "You will need at least $200,000."

People retiring today are very different from the last generation. They (especially early retirees) may not receive a Social Security check for five or ten years, and when it comes it will be a small percentage of their spendable income. These retirees need more powerful tools to manage much larger sums of money for a longer period of time. While some choose to run their own businesses, others do not have skills to be self-employed, nor do they desire to learn a new career, especially in money management. Often retirement incentives look so attractive that the long-term picture is not seriously studied. Financial Engines, an advisory firm, found that only "8 percent of employers think that their employees are prepared to make investment decisions regarding their retirement assets" (*Journal of Financial Planning*, November 2000, p. 28). Whether or not you work after retirement, you will almost certainly need to supplement your income with a retirement account, such as a rollover IRA, which will need to be well managed.

If you are among the millions of workers in their fifties and sixties who plan to have a substantial amount of their retirement income (as much as 70 percent to 100 percent) coming from retirement plans and personal savings, this book is for you. You will need transition planning (from working to retiring) or possibly career planning. In a short while you will go from accumulating income and assets to spending them. People who do not have

$200,000 or more in a 401(k) or TSA, *plus a pension plan*, will most likely fall short if they retire too soon without another job. According to the Social Security Administration, Office of Research and Statistics, as of 1996 new data show a dramatic change in sources of retirement income. For those retired earning more than $31,180 annually, pension and Social Security provide less than half of retirement income on average (see chart below).

Without a pension, many people may not be able to retire until Social Security begins. They need to take a good look at everything they spend money on and save as much as they can daily, going as far as to check the bottom of the washer and dryer for loose change. The English say, "One of these days is none of these days." Do not wait to begin a meaningful savings program. This book is aimed at those who have already begun investing for early retirement or have retired recently. If you're fifty or over, the 2001 tax act allows for higher contribution limits to retirement plans and new "catch up" provisions (see the Appendix).

While we were still in grammar school my mom gave each of us kids a red, leatherbound metal bank shaped like a book. It was about the size of a man's wallet and on top it had a slot for coins and a round hole for bills. After forty-five years I still have that gem. I recall filling it and then bringing it to Cayuga Savings Bank in Auburn, New York. I quickly discovered how money worked for me, rather than me working for money. The bank tagged on a few cents to the balance each time the teller tallied up its coins. I would stare at those "free" additions and smile. My first lesson in unearned, compound interest would have a profound impact; it may have been then that I began to associate a book with money, for I called it my *bankbook.*

For Those Earning $31,180, Retirement Income Sources on Average Income

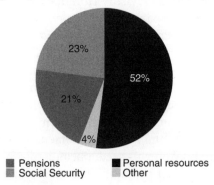

23%

52%

21%

4%

■ Pensions   ■ Personal resources
■ Social Security   Other

Source: *Social Security Administration*

The good nuns in school, with the help of my mother, taught me to share and save before they taught me how to write. Sharing, saving, and writing are alike in one special way: the best way to learn it is to do it. After advising hundreds of retirees, I want to share with you how financial professionals can work with you to help you fulfill many of your retirement goals.

Do You Have a Strategy?

You will learn in this book that investing, like life, is unpredictable, so your planning must be *strategic* in nature. And the best strategy is to maximize your greatest possibility of winning right from the get-go. That approach is not the same as trying to win the most. Many investors wrongly think, "I don't have enough to keep up my lifestyle, so I'll shoot for the highest possible returns." Poor investors seek the highest possible returns, while the great investors seek the highest probability of good returns.

I'm inviting you to use my experiences with retirement planning to better your own planning. The more self-sufficient you are, the less you need to depend on our government, and the more you have to share with those you love. The mistakes of others can be your least expensive lessons—lessons you do not want to learn firsthand at a time when you can least afford the experience. As Laurence Peter said, "Experience is the worst teacher—it gives the test before explaining the lesson."

For example, too many financial advisors are projecting much higher returns than what the markets *normally* deliver. Such projection breeds giraffe-type charts that are overly optimistic, eschewing the amounts people can feel comfortable withdrawing. Why do these advisors do it? Do they want to tell clients what clients want to hear in order to get their accounts? Too many retirees are already feeling the strain of more than moderate future return estimates. Ask yourself: are your own estimations high? "The more time for which you project returns, the greater the possible variance, so it's best to use lower-than-average investment returns" (*Journal of Financial Planning*, October 2000, p. 28). High expectations might make you feel good, but realistic expectations make you live well. After all, a scientist does not make a good advisor. The scientist can say, "My job is 99 percent about failure and 1 percent about success." The advisor cannot be experimental with future assumptions in order to manufacture a more *sellable* outcome in order to hook a client. He must have a process and a plan based on your personal objectives.

A 1999 study done by the Forum for Investor Advice found that only 38 percent of retirees "prefer an *ongoing* relationship with a financial advisor." If you are going to manage your own portfolio, first read this book, and then take some college-level courses on money management theory and macroeconomics. Be advised that you will need to sustain yourself through the experiences of bad judgment in order to learn good judgment. Like the uninitiated teenager learning to drive, few make it through without a costly accident. Successful investing is difficult. It is competitive. In the market, someone is selling what you are buying. Brilliant people work full time getting big money trying to outwit each other and you. As one advisor said, "I wish I had been wrong in the beginning—I would have learned earlier how to be a good investor." My mistakes came early in my career, thank God.

Don't Be Fooled by Past Performance

Many popular investment books offer good information for people over fifty, but some of it is simplistic. One popular book by a well-meaning financial planner comes to mind. The chapter entitled "Keep Your Retirement Bucket Full While Drawing the Income You Need" includes a table showing how a sixty-five-year-old can remove 5.75 percent per year and still make 4.25 percent growth each year. The book does not explain the volatility of annual returns, but simply assumes the account will earn 10 percent year in and year out. The author seriously confuses the average return and the actual return when she makes her case for the continued growth of the retirement funds. Such books can greatly misinform readers about how money is made and can generate foolish expectations.

To be a little easier on my colleagues, I do believe some planners are often misled by the past performances of their own recommendations. The warning label "Past returns are no guarantee of future results" is as well heeded today as the ominous label on packs of cigarettes. I have heard that planners are saying, "Well, you can live off 10 percent per year, can't you?" They neglect to add that there may be months or even years when 10 percent will be absurdly optimistic, and that the client may need to take nothing to save his account from a disaster. Using data from Ibbotson's *2001 Yearbook*, I calculated that from the beginning of 1968 to the end of 1977, $100,000 invested in the S&P 500 Index would have grown to $142,252. With a mere 3.6 percent average annual return, can you imagine what retirees got from their stock investments during that period? Very slim pickins. During that same period inflation averaged 6.24 percent, so subtracting that from the stock returns would have disheartened most investors as they saw their buying power shrink for ten years.

It's wisest to pay yourself first. Putting money in a retirement plan does just that. It's also best to pay for insurance to cover family medical needs and disasters. And everyone has to give Uncle Sam his cut. After giving a nice weekly donation to church or other favorite charities, there isn't much left. Some choose to have a new car every two years and a much larger house than they need. Yes, they can get into expensive clubs and theaters, but the money spent means less put toward retirement. A 401(k) or 403(b) is not as flashy as a Cadillac or a Boston brownstone, but neither does it rust or collect dust. It does not show up as part of your "visual" wealth, and that invisibility takes a little humility to come to terms with. *Humility*: now that's a word you may not have expected to see in a book about wealth, given our consumer culture. I want this book to teach you how to pick your financial advisors just as you would pick your friends—by how much they care about you, and not by the size of their home, car, or boat.

Avoiding Big Errors

The city I work in was the home of one of the larger corporate bankruptcies in U.S. history. By the end of 2000, corporate officers were sentenced to the tombs for misusing investors' funds. Although the company did not initially do business unethically, the courts found that it eventually used money from new "investors" to pay off old ones until the entire thing collapsed. Much of the money lost belonged to thousands of retirees from across the country who parted with it for a promise of a steady 8 percent return. Bankruptcy trustee Richard C. Breeden, a former chairman of the SEC, estimated that investors would get back between 32 and 43 cents on every dollar invested, and *no interest income while they waited.* Some early investors actually had to return some of the money they received in years past. That surprised one retiree I spoke to who had to pay thousands of dollars.

A similar situation unraveling in the Western and Midwestern states as I write this book involves "promissory notes." These securities guaranteed to pay the note holder 8 percent to 12 percent for nine months, and then return to the investor her full principal. Investor confidence was boosted when investors were told the short-term notes were on start-up companies backed by a foreign insurance company. They were sold by over 100 neighborhood insurance salespeople who got an 8 percent commission. Although some interest was paid, the notes came due but defaulted, and more than $300 million of invested dollars so far have disappeared. Insurance agents who did not have the proper training and licensing to sell securities broke state and federal securities laws. They now are facing stiff penalties. (Although there are many legitimate new investment vehicles, two causes for concern are the buying and selling of insurance policies and some questionable investments offered on the Internet.)

Investors in both cases I've mentioned came from all income and education levels, and they all made the first big error that retirees should avoid making: they trusted in an investment that they could not evaluate. If they had been able to see an account value monthly or quarterly, they would have been aware of their net worth. From observing such scams, I discovered a good rule for the investor:

Investment Proverb 1

Be able to see and discuss the value of your
account with your advisor at any time.

This recommendation should keep your account honest and prevent you from hiring an advisor who is just "the nice guy I work with." Remember what is more important than your income: your principal. The tree is your principal, and income is the fruit.

The Why and How of Investing

This book will help you examine why you invest money and how you can invest it better. In this age of computer technology, we tend to place a lot of emphasis on information, as if it were the answer to success. The longer one is in the business of providing advice, the more one realizes that anyone can get information. It has become a commodity; you can buy staggering volumes of it for a fraction of what it once cost. Wisdom, on the other hand, is still at a premium. I look everywhere for it. Turning to his God, King Solomon begged for one thing: wisdom. Famed nineteenth-century English preacher Charles Spurgeon said, "The doorstep to the temple of wisdom is a knowledge of our own ignorance." When I was much younger I once lost lots of money doing what online day traders are doing now—speculating. I regretted my overconfidence and greed and realized I needed to change. Unless you have a great love for mathematics, learning about money management, and spending considerable time researching investments, it is best to find someone who has that desire. You can hire that person as a mentor, as a coach, or as a money manager. This book will teach you how to relate to the professional financial advisor of your choice.

My grandfather, an immigrant who loved this country, retired in 1965. He sweated it out for years at the rope shop where he almost lost his life, being pulled by the arm into a twine-spinning machine. Halfway to retirement he received a gold watch that says on the back, "Presented to Fransesco Netti, 25 years of service." Twenty-five years later—a total of fifty years in the same shop, except for a break to serve in the U.S. Army in World War I—he retired with nothing but the company watch, becoming totally dependent on Social Security income. The timepiece sits on my dresser protected by a glass dome. Although it does not work, it is a functional reminder of why I am a financial advisor. Although many companies offer retirement benefits today, unlike my grandfather's employer, people must nevertheless be motivated to oversee their own retirement plan.

In the late 1990s, IBM tried to change the rules and shortchange its soon-to-be retirees. Not until the older employees rebelled did IBM rescind its new way of paying retirement benefits. Employees of Enron Corporation, a leading world marketer of natural gas and electricity, were not as fortunate. Company shares held in retirement plans could not be sold to diversify risk. The Associated Press reported: "Enron's swift descent into federal bankruptcy court left countless investors burned and thousands of employees out of work and with decimated retirement savings" (*Post-Standard*, "Congressional Probe into Enron Failure Begins." Syracuse, New York. December 13, 2001, section B, p. 5). By law you have the right, by nature you have a duty, and to your family you have an obligation to be a good steward of all your assets. Get copies of your retirement plans, look for any changes, and contact your human resources department (and a financial advisor) if you cannot understand how these changes affect you. When it comes to company stock in 401(k)s or company stock options, many investors make large financial errors. A survey by Fidelity Funds found that 48 percent of preretirees had company stock in their 401(k). "The National Center for Employee Ownership says that employees own, or have options to own, stock worth $800 billion. But while ownership of stock options is at an all-time high, the knowledge and understanding among owners is low"

(*Investment Advisor*, February 2001, p. 72). There have been employees who have done nothing with valuable, in-the-money stock options before they crossed the expiration date (a date after which one no longer can convert to stock), losing tens of thousands of dollars.

Everyone Retires

Some people say they will never retire, and they mean it honestly—but the truth is that almost all of us do. The harder the physical labor or the job stress, the more difficult work becomes as you age. Even those who know this still find that time creeps up on us, catching us off guard and slowing us down. If you say you will not retire, be sure it is not an excuse for not saving now. One soon-to-be retiree told me, "We had a great time; spent a lot of money traveling. Now I can barely afford to retire."

Most financial planning advice is given to people who are staring into a rearview mirror. Thinking that good past performance of the stock market will continue, they underestimate how much must be saved. Any good truck driver will tell you it takes a long time to learn how to properly use rearview mirrors when going forward. One client called me because, he said, "for the last forty years I have had all my money in the bank and now I want to retire in five years. Shouldn't I put everything into the stock market?" He finally had looked at the road and wanted to rush into the fastest lane instead of shifting down immediately.

Jeff Brown, syndicated columnist, wrote that a new survey done by Mathew Greenwald & Associates (for John Hancock) came to unfortunate conclusions regarding the average 401(k) investor. Of the eight hundred participants, "40 percent of those surveyed had no idea what returns to expect from stocks, bonds and other investments, and the remaining 60 percent, on average . . . over the next twenty years, expected stocks to return 19.3 percent a year, nearly double the 11 percent historical return." My six-year-old daughter woke up one morning too tired to dress herself. She said to her mother, "Ma, you let me stay up too late." Much like her, many people will wake up someday and point the finger at somebody else for their own poor choices. It is my hope that you are not among them.

I will share with you vignettes that illustrate the errors people make in planning for retirement and investing retirement funds. While showing you how to establish a successful investment process, I will also share with you the pitfalls I have learned to avoid in this complicated and competitive game.

Today, a financial planning shingle hangs on every corner. "Whom should I listen to?" you ask, even if you have an advisor. "Whom should I trust?" you wonder, because now you are talking about a larger sum than you have ever had to manage. The decisions you make may affect the fate of people for generations to come, as well as your immediate personal income. By reading this book, you will gain confidence in dealing with expectations and uncertainties that are part of investing. And you will better understand long-term wealth management, equipped with the knowledge to keep you from dying broke.

Even the smartest investors can get burned. Remember that Fidelity in the mid-1990s got stuck owning shares of a gold mine salted with not-so-precious metal, yet they still have a great reputation for finding hidden treasures. Your time spent speaking with your financial advisor (or interviewing advisors), as well as reading personal finance books, will give you a feel for an "other world"—a place where there is constant change, at times monumental chaos (as we saw on September 11, 2001), yet some sound rules exist. A wise spiritual writer once asked, "Which has more freedom, the train on the track or the one off the track?" Staying on course does not mean you are trapped in an investment mold, but that you have created guidelines by which you can act rationally. It is the irrationality of investors that causes broad swings in the markets and poor returns in portfolios. Let's look at some examples that illustrate an investment process that, if followed, has its own rewards.

PART ONE

UNDERSTANDING YOUR RETIREMENT INVESTMENTS

"Rest is the sweet sauce of labor."

—PLUTARCH (46–120 A.D.)

1

The Numbers Game and Retirement Timing

"If making money is a slow process, losing it is quickly done."

—IHARA SAIKAKU

Investment projections can help or hinder your understanding of how much you can expect from a retirement account. I can offer some examples that can chill even a day trader. Let's suppose a person places $200,000 in a brokerage account and intends to make it grow to $400,000 in five years. To achieve this, he would need to get an average return of 15 percent per year. From 1995 to 1999 this was not difficult, even if a person owned an 80-20 mix of blue-chip stocks and bonds. But let's suppose the investment went like this: for the first four years, we have three years of 15 percent returns, then a fourth-year return of minus 15 percent:

$$\text{Year 1: } \$200,000 \times 1.15 = \$230,000$$

$$\text{Year 2: } \$230,000 \times 1.15 = \$264,500$$

$$\text{Year 3: } \$264,500 \times 1.15 = \$304,175$$

$$\text{Year 4: } \$304,175 \times 0.85 = \$258,549$$

Since we have shown four of the five years, we have one more year to make money to reach our goal. We note with some concern that minus 15 percent in the fourth year has created a loss. Let's look at the next equation to find out what percentage return we would need to reach our goal of $400,000.

$$\text{Year 5: } \$258,549 \times \text{unknown} = \$400,000 \text{ goal}$$

To solve the equation for the value of the unknown, divide $400,000 by $258,549. The answer? A *55 percent return* in one year!

Doesn't that sound abnormal? We would have to get a return greater than the S&P 500 has had in any year in the past seventy years in order to get to the goal. Weird things happen in arithmetic. In the example above, the *mathematics of compression* crushed our steady easy walk, forcing us to either accept less money after a five-year period or take on too much risk in order to get to what is now, by reasonable measures, out of reach. This compression of returns will happen more often than one can guess, and it is never without great shock when 15 percent is lost in a single week or single month.

Many preretirees come to a financial advisor wanting to retire on a given lump sum or an annuity plus a 401(k), 457, or a TSA. They will make hard choices within the next year or two. They have 80 percent of their 401(k) or 403(b) money in stocks, and the first warning I give them is that we need to look at their current asset mix and try to preserve it from near-term decline (or crisis) if they are firmly set on retiring. I also explain that if the market falls sharply, to get this money back to where the glass is as full as it is right now could take a miracle like the one at Cana. I ask them, "Can you afford to retire if the funds you have now decline 15 percent to 20 percent?" Usually that question is met with uncertainty until it is translated into dollars lost. As I showed in the previous example, it may be impossible to get back the present value in the short time from now until retirement.

The Big Difference: Accumulating Versus Spending

During our accumulation years, we do not need to pay much attention to yearly declines, because they are opportunities to add to the securities at low prices. Low prices and poorly performing markets are a friend to younger folks. They had best wish for good performance toward the end of their saving cycle. The preretirees and retirees who will be or are drawing funds off each year want the opposite market behavior—a big difference. Since they are no longer putting money away, it is best for them to hope for steady, positive returns in the immediate future and most of the upcoming years. When they are older and less healthy, retirees usually use less money, unless they have to contend with inflation or have high medical expenses.

The young investor will make more money if reinvested income and dollar cost averaging are done at low prices rather than high prices. Reinvestment is not as powerful a tool for retirees, because they most likely will be spending some income and gains each year. For them the principal needs to be an income-producing cash cow. The grave danger of changing from an *accumulator* to a *spender* mentality is that many do not do it quickly enough. One prospective client admitted she had gotten greedy. She said, "I saw everyone else throwing money into growth funds in January 2000, so I did too." She lost 36 percent of her retirement a few months before exiting her company. This kind of postponement also hurt a client of mine who decided to stay 100 percent invested in stocks until the very end. He then retired. The month he transferred the 401(k) account to a rollover IRA, he had lost more than $30,000, about 12 percent of his account value. Some people think they need to ride the fastest horse in the race in order to win, and often they wind up losing at a time when they can least afford it.

Although I had suggested he should transfer within his 401(k) 20 percent of the funds into bonds and cash each month for five months before retiring, he did not do it. Having done so, he would have given up a few bucks in upside potential, but he would have substantially reduced his downside risk. Further, it would have given us a more certain dollar amount as the basis of calculations for designing a sound plan to create a retirement income. Greed got the better of him, and he left all his money in stocks. He was just placing a big bet with his retirement account. Clients can drive planners crazy when they do not take the advice they are paying for. The chart of the S&P 500 index, Figure 1.1, shows that there have been large variations in stock market returns during the past fifty-one years, which can be expected in a free economy like ours.

Figure 1.1   S&P 500 Index Change Year by Year Returns from 1951–2001

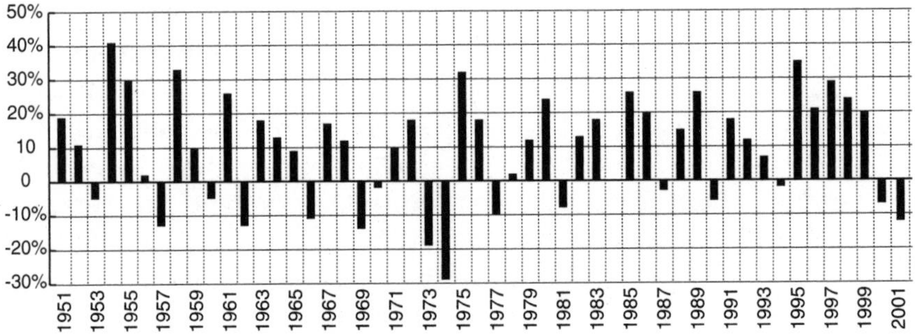

Source: *Standard and Poor's and First Union Securities/Wachovia*

Investment Proverb 2

If you don't know how much you need to live on,
the money you make is never enough.

Some think that they should be making in returns what is being made in the latest investment fad. These investors always feel that they are being left behind, because they missed having all their funds in whatever asset class is performing well. Some actually feel a deep sense of loss and criticize their advisors for not being as smart as everyone else is. They mistakenly see advisors as omniscient and, worse still, think some advisors should make money in spite of any market crisis. These clients make unreasonable demands. After the market has been down several months, I have heard a few clients say, "I am paying you to make me money, not to lose it." Yes, you may be paying a money management fee every month, but it is for advice that leads to sound long-term investments. This does not mean we will stay with an investment come hell or high water; what it does mean is that our economic system is capable of withstanding large shocks and then healing itself.

Uncertainty and Risk Within Our System

In the short run (one or two quarters, or even a few years), anything can happen. Edgar E. Peters has pointed out that our economic system is complex and filled with uncertainty. Capitalism, unlike socialism, rewards those who are willing to take risks, willing to win or lose. He writes, "Uncertainty is the price we pay for the benefits of capitalism" (*Complexity, Risk, and Financial Markets*, p. 207). He explains that our individual freedom helps us self-organize in times of crisis without turning to a central planner, such as government. Thus, many minds are thinking at once, which is far more effective in finding solutions than a few government heads. The interconnection among many people has a way of strengthening our ability to survive. Peters adds, "This process can adapt to a crisis—an ability that comes from the randomness or freedom of the individual participants. It introduces the element of chance into the system" (p. 204).

As products in the marketplace fail and business values fall and stock prices decline, *our system is working*, because failure leads to innovation. New growth comes from pruned branches. Competition for new products keeps this innovation speeding along. Our economy always moves through a cycle, and while new companies are created old ones are either re-created or dying off. In contrast to what financial news networks would like us to believe, Peters writes, "Economic forecasting has become a joke" (p. 63). In spite of the unpredictability of investment success, in the end we survive and many companies prosper.

My clients, of course, are warned about my profound inability to predict the market's next favorite fad or bear market. So what advice do reasonable people look for? Ask yourself: do you want realistic or egotistical advice? Do you want honest information or feel-good fluff? Sometimes the right answer to a financial question is "I don't know." For some investors those words go down hard; they fear that an advisor who doesn't know all the answers can't be trusted. But the inescapable truth is that some things cannot be known—for example, what the market returns will be next year.

For retirees (or others, for that matter) who are living on a fixed income and depending on greater certainty of returns, investing in stocks can feel like walking a tightrope. Yet our economy's stability is derived from the unpredictability and chaos that accompany all free markets. It is important to recognize that although we may be always in the dark, it is the only way that our adaptive economy can survive and prosper. Stock returns are nonlinear; that is, they are erratic because of the inherent uncertainty of our economy. Over the long run stock returns have been much better than returns from bank certificates of deposit (CDs)—almost three to one better. The problem we need to overcome is one of perception: the *average annual return* for stocks (although far exceeding the average return for CDs) masks the highly *irregular actual returns that come each year by investing in stocks.*

Understanding Averages

The average height of a man is, say, 5 feet, 8¼ inches, but in my senior high class there may have been only one young man at that level. Since I was the shortest in the class, I realized long ago that averages do not make sense in describing actual demographics. Not once in the past thirty years has the market made its average return number; each year it has been above or below the average. Financial advisors Matthew Peterson and Scott Welch of CMS Financial Services write about the problem in a traditional analysis of cash flow: "When using projections to show how the prescribed portfolio meets the investment demands, it is common [and an error] to use the expected rate of return as a constant rate of return throughout the assumed life of the portfolio" (*Investment Advisor*, August 2000, p. 78). They add that for an investor, such as a retiree, "With ongoing income or cash flow needs, this is a critical oversight" (p. 80). I can demonstrate how an *average* can destroy the perspective of an investor when looking at returns of mutual funds or money managers.

Let's take some simple numbers to arrive at an average return of 15 percent consisting of five actual noncompounded returns over a five-year period. It could look like this:

Portfolio A

Year	Investment returns
1	8 percent
2	14 percent
3	30 percent
4	28 percent
5	−5 percent
Average return: 75 percent ÷ 5 years = 15 percent	

Suppose an advisor says that because Portfolio A has produced an average of 15 percent and because you need to make only 10 percent per year to create the income that will support your lifestyle, it can be concluded that this investment should work. Note that there has been one minor negative return here, which is not uncommon over any five-year period.

So you begin withdrawing at a rate of $10,000 at the end of each year on a beginning amount of $100,000, and the first five years' returns are repeated. Here is your portfolio:

Portfolio A
Return After Withdrawal

End of year 1: $98,000 (down 2 percent)
End of year 2: $101,720 (up 1.7 percent)
End of year 3: $122,236 (up 22 percent)
End of year 4: $146,462 (up 46 percent)
End of year 5: $129,138 (up 29 percent)

You took a total of $50,000 over five years, which is 50 percent of the original $100,000. You would reason that your portfolio would be up 25 percent, but actual returns show differently. You would be up 29 percent.

Next let's change the numbers around so that they happen in a different sequence, and let's begin removing $10,000 per year in the beginning of the investment period (rather than at the end of the year), which is often the case for early retirees. The average return is 15 percent per year.

Portfolio B

Year	Investment returns
1	−5 percent
2	8 percent
3	30 percent
4	28 percent
5	14 percent
Average return: 75 percent ÷ 5 years = 15 percent	

Here is what your portfolio return would look like after removing $10,000 of the beginning amount at the beginning of each year.

Portfolio B
Return After Withdrawal

End of year 1: $85,000 (down 15.5 percent)
End of year 2: $81,540 (down 18.5 percent)
End of year 3: $93,002 (down 7.0 percent)
End of year 4: $106,242 (up 6.2 percent)
End of year 5: $109,715 (up 9.7 percent)

There are two major differences in Portfolio A and Portfolio B. First, although each has the same average annual return, the yearly return percentages are rearranged. Second, although we withdrew the same dollar amount from A and B, we took dollars from A at the end of the year, and from B in the beginning of the year. Both differences dramatically changed the outcome. Remember, small variables make a significant difference.

Your money would have appreciated only 9.7 percent in Portfolio B over five years (versus 29 percent in Portfolio A), and that would have been less than the accumulated inflation rate. Portfolio B would have lost its buying power, because the principal had not grown enough. Stunning though it may seem, most investors and some planners are convinced that past returns will be repeated, and in the same order. Both assumptions can easily be off the mark. Milton Friedman said, "Never try to walk across a river just because it has an average depth of four feet." I will add that if you cannot swim, you may be sadly caught by surprise, as many investors are.

Investment Proverb 3

Average return does not mean actual return. The expected return each year will be higher or lower than the average, but will almost never be equal to the average return.

Market Returns Are Variable

As you can see, market returns are not like returns from CDs. Although bank yields are usually much lower than stocks, they are more predictable— that is, less variable. The market, because it is uncertain, can be said to be risky. Here risk is not the same as the risk of losing all your money or seeing sizable market correction. It means something far subtler: the unpredictability of year-to-year returns. Often people approach retirement investing with the narrow perception of the recent past. But bias will often hamper investment judgments. You want an unbiased advisor, someone who does not get fooled by past performance.

When you look from afar at Giant Mountain in the Adirondacks in upstate New York, you see the tree-covered slope gradually rising to the top.

But just try to walk the trail. The high boulders and deep crevices make for a long and arduous hike that is not linear. So it is with the market, and so it is with life. You may see several recessions during your golden years. You may go in and out of different careers or jobs after your primary job is terminated. You may not work at all. Many people have completed the twenty or thirty years required by an employer to qualify for a pension check, while others have been through ten different employers, accumulating several 401(k)s or TSAs. You may have the vigor after sixty to have a more active life than while you were working, or you may be disabled. In either case, the meaning of *retirement* is changing for most of us.

It is not clear how these changes will affect the social order, but government and academia are studying these matters. Will long-lived people put stress on our Social Security system? Will people need career counseling at age eighty-three? For those who welcome challenges, life will be more exciting—for example, acquiring new skills and jobs. We must be aware of the forthcoming challenges. If a happy and successful retirement is important to you, read on. Whether you are transitioning to retirement or have just retired, you need to be mindful of important factors and issues that will help you to discern the most dependable plan for your lifestyle.

2

Factors to Consider When Transitioning to Retirement

"Human felicity is produced not so much by great pieces of good fortune that seldom happen, as by little advantages that occur every day."

—BENJAMIN FRANKLIN

Donna (fifty-five) and her husband, Richard (fifty-nine), are happy to see a generous "separation package" offered by Donna's employer, a private utility company. Richard is retired and disabled, and he has no Social Security disability income or pension. He has had two heart attacks. Donna would like to work part-time. She is not in the best of health and wants to spend more time with her husband. Their home is paid for and their children are independent. She knows the income from her 401(k) and cash balance (lump sum distribution) will be enough to pay for her spouse's needs as well as her own. At retirement, neither yet qualifies for Social Security or Medicare, but she has health benefits, paid mostly by her employer, that will cover both of them.

William (fifty-six) and his wife, Cynthia (fifty-three), are recently retired from their primary employers—he from the IBEW union and she from a major telephone company. Through her past employer Cynthia has health coverage for both of them. The company pays 100 pecent of the cost. William now works full time in hotel maintenance—a job with less danger, less pay, more time off, and a health benefits plan. He pays $180 per month for health, vision, and dental. William's major goal is to make sure his wife has enough funds if he dies before her, so he buys a large life insurance policy to cover her needs. He has a 401(k) he will tap later, and for now he chooses to take his monthly pension income on his life alone. They plan to enjoy traveling and vacationing together.

Joe (fifty-five) and his wife, Barbara (fifty-six), agree that Joe should retire early. His job has become more demanding over the past few years, affecting his health—high blood pressure is only one sign, and the stress aggravates his Type II diabetes. Barbara provided day care for children until recently, when state regulations became too difficult to meet. Her health has deteriorated; she struggles with many serious allergies. Besides, she has committed to spend more time with her granddaughter. She has no retirement plan or medical coverage. Joe has a separation package with health and medical insurance coverage that will be paid mostly by his employer: He will ante up about $100 per month for health benefits while receiving severance pay, and about $50 per month after the severance pay period ends. Through his employer he has term life insurance until age sixty-five, when it will begin to decline. With the house paid for, and a modest standard of living, Joe's lump sum distribution and 401(k) are adequate. He still would like to work part-time; he does not want to dip deeply into his retirement plan.

Libby (fifty-one) would like to see her company offer her a voluntary early retirement package that would get her to the corporation's full retirement age of fifty-five. "If they give me four years added to my current age and to my years of service," she says, "I will qualify for all the company health benefits offered people at age sixty-two, plus a large pension." As an active single woman, she feels this would give her the opportunity to begin a dog-grooming business, fulfilling a long-awaited dream.

Are these folks unusual? Or are they representative of the changing face of retirement? When do people expect to retire? According to a study conducted by Cornell professors Phyllis Moen, Vandana Plassmann, and Stephen Sweet, "Unprecedented changes are transforming workers' career patterns, along with the social organization of work and retirement" (*Cornell Midcareer Paths and Passages Study*, 2001, p. 4). The statistics in Figure 2.1 provoke thought about why retirement recently has been considered another life stage rather than a date when we leave our employer close to life's end. The sample consisted of 887 men and women who either worked for one of four upstate New York companies or were the spouses of these workers. They were asked many questions, and one was about their planned retirement age. The study reports, "Americans are rewriting the script—some leaving their primary career jobs in their 50s, most in their early 60s, and a few continuing their primary career jobs into their 70s or even 80s." (p. 7.) Drawing from this study and my years of experience as a financial advisor, I have concluded that many people are retiring younger than previous generations.

These findings prove why in Codger City, U.S.A.—the fictional home of old, rocking-chaired eccentrics—the population has shrunk to one hundred souls: no one is moving in to retire there. Today, when people ask themselves, "What is my perfect day or month in retirement?" Codger City just does not fill the bill. It contains no modern athletic gym for us exercise nuts. Nor are there nearby mountains to hike or rivers to canoe. There is no senior center for learning, or college to keep one's mind alert or to train us for another career. Theater? Forget it—there's no building with a stage. No golf course or tennis courts.

For the first time, lifestyle factors, such as wanting more time to travel, are what leading-edge baby boomers talk about with friends and coworkers when they discuss hanging up their suspenders. At the same time, these preretirees are not kidding themselves. A topic that is not often discussed publicly, and is verboten around the office watercooler, is that many of them really want to get out and do something different, because some jobs are no longer satisfying. But to pack up and leave is another thing altogether

Figure 2.1   Baby Boomers Expect to Retire at an Earlier Age than World War II Generation

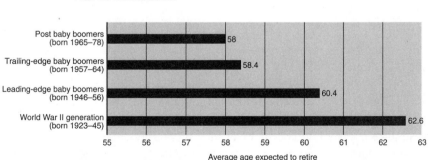

Source: *Cornell Midcareer Paths and Passages Study, 2000*

when we consider what a job offers besides the weekly paycheck. After their blood pressure goes back to normal, some early retirees are ready to work again, while still others pursue long-repressed artistic dreams, creating new lifetime goals. These are all things you should share with your financial advisor.

People may want to live in a housing complex peppered with tennis courts, an earshot away from breaking ocean waves, but these are not often their deeper longings. For most of us, sports do not fulfill our spiritual needs. Many advisors believe that preretirees and the newly retired should seek psychological counseling as they transition to retirement, because many emotional factors come into play. When looking at couples and retirement, Cornell study author Phyllis Moen said, "I was surprised that it was the transition that was stressful on relationships" (*New York Times*, "New Portrait of Retiring Is Emerging," May 29, 2001, pp. 14, 17, 36). One does not just play golf every day and feel fulfilled. Unspoken needs that must be addressed include family and community ties, which make up the fabric of our lives. In general, when asking preretirees and retirees, "What are your important financial goals?" Greenwald Associates, Inc. found several common to every generation. So although retirement is changing dramatically—more time, more choices—Figure 2.2 shows that our deeper goals remain the same, and they need to be addressed.

Taking care of our spouse, or others we love, is important to most of us. Preserving our wealth, knowing it may be all we ever have, is a major concern for the majority of us. Each of these goals takes on even greater significance as we begin to live longer lives, but we may not be able to talk about them easily at a neighbor's social hour, as a way to seek advice. Let us here take the time to address some of these concerns.

Insurance Needs

One of the factors that workers consider most important when choosing a job is insurance, especially if they have a spouse and children. It also plays a significant role when they are considering leaving their jobs. We all need insurance. Some of the questions you must ask are, What will my health and medical insurance cover? What are my deductibles? and What will my insurance not pay for? For many retirees, the traditional date of termination of full employment arrives when they qualify for full Social Security income and Medicare insurance benefits. Social Security is discussed in Chapter 7,

Figure 2.2   Important Retiree Goals

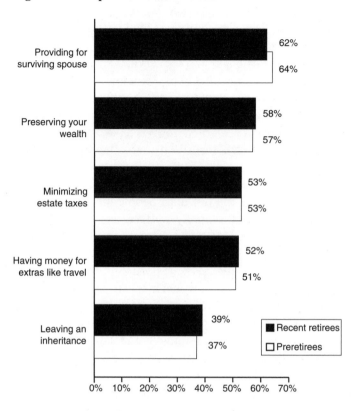

Source: *Forum for Investor Advice, Greenwald Associates, Inc.*

but here I want to focus on insurance rather than on income. Most people planning for an early retirement have included the costs involved with health insurance—an expense often partially paid by their employer—but a little more discussion on the subject can be helpful. Others planning a traditional retirement must review their Medicare coverage, which early retirees will be offered when they turn sixty-five. Here is how Medicare works.

Medicare is a federal and state health insurance program primarily for individuals who are sixty-five years of age or older. Full or partial coverage is offered to those who are disabled before age sixty-five. There are two parts to the government's insurance benefits.

- *Medicare Part A* is hospital insurance. Most people do not pay a monthly Part A premium because they or their spouse have forty or more quarters of Medicare-covered employment. This portion covers inpatient hospital costs in a benefit period; you may pay a deductible and coinsurance charges. Part A also covers skilled nursing home facility care up to 100 days after hospitalization in a benefit period with a coinsurance charge. Home care and hospice services are also available. If you exceed 100 days, you must begin paying the costs of the nursing home stay. In states as large and diverse as New York the cost can range widely. The insurance industry reported that the average cost per day in Chautauqua County (western New York) is $144, while it is $251 per day in Suffolk County to the east. With such a high price to pay, many people consider buying long-term care insurance to cover the possibility of longer, extended periods. If one cannot afford it, Medicaid begins to kick in to pay the bill once people meet the requirements to qualify. Medicaid is essentially welfare, and to qualify one must have few assets.

- *Medicare Part B* is medical insurance. This portion of the plan covers physician's services, inpatient and outpatient medical and surgical services, physical and speech therapy, diagnostic tests, durable medical equipment, and such. Monthly premiums may be deducted from one's Social Security benefit. In 2002, the premium is $54, adjusted annually. There are possible 20 percent copayments due on some Medicare-approved charges. Since some medical costs are only partially covered—for example, you would pay 20 percent of the cost of durable medical equipment—or, as in the case of prescriptions and vision and dental care, are not covered at all, you may need to keep a nest egg set aside for these expenses. On the other hand, you may find coverage for these things by buying insurance plans from a company in your area. To get your copy of a Medicare benefits description call (800) 633-4227.

As well as learning about Medicare, you should look at purchasing a Medigap insurance policy (also known as *Medicare supplemental insurance*) to cover the gaps between your expenses and what Medicare pays. Financial advisors recommend the purchase of Medigap before you sign up for Medicare in order to maintain flexibility in your options. Stan Hinden's book *How to Retire Happy* (2000) has valuable information on the ten different kinds of Medigap insurance policies offered by insurance companies. In addition, you may want to check to see if your employer or union has insurance available for those over sixty-five.

Or you can get coverage through another Medicare health plan under Medicare + Choice, which allows you to go to a private insurance company serving your area. Going this route, there are two types: a Medicare managed care plan, like an HMO, or a Medicare private fee-for-service plan. With either you will still pay Part B premium, and you may pay extra for the private insurance, too. Many people with Medicare choose one of these plans, but they are not available in all areas of the country. You can find out more about Medicare plans by contacting your state health insurance program listed in the booklet *Medicare and You*, which can be obtained by calling (800) 633-4227.

If you spend a little time each day investigating what is important to you, sharing your concerns with others (especially with a financial advisor) may help you with your choices. In the Greenwald Associates study cited earlier (see page 28), 200 preretirees were asked about when they undertook certain planning activities. The activities the respondents ranked first and second were "review medical coverage options" and "estimate retirement income" (*Transitioning to Retirement*, 1999, p. 12). Figure 2.3 ranks the respondents' answers to seven other activities as well as the two primary ones.

We do not know from the figure whether these "activities" are undertaken with thoroughness and with thoughtfulness. Some people do them much too hastily. Overall, I believe, they are done poorly. Many of the people I have interviewed in the past years do have some idea of their insurance coverage, for example, but often wait until just before retirement or just after to get all the details. If you are sixty-five or over, it is important that you sign up for Medicare several months before you retire. If you have turned sixty-five and your spouse is *under* sixty-five, he or she will not be covered by Medicare. So if your spouse is not employed, and you are concerned about his or her welfare, there is a big insurance risk that you need to address before giving up your job.

If you leave your employer prior to age sixty-five, then it is important that you look at your company's summary plan documents to fully understand what insurance benefits are offered. As well, if any separation or early-out package includes an insurance benefit, then ask yourself, What are the terms? For those people who retire involuntarily, there might be no "package" and, thus, no insurance. They will need to consider other ways to be covered, such as COBRA. Since group health is less expensive than individual or family coverage, those without insurance can see a bigger piece of their income going to pay premiums. This cost has to be factored into their budget. On the other hand, the people I have met who take early retire-

Figure 2.3   When Recent Retirees Conducted Planning Activities

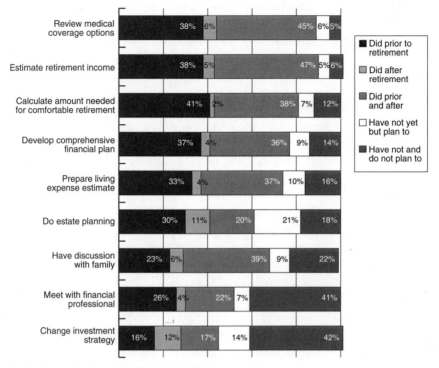

Source: *Forum for Investor Advice, Greenwald Associates, Inc.*

ment have all received some health and medical coverage as part of their incentive package. My own experiences can be summarized in a paper written by Daniel Dulitzky: "The current structure of some private pension plans and the availability of health care coverage provide strong incentives to retire early" (*The Retirement Project*, Urban Institute, 2001).

COBRA

When a person's job is terminated and no insurance benefits are offered, and that person is under sixty-five, then COBRA takes over. You must be working for a company that has at least twenty employees (part-time employees are partially counted in the total) to qualify. A *qualified beneficiary* under COBRA is an employee, the employee's spouse, or an employee's dependent child. In certain cases, retirees do qualify. Qualifying events for an employee are as follows:

- Voluntary or involuntary termination of employment for reasons other than "gross misconduct"
- Reduction in number of hours worked

The qualifying events for a spouse are as follows:

- Voluntary or involuntary termination of the covered employee's employment for reasons other than "gross misconduct"
- Reduction in number of hours worked by the covered employee
- Covered employee's becoming entitled to Medicare
- Divorce or legal separation of the covered employee
- Death of the covered employee

The Consolidated Omnibus Budget Reconciliation Act (COBRA, revised in 1999) allows people to continue group coverage of medical benefits at up to 102 percent of the monthly cost of that coverage. That is, you can continue your company's coverage, but you will pay all the premiums plus up to 2 percent more for administration of the plan. The law allows for this insurance to continue up to eighteen months after your retirement—one of the qualifying events. But you should be aware that retirees may be disqualified from COBRA quite easily.

For example, suppose you retired and were given a retirement package that includes health and medical insurance, and then that insurance was dropped eighteen months later. Since you have used up your eighteen-month period past your qualifying event, you do not get COBRA rights. So, at age fifty-six, Joe gets his retirement package that includes medical insurance. After a year and a half his company goes bankrupt or it gets bought out, and the new company decides to cancel benefits to retirees. Joe cannot get COBRA. In that case, he would have to find his own insurance. If he has serious preexisting health conditions, that could be a challenge.

Downsizing in government and the merging and rightsizing of corporations are hitting the fifty- to sixty-year-olds harder than ever. The corporate motto, "Let's add shareholder value by increasing profits and cutting costs," has found the corporate whipping boy—the older workers, who are more expensive to carry than younger ones. Forget seniority! Besides, those younger workers have new skills, so we hear. I have one client who has been forced to take large premature distributions from his retirement plan in order to meet daily obligations, including insurance. He had to sell his home, his wife had to return to work, and he had to take a lesser-paying job farther from home. The cost in taxes and penalties to take withdrawals from their IRA has made them bitter. Now in their late fifties, they have to begin once again saving for retirement. (It is important to note that you can collect unemployment checks if you have an involuntary retirement and you are seeking another job. But be aware, if you receive checks from your company pension plan, this amount will reduce your state's payments to you. If the pension is high enough, you may not qualify for any unemployment income.)

Today, many early retirees are not forced out, but are given attractive incentives to leave employment that they began to dislike long ago. When the pressure to perform grows to the point that your health begins to deteriorate, an "early-out package" becomes like a carrot held in front of a hungry donkey. Few turn down the opportunity. Retirement has had a positive effect on the health of many of my clients. Makes sense. To their surprise and relief, several found that their blood pressure fell to a normal level not long after leaving their job. One early-out package—$500 per month until the retiree reached age sixty-two, plus time added to their years of service, getting them to full retirement with heath care benefits to boot—seemed too good to turn down. People jumped.

But don't be fooled. Medical and health benefits should be fully understood before you choose any retirement option. If you are not eligible for Medicare, then reading your plan documents and reviewing your deductibles, costs, and coverage may be a complex matter. If you want to be certain about what you have, you may want to hire a financial planner to interpret your retirement benefits and surmise for you any shortfalls in your plan. Important questions to keep in mind are, What happens when or if my benefits disappear? and, How will my family and I be affected? You will sleep better knowing the answers, and so will those who have come to depend on you for insurance coverage.

Investment Proverb 4

If you think good health is everything, then health insurance is next to everything.

Life Insurance and Income Protection

In reviewing many retirement plans, I find that many times too little thought is given to life insurance as a retirement benefit. Too often, preretirees do not even engage in life insurance planning at all. *Why bother? Life insurance is about dying and not about living*, they think. On the other hand, most people want to take care of their spouse after they die, but without the proper insurance coverage the spouse could be left with far less available income.

Many severance and early-out packages continue the insurance policy that the company carried while the worker was employed. The policy face amount is usually pegged at the employee's salary times a multiple, which then is reduced at some future date. For example, two times a salary of $60,000 would give you $120,000 in life insurance coverage, but oftentimes this face amount is reduced by 10 percent per year for every year you pass age sixty-five. In this case, the retiree's insurance will have disappeared by seventy-five. But the need for coverage has not gone away. For some of us, the need for life insurance coverage is even greater as we age. Think of it. As we get older, more things can go wrong, forcing us to spend our savings. A catastrophic illness of one family member is one way we can wind up spending all of our retirement assets, and life insurance can replace those assets.

Trying to explain to retirees that they need to start thinking seriously about adding life insurance—and along with it, another fixed expense, the premium—is not easy. Although we think of our retirement income as being enough for the both of us, we can forget what happens if we die before our spouse. For example, suppose both spouses are receiving Social Security income. If one spouse never had "earned income," would your combined Social Security income remain the same once the one spouse dies? No. For example, the Social Security benefit that you each may have qualified for when you reached sixty-two could be lessened upon death of the higher wage earner. My mother began receiving my dad's Social Security check after he suffered a stroke, because she became his guardian. For the time being, she also continues to receive her own check. When he passes away, she will receive one check that will be less than the total of the two she now gets. Unhappily, his life insurance will not be enough to replace her lost income. That can happen to you, if you do not have a plan to replace income.

How Much Insurance Will You Need?

There are some easy calculations you can do to determine the face amount of the insurance you may need to buy. It is a good idea to do this calculation before retirement for several reasons.

1. If you are working, you may be able to pay higher premiums while you have a paycheck and then scale down the premiums after you retire. There are insurance policies, such as universal life, that allow for great flexibility in when and how much you pay in premiums. Paying more now hurts less than paying more later.
2. You may be able to buy insurance at a group rate and then convert it to an individual policy at the same rate once you leave your job. Or you may have an individual policy aside from work that can be used to develop future income. You may want to add more face amount of coverage without canceling the old policy.
3. Because you are younger than you will be tomorrow, you may not get a better rating if you wait several years to buy additional coverage.

With a little imagination and planning, you may significantly improve your financial outlook. For example, one can replace income lost due to early death using life insurance proceeds. Let's suppose Barbara, Joe's spouse, wants to buy an insurance policy on her husband's life so that she could replace $656 in monthly income if he passes away at age sixty-four (or older). Without the extra Social Security check, Barbara would not feel secure. Suppose Joe does pass on soon after he reaches sixty-four, when Barbara is sixty-five. The $656 per month equals $7,872 per year that will be sorely missed. At today's annuity rate, Barbara could get $656 per month for life by buying a $100,000 life insurance policy now and converting it to an annuity income at Joe's death.

Stay with me. We worked backward to find our answer; working the solution forward looks like this:

Barbara purchases a $100,000 life insurance policy on Joe's life when he is fifty-eight.

Joe passes away six years later at age sixty-four, when Barbara is sixty-five.

Barbara receives, tax free, $100,000 in insurance proceeds.

At the same time, she loses $656 per month in Social Security income.

Barbara invests $100,000 into an immediate life annuity.

The annuity company guarantees that she receives $656 per month for life.

Whether Barbara or Joe buys the policy on Joe's life does not matter; what does matter is that there are enough assets available to create income for the life of the survivor. Listed in Table 2.1 are the monthly income levels for men and for women at varying ages, investing $100,000 into an immediate life income annuity. Note that the income is less each year for women, because women have a longer life expectancy. And remember, annuity payouts vary among insurance companies, so it is wise to shop around.

When looking at old insurance policies to replace income, more often than not you will need to have them reviewed by an insurance expert. Reasons for the review are plenty:

- Old insurance policies may be performing poorly; the returns inside the life insurance that builds cash value by age 100 may not be doing the job.
- The insurance company may be in financial trouble, endangering the face value (what you will be paid).
- There could be a loan on the policy you forgot about.
- Some policies are not earning enough to keep premiums level, which could mean that the policy may be in danger of lapsing.

Table 2.1   *Immediate Income Annuity ($100,000 Invested, Based on Age and Sex)*

Female age	Monthly income
65	$656
70	$723
75	$835
80	$997

Male age	Monthly income
65	$711
70	$798
75	$925
80	$1,102

- Additional "old policy" payment of premiums may be required many years beyond the original illustration.

Investment Proverb 5

*The day when you need insurance is the day it is
too late to buy it.*

To wait until after retirement for an insurance review is not wise. This review should be part of your retirement planning review that is discussed in Chapter 11. If you want to know the cost of a policy, you can find it on the Internet in a few minutes; or, better yet, call at least two local insurance agents for a quote. If you find the calculations discussed previously confusing, you can get an insurance specialist, accountant, or financial planner to help you.

To Cover Long-Term Care, Spend Down

Another important factor for insurance planning is your risk of needing long-term care. Under the current government budget restraints, we now are required to pay for our care in nursing homes or for in-home care for as long as we are able to. In general, the government wants us to *spend down* our wealth to certain limits before Medicaid will pay for our care. There is nothing wrong with that, but if you want to be sure of leaving a substantial amount of assets to your spouse or children or a charity, then life insurance is one way of replacing lost money due to a catastrophic illness. That is, if you are forced to spend money for health care, a life insurance policy can replace some or all of the assets that may be spent before you die.

Clients Ralph (sixty-seven) and Eve (sixty) had enough 401(k) money to care for a major illness that could wind up landing him or her in a nursing home for a few years. However, they feared a prolonged illness could entirely deplete their principal and other assets. Rather than purchasing long-term care to cover the cost of a nursing home, Ralph bought a $150,000 life insurance policy in order to guarantee his children would have an inheritance. Since they each have children from prior marriages, Eve purchased $200,000 of protection. Listing their children as owners on the contracts made sure that upon their death the proceeds of each policy would go to the children *free of income tax and without estate taxes*. Smart planning techniques can create and transfer wealth from one generation to the next, saving taxes to boot.

Another way to protect your assets from the spend-down provision connected with Medicaid is to purchase long-term care insurance. Both life and long-term care insurance may cost less before you retire. It is even possible that you can get group rates on these policies, which may be less than individual rates. But it is wise to get quotes from companies besides your company group administrator. When I wanted to add life insurance protection at age fifty-one, I found an individual term insurance policy that cost me less than my corporate group policy. Was I surprised! I had been convinced that company-offered products were always less expensive. The fact that a group is a "captured" society affects group insurance rates, raising them or lowering them. By contrast, individual rates are set in a more competitive insurance environment with more people insured, possibly reducing premiums below what groups offer.

Some expenses may be cut after retirement. Disability insurance, for one, may no longer be needed, since it is intended to replace income lost from an injury related to work. When transitioning to retirement, you may save money by letting the coverage lapse, unless you feel you are going to work at another career; if so, then see whether the coverage can be moved from a group to an individual. Some can and some cannot. When you are no longer employed, Social Security tax will disappear and contributions to your 401(k) or TSA will disappear, too. The extra money saved from no longer buying lunch or paying to travel to and from work can be diverted toward extra insurance.

Transitioning to retirement should never be done without considering the following expenses and getting a general idea of what your budget looks like. Page 40 lists a summary of what your spending habits may include.

If you have not added up these items before retiring, then you may be surprised when you begin to spend more than your income, forcing you to tap your principal to make ends meet. Ouch! I have seen astute investors have to cut back their lifestyles because they were too loose with a buck. Then again, there are things that are out of our control that eventually must

Summary of Preretirement Expenses

Monthly amount × number of payments per year = annual expense

Auto expenses _____	_____	$_____
Charity/gifts _____	_____	$_____
Clothing _____	_____	$_____
Cleaning/upkeep _____	_____	$_____
Debt payments _____	_____	$_____
Entertainment _____	_____	$_____
Food/dining _____	_____	$_____
Health insurance _____	_____	$_____
Home mortgage _____	_____	$_____
Home repair _____	_____	$_____
Hobbies/sports _____	_____	$_____
Income taxes _____	_____	$_____
Life insurance _____	_____	$_____
Long-term care _____	_____	$_____
Prescriptions _____	_____	$_____
Personal care _____	_____	$_____
Property taxes _____	_____	$_____
Rent _____	_____	$_____
Pets _____	_____	$_____
Travel _____	_____	$_____
Other expenses _____	_____	$_____
Total expenditures		$_____

be factored into a budget—for example, inflation. In Table 2.2 you will find a comparison of the money needed today to purchase goods and services with yesterday's dollar. For example, if you had an income of $1,000 per month in 1950, it would require $7,365.15 per month today to purchase the same goods and services. That is to say, it would take $88,381.80 today to buy the same stuff that $12,000 purchased in 1950. The effect of inflation summarized in Table 2.2 can give financial advisors and investors alike the willies.

Until you get a good feel for your retirement spending, which may take you at least a year after you sever your ties with your employer, stick to a sound spending program. Once you know how much income you will need—reevaluating your needs as your life changes—you can better focus on making the right investment moves to meet your current and future income expectations. The rest of this book will help you do just that.

Table 2.2   The Money Needed to Purchase $1,000.00 in Goods and Services, 10, 20, 30, 40, and 50 Years Later, Using CPI

Number of years	Time period	Dollars needed
10	1990–2001	$1,358.07
20	1980–2001	$2,154.13
30	1970–2001	$4,574.74
40	1960–2001	$5,996.62
50	1950–2001	$7,365.15

Source: *Bureau of Labor Statistics*

3

Why Some Retirement Plans Fail and Others Succeed

"When lost in the woods, use your head and not your legs."

—U.S. FOREST SERVICE

Although annual returns will most likely be, on average, what the returns have been for the past fifty years—about 13 percent for the S&P 500—we cannot count on the ambiguity of returns when managing retirement money. Some think a better bet may be the combination of large stocks, small stocks, bonds, and international equities, but that combination also did about 13 percent. Because we do not know how or when the average market returns will be produced, it is important to look at the withdrawal side of our equation. Regulating how much you draw can be accomplished by setting some minimum withdrawal rate (or dollar amount) to meet your needs. The plan could allow for further withdrawals every couple of years, after you see what the market delivers. Such an approach will make your retirement account your good servant and not your poor master.

Will Your Portfolio Survive?

My study of endowment funds has helped me to form a strategy that can help you manage your portfolio and make it produce a life income. Knowing what endowment funds do to ensure a future cash flow and still allow you to spend today can help you make sense of investing. Did you know that most colleges and churches have between 4 percent and 5 percent annual withdrawal rates even if they are earning 15 percent to 20 percent annually? Even if they have a negative return they still spend between 4 percent and 5 percent of the portfolio, hoping for better returns the next year. Remember that 5 percent of a growing account becomes a larger amount each year. This larger income can offset inflation! As well, after several good years they may have an exceptional withdrawal. (The wealth effect we hear about is the spending of gains made in stocks rather than spending income.) In this manner they do not dictate to the portfolio what it must return, but allow the portfolio to deliver what it can and, naturally, when it can. The variability of returns does not bother the CFO of an endowment fund.

Like the endowment or foundation, the retiree withdraws money in a rather odd manner. Retirees spend what they are not sure of earning and may not earn that year. This situation is different from when the person was a worker. With steady pay, a worker can spend money before he or she earns it, knowing how much is coming in. On this premise, banks will loan money to a young working person with few assets but potential income. Retirees spend money no matter what they earn. This constant drain is a major investment problem that clients want professionals to contend with. It is a mathematical problem, which people like me love to solve—one of the small joys of our business. Face it: the rule you will learn to live with is that you will spend money whether you make it or not.

There is a psychological advantage to being a worker with a paycheck. No matter what happens to the stock market, you still have a job. A retiree once told me, "Now that I'm not working, I'm concerned about the market every day." That may be the reason so many people find it difficult to retire and then wait for that withdrawal check to come in. It may be for this reason that many workers migrate to the larger, nationally known investment firms, believing that these firms offer dependable income and security. But these investment firms are just as likely to do as good or as poor a job as independents or sole advisors. I believe it is not so much the firm, but the process and the person you work with and the relationship you develop that will lead you to feel secure. We will discuss in a later chapter how to find an advisor and monitor your account once you have one. If you have a financial advisor, you can gain much insight into the services he or she should provide, some of which is behind the scenes but important to know.

Let's try to put into perspective the long-term nature of investing after you retire. One perspective that may be honest is that of John Rekenthaler, CFA at Morningstar, who wrote in the *Journal of Financial Planning*, "for most retirees, who have a limited pool of financial resources and no particular desire to amass a large estate, the longer the time horizon, the greater the probability that they will suffer [the ultimate failure]: the loss of all their assets. Time now becomes an enemy, not a friend" (*Journal of Financial Planning*, January 2000, p. 40). True enough, many retirees are not financially prepared to have enough money to last thirty years, let alone forty. And the longer one lives, the more risks one faces. The largest risk is inflation, then poor health, then poor investments, and ad infinitum. Moreover, looking at Table 3.1, we find that as the average person ages chances increase that he will live even longer than his original life expectancy; so those who have long life expectancies and want to maintain their standard of living need to accumulate more money.

Table 3.1 Mortality Table (GAM 83)

Male age	Life expectancy	50 percent will live past
50	29.9 years	79.9
55	24.8 years	79.8
60	20.6 years	80.6
65	16.7 years	81.7
70	13.2 years	83.2
75	10.2 years	85.2
Female age	Life expectancy	50 percent will live past
50	34.9 years	84.9
55	30.2 years	85.2
60	25.7 years	85.7
65	21.3 years	86.3
70	17.1 years	87.1
75	13.4 years	88.4

Source: *1983 Individual Annuitant Mortality Table*

This insured group experience is taken from statistics collected by the insurance industry, but they are changing due to longevity changes in our population. But even these longevity figures are misleading, because they are only averages. Call it "the average longevity blunder," because half of the people reaching a particular milestone will live *beyond* that age. For example, a male who lives to be seventy years old has an even chance of living past eighty-three, while a female at age seventy has an even chance of living past eighty-seven.

On the other hand, we know of a few people who have very low income needs, and hardly any wants more than a simple roof and diet. Somehow they get by on little more than Social Security while amassing millions. The more realistic story is that people learn to live within their income, decreasing wants as income falls and only increasing spending as windfalls occur. It is human nature. I call it the survival instinct. There will always be those who will go bankrupt in old age, because nursing home expenses or serious illnesses can gobble up money faster than most people can make it. Overall, I find that most of my clients still spend less than they make, aware that spending principal is not a wise decision. The good news is that many people are quite flexible in their monetary habits. Too many advisors think people all want more, need more, and demand more. It's just not so. From where I sit, most people have a handle on spending but need guidance on the income side of the balance sheet.

It Is Better to Know the Truth

My experience is that people want to feel that their advisor can be honest with them—even if it hurts. We are not in your life to spin gold out of straw. Financial advisors never should promise to make a retiree rich. That assertion is unethical. Our job is that of a guide in a jungle, not a guide to some unknown gold mine. Our objective is to be realistic and not contrive a rosy future. One client said, "I want to see the spending plan for the next thirty years in the form of a chart. I like to see colored graphs." We worked up a plan that showed exactly what income he would have from year to year and where it would come from. No stratified rock formation looked as impressive. Our certified financial planner (CFP) showed every source of spendable dollar each year—yellow bars for nontaxable money were stacked on green and blue bars for retirement and personal savings. Seeing our illustration, the client's eyes sparkled as if he were gazing at the Hope diamond. Then I put a little water on the fire. "Remember," I said, "markets do not produce returns in a predictable upswing slope. So your principal and even income may vary from year to year. Graphs do not tell this side of the story." If I had not added the warning that returns are not a linear thing, the presentation would not have been balanced.

The really hard message to get across, when looking at graphs, is that forward-looking assumptions had to be made in order for the computer to run the numbers. We have seen these things before. Remember that old insurance policy, the one that was supposed to be worth so much after forty years? Now look at the cash value! Big deal. Same thing here. Because we are addicted to bar charts and graphs, we give them too much weight in an ever-changing and unpredictable future. Computer power can make a few hours of data entry look like a sophisticated life plan, but it's more like a lullaby that lulls some into dreamland. I tell clients, "I will be with you through the thick and thin. We are in this together, and *that* is what I get paid for—not for creating fancy graphs." I then smile, and most nod and smile back with some understanding. A few conclude that I am not the advisor for them.

The 1968 Retiree

Let's look at two different retirement scenarios based on some research done by T. Rowe Price Associates. They hypothetically invested $250,000 at the end of 1968. Sixty percent of the portfolio was invested in the S&P 500 index, 30 percent into U.S. government bonds, and 10 percent in U.S. thirty-day treasury bills. From January 1969 until January 1999 the portfolio had an *average return* of 11.7 percent. In the first withdrawal scenario (A), they started withdrawals of 6 percent (made at the beginning of each year and starting in 1969) with an increase of 3 percent on that amount each year to offset inflation. The first year's draw was $15,000, or 6 percent. In the second year the retiree would draw 6.18 percent, $15,450, and so on. Even with the commonsense idea that big-company stocks and government bonds would have been a good choice for these funds, the account went to zero in the *twenty-seventh year*. For some investors this result would be acceptable; others who want to retire early or want to leave funds to children or charity find it a poor finale.

To Make Things Worse: The Average Return Blunder

In another withdrawal test (B), using the same portfolio balance as we just discussed, T. Rowe Price assumed a withdrawal rate of 8.5 percent per year (with a 3 percent increase on the withdrawal rate for inflation) over the same period, from December 1968 to December 1998. The average return of each of the thirty years was 11.7 percent and is illustrated by the upper line in Figure 3.1. What happened to the portfolio affected by the higher and *more common* withdrawal rate is illustrated in the lower line of Figure 3.1. That is, $21,250 (8.5 percent of $250,000) was drawn the first year, $21,875 (8.75 percent of $250,000) the second year, and so on. Following the lower line in Figure 3.1, the $250,000 account would have been at the zero mark by the *fourteenth year* (in 1983). Hardly a nice picture to watch as the sixty-nine-year-old, retired at fifty-five, goes bust. What went wrong? T. Rowe Price calls this investment problem "the risk of relying on an average return." We will name this problem the *average return blunder*. Assuming an advisor had accurately predicted the average annual return of 11.7 percent for the portfolio over the next thirty years (the upper line in the figure) *and* his or her bar chart had showed that at the 8.5 percent withdrawal rate the principal was safe, then why was the fund so quickly depleted? Why did the account go bust? Every retiree must ask, Can this happen to me?

What's Wrong with Being Right?

Clients, as well as some advisors, confuse the average return projection with the actual return. The average return that was used to create the thirty-year projection was just that: an average. The actual returns on the S&P 500 came in low during the beginning of that time period. Thus, the portfolio was dragged down by the higher withdrawal rate (8.5 percent) in the initial years even though an *accurate annual average assumption* was made. The blunder is that although we may have a good idea of the average return, we have no idea of the timing of the numbers that make that average possible. Returns are not linear. Portfolios A and B had very different results, even though they had the same average return. The greatest mistake made in retirement planning is the average return blunder. It makes you think that you will get this return in a steady fashion forever.

    I find it quite awesome to see that a mighty S&P 500 index portfolio can fall like a once-proud Goliath, which is what happens when too much

Figure 3.1   Average vs. Actual Returns

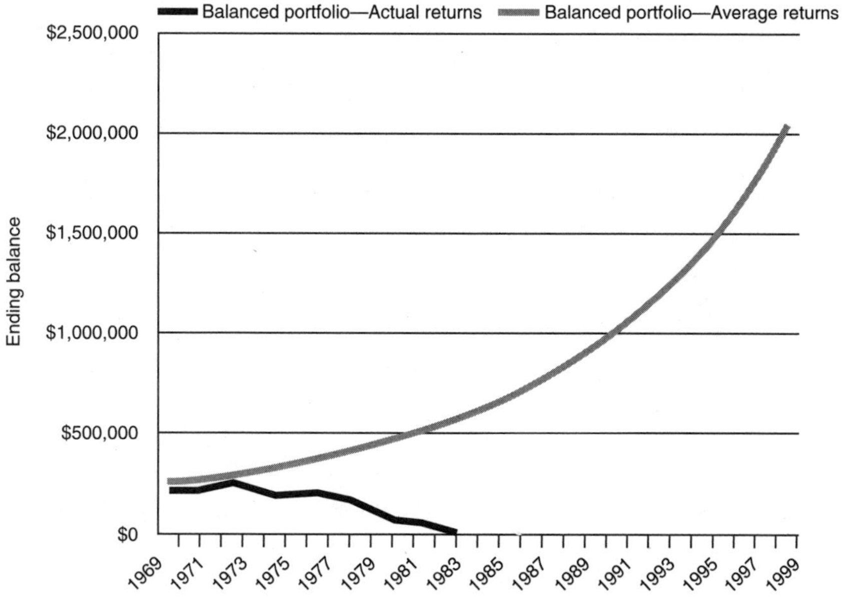

Source: *T. Rowe Price, www.troweprice.com*

is withdrawn because too much is assumed and too much hope is placed on what is unpredictable. I am sure the retiree would have adjusted with some consternation, lowering his withdrawal rate as the account began to fall. Still, much tension could have been avoided by accepting less payout in the beginning, or a payout that was linked to the real return of the portfolio. Even if we hope that the investments will do well, we need to place our bets on realistic estimates. This practice is often hard to follow if one is used to seeing an average return on the S&P 500 of, for example, 18.2 percent, which occurred from 1990 until 1999.

So Easy to Be Fooled

How is it possible that the advisor and the client we discussed earlier could have been made to feel comfortable in choosing a payout of 8.5 percent or even 6 percent? Is it possible that we can be fooled, too? Sure, because our experiences of the recent past can substantially influence our judgments and create a bias that is too optimistic. Following this thought further, I wondered whether the average annual return for the ten-year period just prior to 1968 could have influenced an advisor's projections and the retiree's expectations. My research established that the answer was a resounding yes. From 1957 until 1967, the S&P 500 had an average annual return of 12.81 percent. Was that a surprise! In addition to the average return blunder, which is forward looking, I discovered the *average return bias*, which is backward looking. It goes to show that the advisor and investor could become victims of the times, the investor losing her retirement and the advisor losing an account and maybe his job.

Right from the first draw, the deck was stacked against the 1968 retiree. Not only had the average return assumption not produced results, the past decade became a poor predictor of actual year-to-year returns. Even if good data and a computer were used to generate a hypothetical illustration, that information simply was useless, if not dangerous. The power of the computer to show various scenarios is still somewhat meaningful, but a computer cannot predict the timing of returns. Advisors using such illustrations can mislead clients if they do not caution them about the probability that their assumption can be dramatically off.

Table 3.2 shows how the returns came in during the next fourteen years that caused the retiree to run out of money by the end of 1983 after investing $250,000 in the beginning of 1969.

The average annual noncompounded return during this period was 8.28 percent, which was far below expectations we could have had in the beginning of 1969.

One investor came into my office with an envelope in hand. He shuffled out five different portfolio models and projected returns, all from the

Table 3.2   Large Company Stock Returns

Year	Return	Year	Return
1969	−8.50 percent	1976	23.84 percent
1970	4.01 percent	1977	−7.18 percent
1971	14.31 percent	1978	6.56 percent
1972	18.98 percent	1979	18.44 percent
1973	−14.66 percent	1980	32.42 percent
1974	−26.47 percent	1981	−4.91 percent
1975	37.20 percent	1982	21.41 percent

Source: *Ibbotson, 2001 Yearbook*

same financial consultant. He said, "The advisor told me to choose the one that would suit me best." I asked him, "Is this good retirement planning? Didn't the advisor give you guidance as to the most probable and suitable plan for you? Didn't the advisor give you guidance as to a proper rate of withdrawal so you have a chance of not outliving your income?" The client looked surprised at my simple questions, and then left my office with real questions to ask the advisor. Why pay somebody to spit out illustrations that, in themselves, are insensitive to market turmoil, having beginning and ending dates that are questionable and containing returns that will never be duplicated? Never! This systematic but flawed procedure adds no value to a client's plan. A friend of mine once jokingly asserted, "Let me choose the beginning date and ending date for a hypothetical investment illustration, and I will outperform God."

Investment Proverb 6

The average-return figure for the next twenty years is not as important as when and how much you will withdraw.

The Great Proposal Failure

In the end, many retirement plans will fail for these two basic reasons.

1. Too much emphasis is put on average rate of return found in recent past data.
2. Too often proposals are created to show that a client's wildest dreams can come true.

Consultants should be asking for a client's input into a plan, but should they ask the client to tell them what they think is the most suitable plan? That's like the surgeon asking the patient where to cut. For many people, the big mistake of our time is simulation-based retirement planning that puts little emphasis on the possibility of error and gives little guidance as to the most probable successful outcome. I say to clients, "Use your common sense. If it sounds too good to be true it probably is. Or if it appeals to a little greedy voice down in your soul, then run from the temptation."

Although good advisors never depend on good luck to replace skill, there are times when some retirees can get lucky. For my example, I looked at a twenty-year period from the beginning of 1980 to the end of 1999. If we invested $250,000 into the S&P 500 and withdrew at a rate of 8.5 percent (plus 3 percent increase per year) as T. Rowe had done in their example above, by the year 2000 this account would have been worth $296,173, rather than zero. Examining the same twenty-year period with a withdrawal rate of 6 percent (increasing at a rate of 3 percent per year), by 2000 the $250,000 would have grown to $1,077,908. Rather than running out of money in the fourteenth year or the twenty-seventh year this more recent twenty-year period delivered stunning returns with plenty of money for years ahead and for leaving to charity or to heirs. Even after the major corrections in the market in 2000 and 2001 you would not have lived penniless. While good prevails, there are those unforeseen crises that influence markets throughout the ages. Looking at the events below, ask yourself, Was anyone ready for these shocks?

Event	Number of days until reaction	Loss of Dow Jones
Pearl Harbor, 1941	4	16.5 percent
Korean War, 1950	21	12.0 percent
Cambodia invaded, 1970	27	14.4 percent
Financial panic, 1987	48	34.2 percent
September 11, 2001	7	14.2 percent

In each of these severe declines we suffered both in our hearts and in our pockets, yet in a few years we regained our tranquility and confidence, and the markets returned to prosperity.

Just the Facts, Please

All investors deserve the facts and should not be given puffed-up expectations that can lead to much anxiety and stress. According to Ibbotson Associates, since 1971 through 2000, the S&P 500 had an average annual rate of return of 13.2 percent, Ibbotson Small Company Index did 14.7 percent, and MSC-International EAFE Index did 13.1 percent. In only eight of the past thirty years did the S&P 500 fall below a 6 percent annual return. Yet even with these terrific returns, a 4 percent to 6 percent annual withdrawal may be an appropriate *beginning* withdrawal rate. Some advisors, such as Bill Bengen in El Cajon, California, have argued that even with an optimal stock and bond mix—60 percent large-cap stocks, 40 percent intermediate government bonds—you should begin with a 3.9 percent withdrawal rate the first year (adjusting that rate each year for inflation) so as to not run out of money.

Since 1994 Mr. Bengen has been studying the problem of withdrawal rates versus investment return. More recently, he ran investment scenarios using portfolios ranging in asset allocations of 0, 25, 50, 75, and 100 percent stocks and 100, 75, 50, 25, 0 percent invested in intermediate treasury bonds. These five asset allocations were tested using initial withdrawal rates of 1, 2, 3, 4, 5, 6, 7, and 8 percent the first year. Using actual historical data from 1926 through 1992, he found that an appropriate asset allocation for a retiree's portfolio must include no less than 50 percent (and up to 75 percent) in stocks. He writes, "Stock allocations lower than 50 percent are counterproductive, in that they lower the amount of accumulated wealth as well as lowering the minimum portfolio longevity" (*Journal of Financial Planning*, October 1994, p. 176). Bill admits that such a low initial withdrawal rate, 3.9 percent, may be unacceptable for many people whose number one goal for these assets is to create income during retirement. But since leaving an estate to a spouse (or heirs) is important to most of us, having some assets last a long time is a goal to consider as well. Finding the balance between stocks and bonds and between expected returns and withdrawal rates is the investor's greatest challenge.

Almost all advisors agree that once you start withdrawing, each year you may want to increase the withdrawal percentage by the rate of inflation so that your lifestyle is maintained—unless, of course, your withdrawals are fixed under certain rules that we will discuss in Chapter 7. In a later study done in 2001 for this book, Mr. Bengen used historical market returns and historical inflation to determine his computer inputs for another hypothetical illustration. As you can see in Figure 3.2, making an initial 6 percent withdrawal and adjusting that rate for inflation each year thereafter would give the portfolio a 41 percent chance of lasting forty years. At a 7 percent initial withdrawal rate, plus an adjustment for inflation each year, the portfolio has a 24 percent chance of lasting forty years. Putting it another way, I am sure most retirees would reconsider taking a 7 percent withdrawal, plus an inflation adjustment, if they knew they had a 3 out of 4 chance of outliving their assets.

**Figure 3.2   Probability of Portfolio Lasting Forty Years
                vs. Withdrawal Rates**

*Tax-Deferred. 60% Large-Cap Stocks Fixed, 40% Intermediate-Term
Government Bonds*

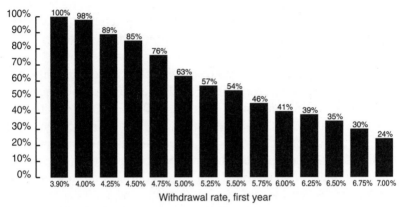

Withdrawal rate, first year

Source: *Bill Bengen, C.F.P., M.S., Bengen Financial Services*

Using good money-management skills, one may increase returns and take a smaller initial withdrawal rate—slightly above 4 percent. The fact that the market has already experienced a large decline in 2000, 2001, and 2002 benefits those who are getting into the market now. On the other hand, since there is no telling how long stock prices will remain low—or if they will go lower—or when they will get too high, timing the market does not give retirees a practical answer. Why? Because people cannot (and do not) time their retirement with the knowledge that it will happen when the market is most favorable.

How much money can one safely withdraw from a well-balanced portfolio? In his book *How to Retire Early and Live Well with Less than a Million Dollars* (2000), Gillette Edmunds writes, "An average, educated, experienced investor can reasonably expect to make 10 percent a year for life." Mr. Bengen would wanly smile at that outrageous percentage, then walk away shaking his head. I arrived at the 5 percent to 6 percent range by studying what foundations and endowment funds pay out annually. For example, Harvard did its own study of the marketplace. These financial academics are what I would call "smart money" people, and they concluded that if one took a payout of 5 percent of the account each year, there would be a 95 percent chance of having principal grow to outpace inflation. Trinity University conducted a study examining and comparing the outcomes of different withdrawal rates from hypothetical portfolios made up of stocks and bonds in which the percent invested in stocks and bonds changed, but the percentages added together always equaled 100 percent. This study found that "at a 6 percent withdrawal rate an investment mix of stocks and bonds outperformed both an all-stock and an all-bond portfolio. And at a 7 percent withdrawal rate, the study found that a 50/50 mix of stocks and bonds outlasted portfolios with higher stock allocations for 20- and 30-year payout periods" (*Bloomberg Wealth Manager*, July 2000, p. 50).

Other more aggressive investment professionals I have spoken with have said a 6 percent (some have said up to 7 percent) withdrawal rate is the highest they would go in order not to outlive income and deplete principal. You may need more, but don't go above 7 percent during the early years if you want to preserve your capital against inflation risk and market risk for the long term. If you go above 6 percent because you retired early, then later, when you begin taking Social Security, you can cut back your withdrawal rate to 2 percent or 3 percent to deplete money more slowly and help maintain your portfolio's longevity. If you are already receiving Social Security, try to maintain a lower (2 percent to 4 percent) withdrawal rate to offset the possibility of poor investment returns. It was reported in May 2001 that Warren Buffet, a legendary investor on Wall Street, said the stock market over the next fifteen years can produce between 6 percent and 7 percent annually. He said that anyone expecting to make 15 percent from the market or by having a broker pick stocks is living in a dream world (*The Motley Fool*, May 28, 2001). Does his expectation make sense?

Figure 3.3 is based on Dr. Jeremy Siegel's work in his book *Stocks for the Long Run* (McGraw-Hill). Shaun Smith, working for Dr. Siegel, updated the data and created a graph to reflect recent market changes. I duplicated his graph to demonstrate the *after-inflation* return on stocks (the top line) from 1802 until December 1, 2001. If you plot points along the solid line to represent the long trend in inflation-adjusted return and then calculate the return of that line, you will find that the average *real return* is about 6.5 percent. (To clarify *real return*: if a stock return is 10 percent and inflation is 4 percent in one year, then the real return is 6 percent [10 percent − 4 percent].) By comparing this real return to the *risk premium* of equities (annual stock market return less the treasury bill rate during the past seventy years), you find the same number! Roger C. Gibson, one of the most respected experts in money management, writes, "The historical equity risk premium of 6.5 percent is a reasonable estimate of what the equity risk premium should be. This has been the historical reward received for bearing risk, based on a long time horizon encompassing periods of both war and peace, economic expansions and contractions, high and low inflation . . . and so on" (*Simple Asset Allocation Strategies*, p. 32). After deducting the loss of money to the hidden thief—inflation—the money invested in stocks returned a *real* return. Getting 6.5 percent (an excess return) above inflation allows you to spend real money and keep up with the general cost of living. *After subtracting inflation from the return on CDs, the real return is near zero and after taxes is negative.* Although you have less volatility in CDs than you have in equities, you have little chance to grow income and protect principal. In Figure 3.3 we see that $1 invested in stocks in 1802 would have grown to $566,270 adjusted for inflation. A dollar invested in bonds, adjusted for inflation, would have grown to $956, and so on. The original investment of $1, adjusted for inflation, left in a mattress would be .067 cents! This is proof that beating inflation should be every long-living retiree's concern.

Figure 3.3   Total Real Return Indices 1802–2001

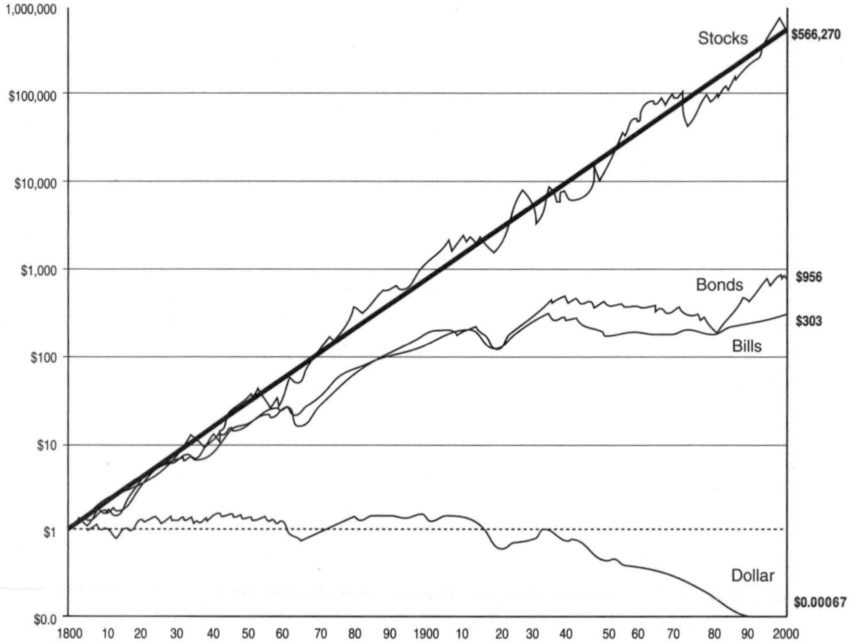

Source: *Dr. Jeremy J. Siegel*

Other endowment funds have payouts of 4 percent of the *previous* year's account value. These experts *plan* for one truism: what happens if people stop giving? Well, when you are retired, *you* have stopped giving. *Your retirement plan becomes your personal endowment and should be managed like one.* If you want to leave a portion to your children or to charity, and be sure you do not outlive your income, then you need to have a reasonable money-management strategy in place. Our goals should be shaped not only by our wants (which must take second place to our needs), but also by an honest assessment of the marketplace.

Investment Proverb 7

Setting a sound investment policy with a reasonable withdrawal rate will create a high probability of long-term success for any retirement plan.

Some could ask whether it would be wiser just to invest in safe, high-yield places like bank CDs, bonds, or fixed annuities, avoiding the risks of the stock market. A retiree should think about allocating more than 60 percent into fixed-income securities or CDs only if she is averse to volatility and does not need to take more than 2 percent to 3 percent out of a plan per year. For most retirees, at least 40 percent in equities for growth is essential; some say even more is needed. When I speak of equities, I do not mean speculative trading in stocks. That is not ownership; that is gambling. My personal opinion is that the stock ownership portion should be placed into a well-balanced, professionally managed portfolio. Prudently, some of that portfolio could be allocated to small- to medium-sized companies chosen by a fund or money manager.

Comparing Performance

To illustrate the drawbacks of fixed-income investing and explain why CFOs do not invest 100 percent in CDs or bonds when running endowment funds, allow me to make a simplified but powerful comparison. This information is not meant to sell you on a plan, but to illustrate that equity ownership is more productive in the long run than lending your money for a fixed return. During a twenty-year period—January 31, 1980, to December 31, 1999—let's suppose we met three retirees: Denny, Penny, and Henny. Each had placed money into three distinctly different portfolios. Although none did the asset allocation that I would have recommended, let's say they each started with a $250,000 investment.

Each had the same goal of removing 6 percent of the account value at the end of the year, no matter what the account was worth. I have listed below first-, fifth-, tenth-, fifteenth-, and twentieth-year withdrawals. Denny's *all-CD portfolio* value each year is also calculated to show year-end balances. I did the same for Penny, who had invested into an *all-bonds portfolio*, and Henny, who had invested into an *all-stock portfolio*. The dollars withdrawn at the rate of 6 percent of the year-end account value will grow only if the account grows from year to year. This arrangement is not the same as taking 6 percent plus a boost of 3 percent of that figure each year, as was done in the T. Rowe Price study discussed earlier. Taking 6 percent of the account is closer to what endowments draw, and in most years that draw will be higher than the draw of the previous year because of the growth of the account.

	Denny's withdrawals	Penny's withdrawals	Henny's withdrawals
Year 1	$16,943	$14,609	$19,899
Year 5	$20,841	$20,980	$22,725
Year 10	$22,206	$30,244	$39,956
Year 15	$20,998	$45,342	$45,342
Year 20	$29,238	$37,542	$109,688
Ending value	$317,057	$588,162	$1,718,915

This illustration should begin to make it obvious why every responsible pension fund owns stocks. Henny ended up with *five times* more than Denny, and more than three times the income. No pension fund that has a fiduciary responsibility to workers owns all bonds or all CDs or all stocks, but some combination of the three. Yet how many of us take the pension fund distribution and roll over these assets into an undiversified portfolio of stocks or bonds or CDs (or treasuries)? This mix would be acceptable only if Denny and Penny were married, and Henny were their live-in son, and they combined their portfolios. Keeping it simple, the household's investment balance (or asset allocation) and time horizon could justify the mix, with Henny having the longest time horizon and the greatest risk tolerance, seeing that he most likely will inherit the fortunes of his parents.

One caution: these were twenty mostly favorable stock market years, unlike what occurred in the T. Rowe example from 1968 to 1999. As well, the results are better when we take a *fixed percentage* of the account annually, rather than a steady, growing percentage of the account, as was done in T. Rowe's example.

We will get into diversification later, but for now the idea of allocating money to different asset classes, especially stocks, is a fundamental one that has been tested and used by the largest money managers. It is the stock portion that has the most potential to increase income, but it can also sustain greater losses in any single year. The CDs and bonds bring in steady income, but the riskier bonds do somewhat better than CDs to grow income and principal over long periods of time. A reliable money-management program with a combination of cash, bonds, and stocks should truly become the golden goose of your golden years. Investors are paid to own the risky asset class—stocks. They are paid well, because they are willing to accept the volatile nature of equities. Bonds do better than cash, but less than stocks, over the long run. The cash owners had little market risk, but pay for it with little growth of principal to offset inflation.

You Can Bet on Yourself

In the era of the do-it-yourself and self-management, security selection is not as simple as going to Home Depot to pick out garden plants. One needs to be objective (disinterested, even) about money in order to manage it best. Many times the investor must go out on a limb to pick the fruit, and unless a person is well trained and doing constant research he or she will not have the courage and wisdom to make quick moves to buy or sell. With new Internet services arriving, there is some expert advice to be found on the Web, but it does not have the human touch that retired clients enjoy.

Psychologists and priests know that people like to hash things out with people, not machines. Neuwirth Research, Inc., of New York reported that 72 percent of people surfing the Internet for financial advice still use a professional advisor. When money becomes a significant asset, most of us need a significant other. Like an endowment fund CFO, you can hire a financial advisor to help you strategically allocate your assets, develop an investment policy, and then monitor and review your investments in a timely fashion.

Investment Proverb 8

Without consultation, plans are frustrated, but with many counselors they succeed.
(PROVERBS 15:22, NEW AMERICAN STANDARD BIBLE)

From the examples we've discussed, one thing should now be clear: *By taking a fixed percentage of the portfolio, the retiree will get an increase in income as the value of the portfolio rises.* So if you take 6 percent per year, and your portfolio rises 10 percent, the following year you are going to take 6 percent more money than the year before, which offsets inflation. That is, if you are worth $500,000, then 6 percent is $30,000. If the $500,000 grows 10 percent, the portfolio value is now $550,000, so 6 percent is $33,000. Although the percent withdrawn remains the same, your income goes up as your wealth goes up. If your wealth falls, then take a fixed *minimum* that will not stress the account in a bad year—possibly 4 percent. You need to work out this percentage with your advisor. For people over fifty-nine and a half and younger than seventy-one, this method is a good one to discuss with your advisor. Whether you begin with 5 percent or 6 percent, if your portfolio doubles in seven years, your income will double too. For retirees under fifty-five, a fixed dollar amount may be required to escape the 10 percent penalty rule. Setting the fixed rate is a critical decision that we will discuss in Chapter 7.

After one turns seventy and a half there are important rules regarding minimum withdrawal rates that may exceed the percentage you are taking, but when you *must* begin to draw more there are easy ways of saving part of this income for later use. You may even use this income for funding trusts or for protecting the estate with insurance.

A sacred bond exists between client and advisor. An advisor should not be fabricating returns or creating illustrations that may mislead the retiree regarding what can be expected. An advisor makes a commitment to serve the client in good faith and with the highest ethical standards, putting the client's best interest first. Although there are many new Internet services arriving, this highly personal advisor-client relationship cannot be replaced. Actually, the Internet is used as a tool by many advisors to better their delivery of services.

A good advisor will look beyond historical numbers and help clients form unbiased and accurate return expectations. With a sound withdrawal plan, a client will not go through emotional turmoil during a financial crisis. When there is a lot at stake, such as your financial future, it takes a strong will to keep reason and emotions in a calm state. Human nature does not change when it ponders the complexity and seriousness of producing years of income from retirement assets. We all can admit that sometimes things can get scary, but we need not give it legs.

C H A P T E R

How to Improve Your Money-Management Decisions

"If you don't know where you're going, you'll wind up somewhere else."

—YOGI BERRA

On the eve of writing this chapter I got a call from my alma mater, Syracuse University. The young woman explained that the college had decided to create a "permanent scholarship fund for senior honor students." SU wanted to "endow" the money, so as never to go back to the alumni and ask for more funds. The money would earn enough each year to give out scholarships perennially. This call reminded me that I am going in the right direction with this book. The university's plan is not so different from what most of my retirees want—if not now, then in a few years. Isn't the university's goal very similar to that of a person who does not (or cannot) go back to the workplace in order to ask for more retirement money? Doesn't the retiree want to spend money each year in perpetuity? Neither the university nor the retiree wants to run out of money! So strikingly similar are the investment objectives of the retiree and the endowment that the *process and method* that universities use to manage money could be applied to the management of 401(k)s, rollover IRAs, and so on.

Other books and articles contend that retirees should adapt an endowment fund management style for their money. A top columnist and money manager recently wrote a book that has received high praise for its commonsense approach to managing retirement money in this way. In one chapter the author reiterates that foundations, like the Ford Foundation, plan to withdraw a small percentage each year as endowments often do. Although implying that these foundations buy mostly stock funds, the book does not show what asset classes foundations typically own. That is no small loss to the reader. There is no explanation of the *process* by which the CFO or CIO of the Ford Foundation (or any foundation, for that matter) creates an investment policy or what asset classes it owns. (In fact, a call in the beginning of 2003 to Linda Strumpf, CIO of the Ford Foundation, revealed that she has 36 percent invested in U.S. equities, 14 percent in international equities, 11 percent in private equities, and 39 percent in fixed income.) In the book there is no hint as to how the foundation hires and monitors the money managers who make many of the investment decisions. The book goes on to say that the average retiree can easily make investments without professional help by developing his or her own simple strategies. This way of thinking is quite contrary to procedures that endowments take to make consistent returns. Not only do endowments spend time analyzing risk/reward assumptions, but they also have an investment committee that sets diversification policy and hires and monitors money manager returns.

What Is the Process That Endowments Use?

Because endowments have a fiduciary responsibility to set investment objectives and then take the least amount of risk to obtain those objectives, the trustees first embark on a search for the correct mix of investments. That is, they first create the best *asset allocation plan* (or *strategic asset allocation plan*). The Uniform Prudent Investors Act has made the fiduciary responsible to document the process taken for the proper diversification of a portfolio. However, if they do not meticulously take this step, they might later be sued for breach of trustee duties. It is this systematic investment process that guides the trustees in defining suitable investments for the fund. No investment is made until the planning is finalized. That is, before buying any stocks or bonds, they determine the limits of their exposure to risk, find an acceptable target rate of return that meets their needs, and create a well-formed investment plan that will be reviewed yearly—if not more often during unusual economic events. Much like blueprints of a house, the plan lays out the structure that, if followed, will aim for the highest probable rate of return at the least risk.

At an investment seminar I taught in the beginning of 2000, an ex-engineer raised his hand and said, "I just left all my 401(k) with Fidelity and forgot about it." It is quite common that people stay where they are planted, and there is nothing wrong with that if they monitor their accounts closely and their money managers are doing an acceptable job. It is another matter if they are offered only a few investment choices or their fund managers begin to change their investment philosophy. Unknown to this ex-engineer, one survey done by the Financial Research Corporation (reported in the *Journal of Financial Planning* in May 2000) found that although Fidelity Distributions was ranked second by individual respondents (the public) for one-year performance in managing funds, the company was ranked thirty-fifth in actual performance. The survey found that for many funds, reality differed from public perception. The advertisement media can create favorable perceptions of any investment firm or strategy. (Look at the online trading commercials that were castigated by the Securities and Exchange Commission in the summer of 2000.) Therefore, what the ex-engineer owns may not be what he thinks he owns. Sure, some of the Fidelity funds are suitable for his retirement plan. They have had some terrific managers, including Peter Lynch, who ran the Magellan Fund (now run by the highly skilled Robert Stansky). But the financial advisor must ask herself, Which funds make the best fit into a client's asset allocation plan? Which asset classes do they fill? Are there investments that can do better? Remember that the provider of your 401(k) or 403(b) will not call you to say, "Now is the time to buy growth fund A and sell growth fund B." They leave that decision up to you! Then again, your 401(k) plan may offer only one growth fund. On the other hand, if you are offered two or more growth funds, do you know the differences? No money manager is identical to another. Whatever the case, you can see why people move money to rollover IRAs—they can have more choices within each asset class and get help with making those choices.

Owning More than One Fund Reduces Risk

Let's suppose you own $100,000 of Top Growth fund, which dropped by 50 percent in one year. Your loss was $50,000. Now imagine instead that you owned five funds you had invested equally in; obviously, your risk exposure with each fund is lowered (compared to the risk of owning one fund). In our example, suppose only $20,000 was invested in the same Top Growth fund, and the remaining went into the other four funds. If a decline of 50 percent occurred in the Top Growth fund, the account would have fallen 10 percent, or $10,000, rather than 50 percent. This shows how important it is to look at the *weight* of each investment within a portfolio. The calculation here is:

$$\text{Investment value} \div \text{total portfolio value} = \text{weight}$$

If you have a $20,000 fund as part of your $100,000 portfolio, the calculation would look like this:

$$\$20,000 \div \$100,000 = 0.2 = 20 \text{ percent weight}$$

You may think you are well diversified, but if you do not do the weighting calculations you cannot be certain whether you own too much of something. Too often people think that diversification simply means *the greater number of investments, the better*. As you can see, without a weighting calculation you can own too much of any one investment. At some point, that can be dangerous.

A new house is the product of many important decisions, and so too is your portfolio structure. First you select blueprints, and then building materials that will create a house that can weather the storms of uncertainty and change. When you have a portfolio, the question to ask is, "How did you arrive at these investment choices?" Just like an endowment fund CFO, a good financial advisor can spend hours telling you about the process he uses to pick the portfolio for you. This important process is the reason we can ask for a commission or a fee for the work that needs to be done. It is work not much different from that of a carpenter selecting the proper size and grade of lumber. It is qualitative and quantitative. The results will strongly depend on the effort set forth. Using experience, knowledge, research, wisdom, and intuition, the advisor can put you on the threshold of a successful investment plan. Like the homeowner, your input as the client is necessary, and you do not need to be a financial wizard to be part of the team. Your advisor will walk you through the process to get you to the properly diversified portfolio mix.

Although the idea of diversification is not a new one, many people tend to think that it is easy to accomplish. One might say it offers more than the cliché "Don't put all your eggs in one basket." Many investors think that because they own seven different mutual funds or CDs, they are getting enough diversification. In truth, they may own one asset class, and that one may do very well in one or two given years, but not every year and not forever. Your attempt at diversification breaks down if the mutual funds you want to buy have similar characteristics to other securities you already own. You may own six funds, but all can have large positions in the same stocks, and that is not diversification.

One diversification tool to consider is a *large value style discipline.* When a mutual fund buys primarily stocks of companies that have financial problems, or are out of favor with investors, with the expectation that these stocks will increase in value, that fund is described as a value fund. *Large value* means the stocks will be chosen from the largest publicly traded companies—such as those making up the S&P 500—at exclusion of smaller stocks. *Style discipline* means the manager will use a particular, well-defined analytical process to pick stocks from the values he or she finds in the market.

One client told me, "My sister owns six funds, and none made money in 2000." I had counseled her sister about proper diversification, suggesting she switch some of her funds to a large value style discipline to complement her other growth-style holdings, but she didn't take my advice. By the end of 2000, the sister was calling her fund company twice a day to check the value of her account. Since funds are priced only once a day, the second call did nothing more than confirm the truth, further shaking her faith in the safety of her principal.

The essence of asset allocation is that every asset class brings its own risk and reward (that is, investment opportunity), and as you limit your exposure to investments you begin to set limits on opportunities.

Investment Proverb 9

Four things never come back: the spoken word, the spent arrow, the past life, and the neglected opportunity.

(ARAB PROVERB)

Note that you need not own investments in every asset class. For example, good ideas are not to be found just in large growth companies. When bonds are paying high yields, that's not the only place to look.

Setting Return Expectations and Standard Deviations

Before you begin your first step toward diversification, a financial advisor has some work to do. Before you visit her office, the advisor has examined the historical data of many investments and looked at the current economy in order to peer into the veiled future. That is, she has investigated different asset classes and created risk and return assumptions about these asset classes. You should not expect perfection—no one can be 100 percent certain about the future—but there is a quantitative percentage of expected return and a risk factor that is given to various asset classes, depending on the advisor and the firm. Avoid a financial advisor who finds it easy to give up on this difficult work or who does not do it at all—for example, one who recommends laddered CDs or bond portfolios (investing in a portfolio of fixed-income securities that mature in stages, for example, one-year, three-year, five-year, seven-year, and ten-year CDs) for everyone, or a 100 percent equity index portfolio, no matter what your goals. Just as everyone does not live in the same type of house, you have unique life income needs, and your advisor must construct a plan tailored to those needs. Although many novice investors base investment decisions on wishful thinking, you are going to an advisor for something worth more than that.

The endowment fund manager with investment acumen and objectivity first estimates the long-term average returns expected for each asset class. For example, large capitalized companies, such as those in the S&P 500, may be given a 9 percent average return projection over the next five to ten years. Corporate bonds may be given a 6.5 percent return projection, and CDs 5 percent. Most take this work further and break down stocks into seven asset classes. They assign a risk factor known as a *standard deviation* to each asset class they use so that they have a firm foundation to build a portfolio on. In general, the higher the return expectation, the higher the standard deviation. Thus, statistically one can say that in any one year, a large-cap growth fund with an expected average return of 12 percent and a standard deviation of 17.8 percent has a 95 percent chance of returning somewhere between the following:

12 percent − 2 standard deviations (2 × 17.8 percent) = −23.6 percent return

or

12 percent + 2 standard deviations (2 × 17.8 percent) = +47.6 percent return

Note that, in general, the higher the return expectation, the higher the risk factor. Don't you just love statistics? They can make a blue sky in August look cold.

In Table 4.1 below are examples of returns expected on asset classes and their risk factors.

One can add other asset classes, such as high-yield bonds, private equity (risky venture capital investments), foreign bonds, mortgage-backed securities, and so on. The point is, there is a meaningful and disciplined approach to building a portfolio in a professional manner. This investment process has been evolving in the past thirty years, and technology has refined it in the past five years. The risk factor (standard deviation of returns) and how closely these asset classes track with one another are

Table 4.1   Expected Returns and Standard Deviation per Asset Class

Asset classes	Future return expectation	Risk factor*
Large-growth stocks	9.0 percent	17.8 percent
Large-value stocks	9.7 percent	14.0 percent
Midsized value stocks	11.0 percent	18.0 percent
Midsized growth stocks	10.5 percent	17.5 percent
Small-growth stocks	10.8 percent	24.0 percent
Small-value stocks	12.1 percent	21.0 percent
Foreign stocks	10.1 percent	15.5 percent
Corporate bonds	6.5 percent	6.0 percent
U.S. treasury bonds	5.5 percent	5.0 percent
Cash and short-term CDs	2.0 percent	1.0 percent

*The standard deviation is called the risk factor.

Note: *These figures are based on my assumptions for the long term. The numbers are used for illustration purposes only, may change annually, and differ among advisors. Many experts today feel that the expected returns on stocks listed in this table are much too high—see the November 6, 1999, edition of* Fortune, *where well-known stock picker Warren Buffett forecasts the long-term return on stocks to be 6 percent per year.*

meaningful to the professional in calculating the correct mix of investments, giving the proper weight to each. Like a carpenter's specialty saws and planes, these investment tools are not so easily used by the do-it-yourself investor. On the other hand, an investor with a CFO frame of mind can work with advisors who will explain and use these statistics as a means of constructing model portfolios.

Only Time Will Tell

Clients ask, "Why not buy all corporate bonds, if the risk factor is so low and the yield is good?" Or, "Why not buy all CDs when there is no chance of losing money, especially retirement money?" "Good questions," I say. And the answer lies in the next stage of the investment process, which starts with more questions: "How long is your life? Your spouse's life? Your children's lives?" Since it is against our nature to say, "My time horizon is short," most new, healthy retirees should have a long-term outlook of at least thirty years or more of life to be lived. (Now that I am fifty-three, middle age is no longer forty-five, but fifty-five—and moving upward. Then again, maybe I am biased.) Looking for the *time horizon*, we ask how long this money will need to last, producing a growing income to offset inflation. A study by the Forum for Investor Advice found that 62 percent of retirees want to leave money to their spouse. But how could one do this if his advisor has set up programs that will run out of assets at age ninety-five? Will your spouse need more income thirty or forty years from now? Do you want to leave something to charity or children? In most cases, the answer to these questions is yes. If you have no spouse or children, then your time horizon is your own life, but even that time period, in most cases, is unpredictable. Then there are people who want to go out of this life, as one fellow told me, "without a gallon of gas left in the tank."

So the retired person who keeps his entire 401(k) plan in company stock, rather than getting counsel and learning to diversify, must ask himself the following questions:

- Is my company going to outperform other asset classes over my time horizon?
- Is my stock more volatile (risky) than that of other companies?
- Is my company going to find every opportunity that exists to grow?

- If I need money, and the company stock is down, will I sell it at a loss?
- If I leave it to my spouse, will she feel sentimentally attached to the stock?

People planning to retire should begin creating an investment strategy that includes their company stock. Once retired, a person's best approach is to ask questions that force her into making hard choices. Employers do not provide employees with much education regarding the management of 401(k)s, and when it comes to company stock they would rather see you own more than less. One client was approached by his firm and was asked to buy another $25,000 in company stock in his 401(k). He did not buy it. Within a few months the stock declined 50 percent; his decision saved him $12,500. Most recently, a Senate subcommittee began investigating Enron Corporation, a major gas pipeline, which filed for bankruptcy in 2001. The major complaints against Enron so far have come from retirees who invested large portions of their retirement money in company stock. Their complaint is that at the same time many corporate officers were touting their company's future and encouraging employee stock ownership, the insiders were selling their own stock. One retiree on the Senate panel who lost $1.3 million blames the company for having misguided him.

I am not discouraging ownership of the company you work for, but there are good reasons to have someone give you an objective opinion as to how much to own and when to sell. When to exercise stock options purchased in an employee stock option plan (ESOP) is another difficult financial decision with investment and tax ramifications. With ESOP, stock investors can be greatly assisted by professionals who specialize in these matters. Without help, employees may lose money they did not know they had by allowing valuable options to expire worthless.

Do You Have Investment Experience?

Because your employer selects the investments to place within your 401(k), many employees must choose from a limited number of funds. If you are in that situation, you can request that your company offer more investment options. On the other hand, some employer 401(k)s give you no selection whatsoever; in that case, your money is pooled into one account and managed by one firm, and you have no say. Such plans do not allow the investors to learn how to make security selections. I find that most investments chosen outside of retirement plans are bought with little due diligence or research on the investors' part. Thus, the lack of investment education in the workplace spills over into the marketplace, where people scramble for the newest money magazine. Whether it is retirement money or other savings, investments often are made after one reads a magazine or watches a television commercial without personally researching how well the investments fit into the personal overall asset mix. While working you might get away with haphazard investing, but once retired a better approach is to ask questions that force you into making hard choices. Some examples include, What asset class can bring income to my portfolio? What asset classes do I need to complement what I already own? What asset classes can outperform inflation? When you were working you did not care about stable income; your clarion call was "Growth, growth, growth." Concerns change at retirement. The older you get, the more your eyes begin to focus on preservation of income and principal or growth of principal, but with lower risk. For decades endowments have been eyeing the concept of preservation of capital and growth of income; and, like them, you can't afford to lose all you have. Endowments have concluded that in the marketplace lie many investment opportunities. With a proper asset allocation mix and a good stock and bond picking discipline they have found that stable returns can be made that far exceed investing in bank CDs. You may want to take their cue.

Why Asset Allocation Works So Well

Studies have shown that there is no perfect correlation between two different asset classes. Stocks of large companies do not move in lockstep with stocks of small companies. Bonds do not move at the same time as stocks. Therefore a portfolio with one asset class will not behave the same as a portfolio with two or three asset classes. In Figure 4.1 we see real returns on stocks, bonds, and treasury bills for the year 2000. Note that the returns vary widely. Contrast those returns with the returns on the same three asset classes in 1999 in Figure 4.2 and you see yet another picture.

The closer we look, the more obvious it becomes that one asset class can complement another, and the greater the number of asset classes that are not closely correlated, the better. I like the metaphor of the eight-cylinder engine. You get a smoother ride with a V-8, because as one cylinder is coming down another is on its way up, while another is bottoming out, and so on. In Figure 4.3, the 50 percent stock/50 percent bond line shows a steadier return compared with the 100 percent stock line or 100 percent bond line. "Poor performance in one investment can be offset by good performance in another," writes Frontier Analytics, a leading firm in asset allocation, regarding this graph. Add more asset classes and you may further reduce volatility. More does not necessarily mean better; so the added value of an advisor is to achieve the right mix.

Still, much of the work regarding proper diversification is based on academic studies. This is called *modern portfolio theory (MPT)*. One of the important assumptions MPT is built on may also be called the *butterfly effect*. It suggests that there is an interaction of all things, so that a butterfly flapping its wings in Florida affects, if only in a small way, the air in New York and California. If there is an interaction among assets, and if there is a way of putting this interactive denominator to work in portfolio design, then we may be able to develop a plan that is less risky than the portfolio's riskiest asset. Strange as it may seem, we may get a free lunch. At the same time, we may produce more return than cash, short-term bonds, or CDs, which are highly predictable assets but have poor long-term results. When securities get into oversupply in one sector of the economy, money begins to move to another sector or asset class that has less supply. When securities go down because few people find them attractive, they eventually become cheap enough to begin to attract bargain hunters willing to take the risk of owning what others do not want. Although we do not know when and where money will move next, diversification helps keep us invested

Figure 4.1 Total Real Return Indices: Stocks, Bonds, T-Bills 2000

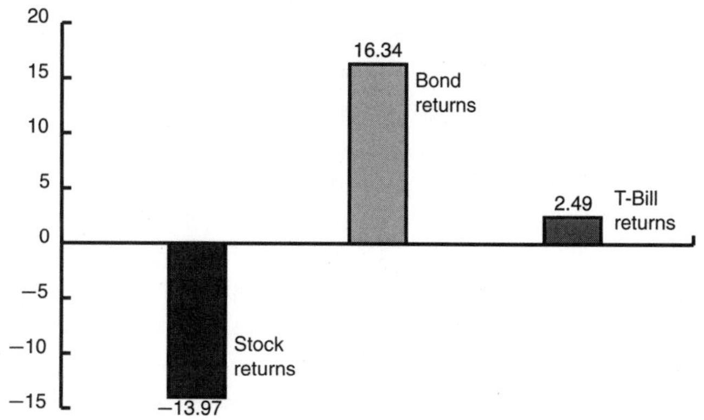

Source: *Dr. Jeremy J. Siegel*

Figure 4.2   Total Real Return Indices: Stocks, Bonds, T-Bills 1999

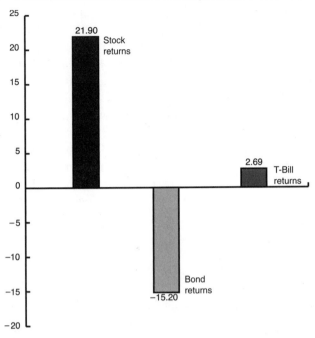

Source: *Dr. Jeremy J. Siegel*

without having to guess or to think wishfully. No carpenter in his right mind would avoid putting a beam under a weight-bearing wall, but wishful thinkers do that sort of thing when they fail to diversify.

Moreover, we are not afraid to look for opportunities in riskier and unlikely places, because we have made less risky investments to complement our aggressive ones. We try to identify how closely the asset classes move (or do not move) in lockstep with each other (known as *correlation*). The less correlated two asset classes seem to be, the greater the likelihood that owning both assets classes in one account will reduce swings in the total value of that account. If you own two asset classes that are perfectly positively correlated, then there is no diversification and no reduction in portfolio volatility. "Do you mean to buy high-tech stocks in our low-risk retirement account?" you might ask. Possibly, I say, because some risk can be diversified away by owning an asset that is not perfectly correlated with high-tech stocks. A good plan, then, would suggest that high-tech stocks mixed with less volatile equities and bonds could create growth without adding a lot of extra risk.

Figure 4.3   Combining Investments Creates Stability

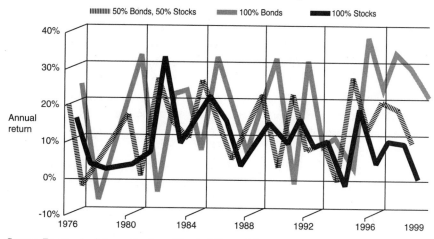

Source: *Frontier Analytics, a division of Sungard Expert Solutions*

One bewildered investor said to me, "It seems like after several good years of a market that favors growth stocks, I buy more and more of these stocks. The longer the trend lasts, the more I buy. Then I wind up with all my assets in growth stocks, only to see the whole thing collapse when growth falls out of favor." A common blunder, I may add. I experienced this personally. Looking back, I see it as my greatest error. I experienced terrific returns from small company stocks versus large, and then over several years I ended up with 90 percent of my portfolio invested in small companies at the top of the market. I erred this way with foreign investments as well. Healthy *planned diversification* sets up an investment discipline so as to rein in our greedy ambitions, leaving us with a portfolio that does not drift out of balance. You will find that proper asset allocation—better known as diversification—will be the primary goal in building a sound portfolio.

What Can Be Learned from Fiduciaries?

Any fiduciary is not considered a good advisor unless she considers how each investment interacts with the total portfolio, placing a secondary consideration on the risk and reward of its individual parts. The Uniform Prudent Investors Act guides fiduciaries in their responsibility in the

management of trusts, including endowment funds. Trust officers managing pension plans follow guidelines as well. The Department of Labor (with
the guidance of the Employee Retirement Income Security Act, ERISA)
wants to see diversification meet the time horizon, market risk, and inflation risk of employees. If you examine how pension funds are managed and
diversified, you will see a similar asset allocation strategy as found among
endowment funds and foundations. If you think more like a CFO, who is
given the fiduciary responsibility to oversee someone else's money, you
will become more objective and more successful in managing your own
retirement dollars.

So let's look at the way two endowment funds have allocated their
money so as to take advantage of the various markets. Note here that they
have a *risk tolerance* that is unique to each, as it is to each retiree. It is this
factor in the investment strategy that is hard to quantify for both the retiree
and advisor. An example of a risk question is, "How comfortable would you
be if your retirement portfolio went down 15 percent in one year?" More
specifically, "If your $500,000 dropped $75,000 in three months, would you
feel a lot of anxiety?" I have watched some people's eyes squint and their
brows furrow with fear. They have a low risk tolerance. Everyone wants to
make abnormal returns at no risk, and that is like fitting a square peg into
a round hole.

Investment Proverb 10

*People do not plan to fail but fail to make a
coherent investment plan.*

When clients come to me with a 401(k) and several IRAs, I begin by
asking whether they want to combine the retirement plans into one analysis or to create an asset allocation plan with the funds in only one account.
Some people have enough money from other sources and do not need
income from the funds they want us to manage. A plan review can include
their total assets or a portion of the assets. Those assets that are to be placed
under our guidance may be put in one asset class to *complement* what they

already own. That is, if they own many growth stocks or growth funds, then they may want to buy bonds in their account with us. I find that one could split 401(k) and pension money into two rollover IRAs and then manage them as if they were one portfolio. This choice would mean that one rollover account would hold part of their total assets and a second rollover would hold the remaining. It is, I believe, simpler for reporting and analysis purposes to have all retirement assets in one account. The asset allocation program is more easily implemented; and, more important, fees can often be reduced when larger amounts are placed into one program. (The Economic Growth and Tax Reconciliation Act of 2001 has brought many beneficial changes. Under the new law you can comingle your IRAs and still be able to roll over tax-free these dollars into employer-sponsored plans such as 401(k), 403(b), or 457 plans at a later date. Most of my retired clients *do not* intend to have another retirement plan, so they roll over *all assets* into an IRA, and we call it a rollover IRA.)

How Do Endowments Allocate?

Comparing how an Ivy League college endowment, a church endowment fund, and a multibillion-dollar pension fund are invested will help us see how our own investment strategy can be designed. These plans are shown for illustration purposes only and should not be confused with a recommendation or verification of anyone's own asset allocation plan. Each individual's retirement plan must go through the same rigorous process as the one that universities take. There should not be a casual or impulsive purchase of a stock if you employ the process endowments take to invest money. One mistake I used to make, which you can learn from, was to buy a stock before pinpointing which asset class it belonged to. It took me a long time to learn not to buy a stock or a fund until I ascertained where it fits into the larger scheme of things. Buying a stock or a fund is an *investment decision* and not an *investment management decision*. The latter comes first, because it is step one of the original planning process that leads to a well-balanced portfolio. Once per year the endowments will review the *weightings* of the asset classes and whether rebalancing assets is called for. Here are two examples, which include the percentage of the portfolio invested in each asset class:

Ivy League College Endowment Fund

Percentage	Asset class allocation
24 percent	Domestic stocks
15 percent	Foreign stocks
9 percent	Emerging markets
3 percent	High-yield bonds
6 percent	Commodities
7 percent	Real estate
12 percent	Private stock
10 percent	U.S. bonds
4 percent	Foreign bonds
6 percent	Guaranteed investments
4 percent	Cash

Church Endowment Fund

Percentage	Asset class allocation
12.5 percent	Large-cap growth
12.5 percent	Large-cap value
12.5 percent	Mid-cap growth
12.5 percent	Mid-cap value
20.0 percent	Foreign stocks
15.0 percent	U.S. corporate bonds
15.0 percent	Foreign bonds

Corporate Pension Fund

Percentage	Asset class allocation
17 percent	Common and preferred stock
24 percent	S&P 500 index
11 percent	Foreign stocks
15 percent	Corporate bonds
14 percent	Real estate and private equity
19 percent	Cash and U.S. treasury bonds

Once you know where your money is allocated, you can be calm in times of turmoil. The Japanese saying "When you're dying of thirst it's too late to dig a well" helps visualize the concept. When the market is down, it is never easy to raise cash. Yet in a well-balanced portfolio, you can justify why you are partially invested in cash or short-term securities. Looking at how the total portfolio could behave in different economic situations shows that cash adds liquidity, reduces risk, and can be opportunity money. Since you have agreed to take a calculated risk, you are comfortable owning what you have. Staying balanced will prevent you from taking positions in equities that are tempting but may be overvalued. It will be easier to buy something that has come down in price or has had a poor performance (because it was out of favor) but remains an attractive company or well-managed fund. It will be easier to sell high when the value of an asset outweighs its assigned weight in the portfolio. You will have a sense of peace when money is managed with this method. You will have what I call a "peaceful portfolio." Would an active retiree want anything more?

All people tell me they are interested in buying low and selling high. But they do not follow through with this claim. They tend to criticize the equities that have gone down and buy more of the equities that have gone up. Several of my clients in the beginning of 1999 said, "My international funds are terrible. Sell me out." Of course, they missed the best run in that asset class in many years.

Investment Proverb 11

To buy low and sell high takes cool self-discipline; a plan tempers fear and greed.

Stop Trying to Predict the Market

At the end of 1999 I visited an investment club as a guest speaker. After explaining asset allocation, I had a feeling that they had missed what I was saying, because most of them were falling asleep when I spoke about buying stocks that were out of favor. Because the members seemed very pleased with the way their portfolio had grown quickly, I sensed that it was loaded with large-growth stocks. Certainly these people did not *need* to hear the words like *value* or *small company* as these terms referred to stocks in which they had seen no recent success. I was a bore. I had explained to them a way to discipline their buying habits, but they knew better. "Look at your stocks," I suggested, "and assign each to an asset class, then, as you take profits, reallocate the money to asset classes you do not own." I could see in their eyes that they thought, "We already own all the good ones."

At the end of my talk I realized that some had gotten the point. One woman said in a sad tone something to the effect of, "That means we will be forced to sell something that has done really well and buy something that has not moved." "Yes," I said. "You can give yourself permission to sell *some* Microsoft and buy a financial stock, oil and gas stocks, or an insurance company that will better balance what you now own." As I walked out of the meeting, I realized that not until their stocks fell substantially would there be any progress made in proper diversification. Then the last half of 2000 and the first half of 2001 brought the big correction in the large-cap growth stocks like Microsoft, Lucent, and Cisco, and value stocks such as Philip Morris and Exxon Mobil moved up nicely.

From another client I heard that everyone had bragged about his or her 401(k) portfolio at a recent corporate party. They all had been making oodles of money, and they did it *themselves*. What exhilaration they had. Nothing like success to make one proud, I thought, especially for those who were doing it themselves. I asked her, "Do you want the *risk* they are taking? If so, we can move all your bonds into those types of stocks. In any one year," I explained, "there will be an asset class that outdoes all the others. Sometimes it's cash. Then the next year it's bonds or international stocks. No one knows for sure." It's been said that a wise person knows that wisdom is most needed when it is least heeded.

Ibbotson studied four U.S. equity asset classes from 1928 to 2000 and found the following best and worse returns of each. The results were not predictable (see Table 4.2).

Can anyone accurately forecast year-to-year returns? Listed in Table 4.3 is the asset class with the best return for each year from 1984 to 2001. I used popular indices, such as the Lehman Brothers Aggregate Bond Index, to represent a fixed-income asset class. To represent the stock market I used four equity asset classes:

Table 4.2   Best and Worst Returns, 1928–2000

Asset class	Maximum return	Year	Minimum return	Year
Large-cap growth	50.18 percent	1954	−35.70 percent	1931
Large-cap value	115.50 percent	1933	−58.70 percent	1931
Small-cap growth	158.10 percent	1933	−46.29 percent	1937
Small-cap value	118.08 percent	1933	−52.19 percent	1931

Source: *Ibbotson Associates,* 2001 Yearbook

- *Large-cap growth: S&P 500/Barra Growth*, companies with higher forecasted growth
- *Large-cap value: S&P 500/Barra Value*, companies with lower price-to-book ratios
- *Ibbotson Small Cap Index*, companies chosen by Ibbotson and picked from the smallest 20 percent of the market weighed by market capitalization, i.e., the smallest of publicly traded companies
- *International: The Morgan Stanley International Europe, Australasia and Far East Index*

Each of these popular indices is used as a benchmark for returns. If you hold your hand over all items in the following list and move it slowly down the page, can you guess which asset class performed best the following year? I doubt that you have the foresight to be accurate even 20 percent of the time. As you move your hand down the list, try to anticipate the return that the winning asset class produced.

Table 4.3   Annual Returns—Five Asset Classes (1984–2001)

Year	Asset class	Annual return
1984	U.S. bond index	16.6 percent
1985	International	56.1 percent
1986	International	70.2 percent
1987	International	25.3 percent
1988	International	28.6 percent
1989	Large-cap growth	35.9 percent
1990	U.S. bond index	7.1 percent
1991	Small cap	44.6 percent
1992	Small cap	23.3 percent
1993	International	33.0 percent
1994	International	8.1 percent
1995	Large-cap value	36.9 percent
1996	Large-cap growth	23.9 percent
1997	Small cap	22.8 percent
1998	Large-cap growth	42.1 percent
1999	Large-cap growth	28.6 percent
2000	U.S. bond index	11.6 percent
2001	Small cap	22.8 percent

Source: *Ibbotson Associates,* 2002 SBBI Classic Edition Yearbook

Many advisors and individuals think that they are smart enough to know where to be before the move. Many market timers think that they are the Wayne Gretzky of Wall Street. The great professional hockey player once boasted, "Everyone else goes where the puck is; I position myself where the puck is going." I know it is much easier to predict the direction of the puck than the direction of the market. The markets give few discernable signals as to the long-term direction they are headed, and yet tens of thousands of Gretzkys are vying for the same puck. Far better that our investment projections be made for a much longer term than annually; then we won't get hit in the teeth by a puck going in the wrong direction in any one year. If your primary goal for your portfolio is that it pay you an income without undue risk to your capital, then proper diversification, similar to the choices made by the CFOs of endowments, is worth the money and time it will take to create.

PART TWO

BUILDING THE WEALTH YOU NEED

"The winds and the waves are always on the side of the ablest navigators."

—EDWARD GIBBON (1737–1794)

5

Portfolio Lessons
for a Lifetime

*"The first step toward discipline is the very earnest
desire for her."*

—Solomon (Book of Wisdom, 6:17, New American
Standard Bible)

The law of unintended consequences says that things happen beyond our
foresight and the control of our good intentions. Unlike many individuals
who were buying large-growth stocks at the end of 1999, the college endowment fund representatives I spoke with were cutting back their ownership
in this asset class. The large-growth stock portion of their endowment had
exceeded its allotted percentage. They sold high. They took profits, placing
money in other pieces of the pie. They bought low. Their rebalancing discipline was admirable. They cut their chances of getting more growth in a
hot area for the alternative, which is reducing risk by taking money off the
table. They placed more money into an asset class that had not done as well
but still allowed for good growth opportunity. They were reducing their
chances of bad "unintended consequences" by controlling the risk of own-

ing financial assets. They were content to meet their *target rate of return* (or happy index), from which we derive an annual target dollar amount. They were not greedy. As my mentor, the late money manager John W. Burns, once said, "They are not two-headed people hoping for three-headed people to come along to buy what they have to sell."

Although the discipline of professional money management keeps human emotion in check, there are irrational investors. Irrational markets do often occur, which goes against what many academics believe—that the markets are always efficient because people always act rationally. *Efficient market hypothesis (EMH)* states that all investors are always rational, reacting intelligently on all the information known at the moment, so that securities are always fairly, or efficiently, priced. Making the assumption of EMH is a simple way to support modern portfolio theory. But an efficient market does not make sense given the sizable declines we have experienced, such as the one that happened in October of 1987. First, information is not known by all investors at the same time, although the media likes to make us think so, because facts need to be deciphered and made into something that can inform. Second, much information is not reliable; we have witnessed CEOs exaggerate their companies' growth prospects, and executives "pad" accounts receivables. Remember, companies are made up of imperfect human beings, and some are unethical at times. Third, the market is made of multimillions of humans around the world who have feelings, and these feelings are interacting with their minds during their decision-making process. Fourth, investment bankers compete worldwide to gain the attention of investors, so *hyping* a stock is unfortunately all too common in underwriting an initial public offering (IPO). Sometimes millions of people are caught in the teeth of speculation, and at other times they run for cover beneath a safety blanket of U.S. treasury bills.

In the midst of this mass confusion, which occurs almost daily, there are those professional investors who can distance themselves from strong emotions that could negatively affect their judgment. Their investment plan would be more likely to succeed because it is more rational in its implementation. Getting an estimate of what an asset class can do for you is what experts are hired for. If they can create models that are built on reasonable expectations, then they are going to be successful. Just as a good psychologist knows that you do not need her until you need her, the money manager knows that his best work shows up not when times are good, but when they're bad—when reason must stand its ground. I believe modern portfolio theory does not need the support of EMH to be advanced, because MPT does help us in irrational markets to keep our heads clear and our portfolios in balance. Keeping a sound, objective perspective is the psychological goal of the successful investor. Any CFO would agree that this perspective can help you sleep in the midst of a storm.

Some Assumptions Can Be Off

Critics point out that in asset allocation, making risk/reward assumptions weakens our investment method. Since we identify asset classes as a way of breaking down the portfolio into workable parts, do we know enough about these asset classes to give them dependable characteristics, such as return and risk numbers? Some argue that the returns on small-company stocks have not been properly documented. Historical data is based on a limited number of small stock funds or the definition of small stocks has changed. Whatever the case may be, they argue that small-company performance over a long period of time has not been properly measured. Others argue that large-company growth stocks have become multinational in nature, so that more than our own economy affects their earning and price performance. The world is getting smaller, and companies are getting bigger. There may even be new asset classes emerging, not yet recognized, that would improve diversification. Some would argue that standard deviation is not a true measurement of risk, only volatility. Volatility is not risk when the stock is going up, they point out, yet an upward swing in the stock price is part of the calculation of the standard deviation. These controversies will be addressed as the practice of managing money evolves.

The good that asset allocation accomplishes by its discipline far outweighs its weaknesses. The law of large numbers is a statistical law that says in a large group of numbers, conclusions can be drawn that accurately characterize the data you are examining. For example, going back 150 years and over any *rolling period* of twenty years or more, it has been found that stocks have always outperformed U.S. treasury bills. The law of large numbers allows us to assume that even if the stock market underperforms bank rates in one or two years, the market will soon return to equilibrium. That the market will outperform, and even make up in performance where it lagged, is a powerful assumption. The law favors asset allocation and thus works well for most retirees. The truth is in the results. My clients who have asset allocation programs are less anxious over their holdings than those who do not. Knowing that some sound method has been incorporated into an investment process, they do not feel that they are gamblers.

The assumptions made by investors when they invest in anything is part of the risk of investing. All consumers are assumers. I have seen people put money into a guaranteed CD for five years with a promised rate of return of, say, 7 percent. After the second year the bank gets bought and merges with another bank. The CD is cancelled, and the investor must reinvest at a lower rate. What was assumed to be a no-risk investment has now experienced what is called *reinvestment risk*. Remember: the higher the chance of *not* getting the anticipated return (the risk), the higher the reward potential must be to attract the money to the investment. Called the *risk premium*, it is that amount of return above the return one could get in a no-risk investment, such as three-month treasury bills. The risk premium is an assumption of the future return and not a guaranteed return.

At What Risk?

Investment risk and volatility are a big part of what asset allocation tries to measure and reduce. It assumes that the client is seeking a return, and that the most efficient way of getting it is with a portfolio that has the lowest risk. For this reason, consultants create more than one model portfolio. Not that they offer them to all clients, but they need to see investment models that span the spectrum of risk and return. The conservative investor who needs income immediately will not usually own the most aggressive investment. The riskiest portfolio will be offered to someone who has the means to get on without dipping into the funds and may have other investments that are guaranteed, like a pension annuity.

Once you see that different portfolios carry different levels of risk, you will understand that there are wrong ways of offering investment services to a retiree. More to the point, one client came in with a pursed-lipped friend. The concerned friend insisted that the annual 10 percent return we had been getting for our client was half what it should have been, and that her firm could do better. The question I asked was, "At what risk?" The client's funds were diversified into CDs, stocks, and bonds. Soon after the meeting, my client transferred the account, and the three stock funds that were sold went up an average 45 percent in one year, and the investment the friend favored went up 11 percent that same year. What they expected to happen came in reverse! Now what? The answer I usually hear is, "It hasn't been long enough to determine whether the new manager is good." Again, I ask, "At what risk?" Waiting is risky. Unless you have a Warren Buffett–

sized portfolio of money, you should not choose one investment style or asset class. As the Bible warns, "Many who are first will be last" (Matthew 19:30, New American Standard Bible). The quote is out of context, but I know you get the message.

Success: It's All in the Discipline

Some people think investing is gambling. It is not, but even if it was, professional gamblers at poker tables are highly disciplined, and investors must be as well. Although you own something in the form of a stock or equity fund, or you lend your money in the form of a bond or fixed-income fund, you still need a solid strategy to succeed. I believe investing is becoming a gamble when you can no longer describe what the company does or know which asset class it belongs to. Day traders do not care to know about the company. They care more about missing an earnings forecast or a sound bite than they do about a balance sheet or a potential new product. They want to make money on a daily price move, not on the rewards that come with being a long-term investor in a company that is profitable.

The models investment consultants create are not for the gambler. A book titled *The Warren Buffett Way: Investment Strategies of the World's Greatest Investor*, written by Robert Hagstrom, hit the shelves in 1997. The *Wall Street Journal* stated, "An extraordinarily useful account of the methods of an investor held by many to be the world's greatest." By the end of 1999, Mr. Buffett's Berkshire Hathaway fund had fallen 19 percent, far *underperforming* the S&P 500. A stock-picking style can go out of style, even for the best investors. Of course, when the growth stock market faltered in 2000, Mr. Buffett's portfolio climbed 25.6 percent, proving once again that asset classes and managers do not walk in lockstep with one another.

Realistically, can you accept more than a 15 percent loss in any given year? Will you feel uncomfortable if it takes eighteen months (the length of a long recession) to wait until your funds start to grow again? It is not a gamble to take that kind of risk, if it is commensurate with a large enough reward. In my studies, I discovered another general rule of thumb: people are much more responsive to the pain of losing a dollar than to the pleasure of making a dollar. That rule may not pertain to billionaires, but it does to most of us. My conclusion comes from one study that asked more than ten thousand people how many dollars they would want to earn in order to risk a loss of one dollar. On average, people wanted three dollars to make the bet. Give up one or make three! Interesting; it may be the reason why stocks fall faster than they rise. Damage comes quickly, while healing comes slowly.

An *asset class designation* gives us at least some guidance as to the universe of stocks that fund managers examine when filling their portfolio, while a *style* tells us the kind of method that will be used to analyze that universe. A *style box* (a term coined by Morningstar of Chicago) tells us both the asset class and the style. In a time of specialization, the asset class and style distinction helps managers compare themselves to other managers who claim the same universe and are trying to meet or exceed the same benchmark or index. These benchmarks also help investors, financial advisors, and investment consultants to get a reference point to compare one manager to another.

A client asked me to find a "go anywhere, buy anything fund" ignoring all style or class description. The answer I gave him is that in the past fifteen years there has been a movement away from that kind of management skill. A manager with an investment style known as *deep-value*, or *relative-value*, will run a portfolio very different from a *momentum* growth manager, who will differ from a *growth-at-a-reasonable-price (GARP)* manager. They each may look at a similar universe of stocks, but they use different tools to measure risk and reward within their portfolio choices. Financial advisors and investment consultants do the *due diligence* that helps them know a manager's investment style and discipline. As well, in searching for a company to put into their portfolios, money managers and funds have their own investment discipline governed by their own stock-picking criteria.

There are many different schools of thought regarding how to evaluate a company before and after buying it. The future value of a bank stock, for example, is not dependent on new product development as much as that of a high-tech growth company. You cannot use the same evaluation method on a computer company that is not planning to pay a cash dividend as you would a high-yielding insurance company. Different evaluation techniques cause different managers to take radically different approaches. Each tries to hold itself out as unique. The analysis of stocks evolves as mathematical and computer tools progress and as new industries are formed, such as the Internet. One stock-picking method can become so common that efficient markets develop, taking out much of the potential abnormal gains that a manager may brag of getting. While working with an advisor you can discover the process by which she picks funds or money managers. Asking about her due diligence efforts can calm the fears you may have that you are taking a gamble.

The statistics show that if you are a very good large-company money manager buying growth stocks, your return can be compared to that of others who share the same benchmark, usually the S&P 500/Barra Growth Index. Using Wiesenberger Mutual Fund or Morningstar data, an advisor can screen large-cap growth funds and find how many are within that particular asset class. Often you can check their work at your local library, which may have one of these databases. The range of return within that category is meaningful when you see how many managers fall in the upper quartile (upper 25 percent) of their peers, while others are at the bottom.

Another value added by a good financial advisor is that he can prevent you from purchasing poorer managers in a particular asset class, so that you can be sure of owning the more talented ones. Between the best and the worst funds can be a tenfold difference in performance. Checking the domestic growth and income funds in April of 2000, for example, I found that some funds returned as high as 22 percent, and others as low as 2 percent, in the same year. What may lead the pack this year may miss the lead the next; for this reason you need to be monitoring your investments while you own them. A red flag should go up if the manager or team leaves the firm; this could change future results in a dramatic way.

As well, the advisor can help you avoid one of the major mistakes the uninitiated make by analyzing a fund to see whether it's truly what it claims to be. For example, although a fund could be named as a large-cap growth fund, it may be overweighted in one sector of the market, and therefore lack proper diversification. There are 179 microeconomic business sectors that fall into 12 macrosectors. Often I hear of managers getting rave reviews because of the success of their funds, but nothing is mentioned of *what* the managers owned. Were they lucky to be in one stock that went to the moon? Will they be so lucky again? The advisor can clarify conflicting information. For example, the New York Opportunity Fund in 2000 was considered a large-cap growth fund by Morningstar, and Lipper Services placed it in the large-cap value fund style box. The fund managers say it is a core fund, trying to outperform the S&P 500 rather than the growth or value indices.

Figure 5.1 reminds me of a pizza with everything on it. In a rather dramatic simplification, it splits the world of investments into twelve sectors. A sizable overweighting in any one sector could cause an investor to have

Figure 5.1   Total Investable Capital Market

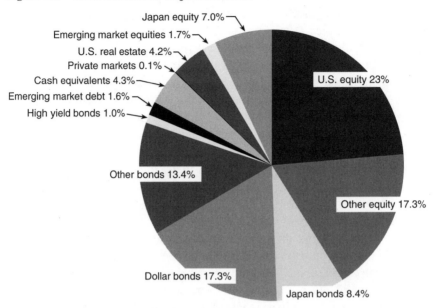

Source: *Frontier Analytics, a division of Sungard Expert Solutions*

a terrific return when that sector is hot, or a terrible return when that sector is not. No asset class or sector will always be the winner each year. To buy into only one asset class could be a gamble. Rather than trying to guess the next hot sector, one should build a more diversified portfolio, because it spreads risk over more sectors and securities. Insurance companies coinsure with other companies to spread risk so that no one company gets badly burnt. Here again, the financial advisor earns her keep, trying to find a balance of investments to reduce the risk of owning financial assets. *That is why we must look not only at a track record, but how this track record was produced.*

Investment Proverb 12

No one company (or country) has a lock on all the good ideas; diversify to reduce risk and increase opportunity.

It Takes Discipline to Remain Diversified

The chief investment strategist with Wachovia Securities, Rod Smyth, once said, "Diversification is always owning something that is underperforming, because one day it will be the thing that is outperforming. I do not believe that anyone can predict the best-performing investment category in any coming year." He means that you should diversify among asset classes and style categories because you are working with the unpredictable. Thus, it is most important to accomplish at least a two-step process (if not more) before an investment is made. First, your advisor will try to find which asset classes you need to own that combine in a way that will best meet your risk tolerance and goals. Next he should find at least one or two top managers in each asset class that are true to his style and consistent in returns. Portfolio creation should be a well thought out process. Many who read this book and who, until now, have managed their own IRAs, 401(k)s, or 403(b)s will find my conclusions quite surprising. At retirement it is more important than ever that this two-step process be taken, because there is too much at stake not to take it. If your portfolio is to last, you need to carefully weigh all your bets.

The difference between diversification and a strategic asset allocation program is like the difference between a guy who can hammer and a guy who is a master carpenter. One swings at the nail, while the other knows which nail to use and when not to use nails. What takes skill is that a percentage weight of the portfolio must be allotted to each asset class to bring about a strategic plan. The great secret of strategic asset allocation is that diversification is accomplished in a special and contrived way so as to produce the least volatile portfolio for a given return. Chance is reduced. Volatility is cut. Confidence in hitting a target return is increased. What more can a practical person want?

Such a discipline may make you buy what you do not want to own, or hold you back from buying too much of what looks great at the time. Sometimes it does both at the same time. Since you are working in such a world of unpredictability and change, the best approach is to see that there is opportunity in the neglected stocks as well as the popular ones. Markets tend to push things to extremes, both up and down. That is to say, the system is not perfectly efficient. The popular will have its fall from grace. No one will ring the bell at the top. (Ownership of the popular stuff can be counterbalanced by an investment moving in not so similar a pattern.) No one will ring the bell at the bottom, either. Although many have claimed that they can hear bells, no one has proved to be right all the time, because no one has a direct line to the Almighty.

After experiencing several equity investment bubbles (Japan in 1990, the emerging markets in 1993, and Internet stocks in 2000, when over 250 dot-com companies folded) due to foolish speculation, I have learned some lessons. After seeing the high-yield bond selloff in the 1980s, the sharp stock decline in the Gulf War, and another tumble after the terrorism in New York and Washington, D.C., on September 11, 2001, I came to the conclusion that there will always be people and events that will cause extremes in the stock and bond markets. Extremes happen. The only way I have come to understand how to avoid getting caught in these swings is to use a strategy that anticipates the worst but can participate in the best. Conservative retirees using this plan will fear less about owning stocks. Those retirees who hunger to be where the action is can feel comfortable, too, knowing that not all their funds will be gambled away. The endowments and foundations can do it, and so can you.

A better way of seeing the bigger picture is to look at Figure 5.2.

In Portfolio 1 the two investments (A and B) that are *perfectly, positively correlated* do nothing for your portfolio (the dotted line) to reduce risk. Investments A and B move together in lockstep. Downside risk has not been reduced, even though we have two investments. Portfolio 1 is poorly diversified, and it may happen when you own two large-cap growth funds. But in Portfolio 2, where there is *perfect negative correlation*, Investments C and D complement one another, creating a smoother upward-moving line. In Portfolio 3, where there is *imperfect positive correlation*, Investments E and F do not move in lockstep, creating a portfolio that produces more consistent results. In both Portfolios 2 and 3, diversification reduces the risk, yet captures a good deal of the return. In my 401(k) I once owned 50 percent in foreign stock companies and 50 percent in U.S. small-cap companies. I was getting very volatile results! Then I got older and smarter. When I began to invest in more asset classes and added fixed-income bonds, large-growth companies, and undervalued blue-chip companies to my total mix, my roller coaster turned calm. It takes discipline not to follow the crowd in one popular direction, whether buying or selling, or when weighting your investments. I got off the stomach-churning Magic Mountain ride and boarded the relaxing Adirondack Railroad—a mountain ride retirees can enjoy.

Financial advisor Lynn Brenner writes, "Managing retirees' portfolios has become the most complex task in financial planning. The challenge: to balance withdrawal rate, investment risk, and investment return deftly

Figure 5.2 Diversification from Combining Investments

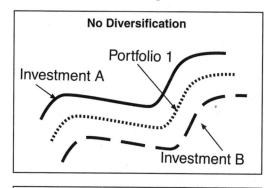

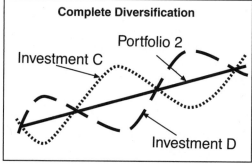

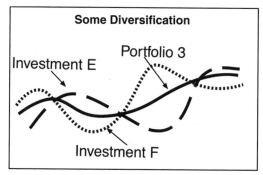

Source: *Frontier Analytics, a division of Sungard Expert Solutions*

enough to ensure that your clients get the income they need without running out of money" (*Bloomberg Wealth Manager*, August 2000, p. 49). Add to the uncertainty the fact that people do not know how long they will live—longer than we may ever guess—and you get one humdinger of a problem. The experienced and intelligent financial advisor is quite aware of this conundrum and its monumental solution. Those retirees unaware of the challenge will come to a better understanding of its complexity by the end of this book. Most books that address the investment process used by endowments, pension funds, and foundations are written for professional money managers and CFOs. In addition, even some financial advisors have come to pity the poor asset allocation pioneers and have pooh-poohed their strategy as an outdated one. But behind the scenes, during the last five years, computer power to crunch larger vats of data—data that is ever more precise and changing—has raised asset allocation to rocket science. Today, better understanding of the correlation among the various markets and the greater creativity allowed in money management have turned asset allocation into an art form. Nevertheless, only a minor number of retirees are fully aware that money management is not for the do-it-yourselfer or for those who are looking for a quick or easy answer to lifetime income.

The CFOs of endowment funds do not make many investment decisions, but instead set investment policy, interact with consultants to develop an asset allocation strategy, pick money managers (and funds), and make periodic reviews of the plan. In retirement, the agonizing gap between making money and spending it is narrowed if retirees take an active part within the investment process like a CFO. Rather than being an impotent observer or solo flyer, you feel more in control of your retirement if you become a part of an investment team.

6

Why You Need to Act Now to Live Happily in Retirement

"What is life? It is the flash of a firefly in the night. It is the breath of the buffalo in the wintertime. It is the little shadow that runs across the grass and loses itself in the sunset."

—CROWFOOT

These are the last words of the famous Blackfoot warrior and orator. It seemed forever to get through my childhood, but life for me moved ever faster after getting my driver's license. From what I have learned from my retired clients, a slow life on Golden Pond is a myth. One retiree said it succinctly: "I thought retirement meant to just relax, but then my kids have problems that they bring back to us; then you or your friends or your family get ill. It doesn't end. There are many joys, too, but there are demands."

In a Daffy Duck cartoon titled "A Dime to Retire," Elmer Fudd rents a room at Daffy's hotel for ten cents a day. Soon, a mouse bothers him. He tips Daffy, who then hires a dog to get rid of the rodent, then a lion to get rid of the dog, and then an elephant to get rid of the lion, and finally a mouse to get rid of the elephant. The cartoon reminded me, in a painfully funny way, that inflation is a similar pest, costing retirees more as the years go on, disappearing only to creep in again. For most of us, retirement is not a stroll down the proverbial Memory Lane, but just another stage in life's journey with its pleasures and chores, meeting demands of the day.

Besides those uncontrollable events in one's life, there are the problems created by poor planning. An article called "The Decision Decade" by Michael Stein, certified financial planner (CFP), highlights the ten-year period—five years before retirement and five years after retirement—"that is the most critical to the success of any retirement" (*Journal of Financial Planning*, June 2000, p. 36). Mr. Stein sees *lifestyle creep* as a serious problem. I, too, have found that many retirees have planned well and have saved in order to maintain their lifestyle after the last paycheck. The problem that evolves can happen in two ways.

First, people with three to five years from retirement find themselves flush with cash and begin to spend it—buy a larger boat, a condo, a new car, and so on—and the monthly bills begin to rise above the reasonable budget they held to for thirty years. This bloated spending floats like a dead log into their retirement years and becomes a real obstacle to healthy balance between income and expenses. They see the cash building, and they can no longer deprive themselves of their "wants." Psychologists have testified that people have anxiety about newfound money. Seeing it build up more rapidly—kids are out of college and the house paid down—burns a hole in their pockets. Spending habits change often for the worse.

If you have not committed the first no-no before retiring, the second is more tempting and opaque. After the retirement party, the healthy go on a long-planned vacation, spend more than they had anticipated, and continue to spend more: they are the ones who see retirement as an unending party, and their lifestyle creeps up, up, and away. They may enter a "second childhood"—but without parents to control unbridled desires, they buy the most expensive toys in the store. They conclude that if Mr. and Mrs. Jones, who never had the income we had, can afford a forty-foot RV that gets eight miles to a gallon, then they can too. Another similar temptation is to think, "If close friends are buying a condo in Arizona, why can't we?" No one wants to feel left out of the fun. Continuing to compare our plans with what others are doing is misguided. Because we do not stop being human, we are all influenced by the commercialization of anything, from desert survival to lush retirement. All one needs to do is to look at the ads placed by any of the thousands of retirement communities. Smiling faces riding horses, golfing, or playing shuffleboard fill the billboards from New Jersey to the Keys.

These two groups try to reach for the sun, only to see their wings melt. As their spending goes higher, their income disappears and some of their principal wanes. Then one day they awaken to the tune of "Auld Lang Syne" and realize they have been on a binge and have another twenty or thirty years of going from hand-to-mouth. Soon enough they show up at the local mall looking for an easy job. Retirement should be a time to marshal your assets, yet most people who retire put off important, life-planning decisions, because the I've-got-plenty-of-time mentality sets in. I cannot pinpoint a more critical time than now to review your estate plan with an attorney and your financial plan and investments with an advisor. I have witnessed the devastating effects of poor decisions and want to share with you vignettes that will impress on you the necessity of finding a good elder care and estate attorney, remembering to review your plan with them as laws change. Include your investment executive, financial consultant, or financial planner (whatever title or designation this person goes by) and your accountant into the process of developing a plan for the management and eventual transfer of your assets. Even if you (and your spouse) feel that you are financially independent, you are not above making grave errors. Without planning you (and your spouse, and most likely your children) and your executor may find a big mess created by your procrastination in finding professional guidance.

When I want to warn people that it is easy to neglect even basic planning, I can hardly stop the stories that flash through my mind. For example, an attorney in my town died and left a five million dollar estate, half of which went to the U.S. government. Ridiculous! How much better if a local charity could have benefited from a generous gift upon his death! Among professionals it is understood that retirement assets are the best part of your total net worth to leave to charity. In another case, a dentist's wife went into a nursing home, and the daily cost plus his own expenses *wiped out* his half-million-dollar estate. In his seventies he had to go back to work because he had not received the proper advice. Each of these financial disasters could have been easily avoided with just a couple of visits to an attorney trained in elder law.

Why Do Retirement Assets Need Protection?

A man I will call Jerry goes into the nursing home, leaving a healthy spouse at home. Although he hoped his retirement plan (worth $300,000) would take care of his wife's income needs and leave an estate to his children, it is now too late to protect a majority of his plan assets. With no long-term care insurance already in place or a properly funded, irrevocable trust, not much can be done for his heirs. Without insurance protection the only recourse to save income for Jerry's spouse or family would be for him to immediately buy an insurance annuity with the retirement funds. When the annuity company begins paying a guaranteed monthly income, the principal is no longer available to Jerry or his family, and it is not available to the nursing home. Let me explain this in more detail.

The monthly income from the insurance company will be paid out according to an annuity table over a set amount of time (known as the *term-certain* option), such as a twenty-year period. Or the monthly payments may be made over a person's life only, known as the *life-only option*. If Jerry dies after, say, five years, under the twenty-year term-certain option the remaining annuity payments can be made to the beneficiary of the annuity, such as his spouse, for the next fifteen years. Under the life-only option the income stops on Jerry's death, unless he had a joint annuitant. The income from the annuity may be needed to pay for care, but the government, which pays for nursing home care when we are no longer able, cannot force Jerry to spend assets (his retirement plan) he no longer owns. That is, if the $300,000 is spent on the nursing home care, the estate is left with far less money, but once the $300,000 is converted to a monthly annuity, the income from the annuity can be paid out although the principal is now gone. *The transfer of the assets (held in a retirement plan) to an immediate annuity in order to receive an income payout is often not recognized as a way of protecting retirement income for the spouse or heirs.* Don't try it without first checking with an attorney prior to entering a nursing home situation. Although people may begin to gift money to their children to reduce their assets, they often lose much of their ability to do so once a long-term illness occurs. Once a person is disabled, it is too late to buy insurance to cover in-home or nursing home care. Too late comes too soon for too many retirees. Without a doubt these choices are easier to make when you are still young and healthy, and you have the wherewithal to create a durable financial plan.

Although I believe estate planning should start once you have children to support, it is most necessary to begin interviewing professionals in the field of retirement and estate planning before or soon after your retirement. When it comes to estate planning, truth is stranger than fiction, especially when there is no family nearby to care for your needs. One of our wealthier clients is slowly becoming mentally disabled. He dropped into a bank and tried to cash a grocery voucher, thinking it was a check, and this instance of his poor judgment is only one of many similar ones. Without a trust and a trustee he will eventually be assigned a guardian by a judge, perhaps someone he does not even know, to control his affairs.

Another elderly person we know calls the police each time her car is "stolen." The police find the vehicle each time in the parking lot of the doctor's office she last visited. If she so easily misplaces her car, how does she balance her bank accounts? All of us age, but are we preparing for changes? In both of the cases I've just mentioned there are no relatives or friends living near to step in to help these people with their daily affairs. Although most people have a few helping relationships, others have none. People let things go by, or they want a level of independence far beyond their ability to perform actions responsibly. There will come the time for each of us when we either become disabled or die. You do not have a choice. Are we thinking ahead, or are we walking into the future like an ox with blinders on?

Don't Wait to Learn the Terms

If you think the term *life expectancy* means how long you will live, then read on. If you have not heard of the *stretch-out provisions* for rollover IRAs, please keep reading this chapter. If a *spousal rollover* is an account that you have not learned about, you need some terminology clarification. There is nothing like ignorance of the law to make life seem blissful—until the law comes back to haunt you, depriving you of money or complicating your estate. Laws are made to give the government power of choice over our affairs if we neglect our duty to be good stewards of ourselves, others, and our assets. If you decide not to make those choices yourself, you have given the government the right to make them for you.

Although government is created for the good of its citizens, at times the state makes laws to favor the state. So if you die without a will (intestate), a judge is going to choose an administrator for your estate—maybe someone you would never have chosen yourself. Each state has its own laws for those who die without a will, which are used to decide where their assets will go.

When your assets are in two different states, probate without a will becomes a real nightmare for your heirs. If you move from one state to another and have a new residency, it is a good idea to see a lawyer in that state to update your will so that it complies with the new residency regulations.

The laws regarding retirement plans are very complex and often are changed by state and federal governments. Company 401(k)s do not give you many estate planning options, because the administrators of these plans do not want to create more headaches for themselves. Some plans offer better investment choices than other plans, but most plans are not up to the demands that you will have to meet long-term financial goals. For example, although there are no longer many different methods to calculate *required minimum distribution (RMD)* [see IRS code 1.4019(a)(9)-1], you still need to take a minimum distribution by April 1 of the year following the year in which you turn seventy and a half. If the calculation is done incorrectly and you remove too few funds, then you can be hammered with a 50 percent penalty on all withdrawals. Many retirees lean on plan sponsors to help them with calculating distributions, but few have the capabilities and time to properly assist you. If you die with a retirement plan that designates your spouse as heir, knowing the rules will help him or her save taxes and properly roll money over. As well, it will not be the employer's money on the line if you get audited. One client asked, "Why doesn't the government tell you about these things?" They do not tell you what to do, because that is called advice, and you have to pay for that.

Here is a good example of poor advice given to a person who did not know what his options were. Mr. Berry (a fictitious name) and his wife retired, and soon afterward Mrs. Berry died, leaving her husband her IRA. He was told by a poorly informed advisor to leave it in her name and continue to take payouts from the IRA on his wife's life expectancy so that the minimum distribution would be less. Sounds good—but the catch was that when he died, the total would be paid out to his estate, creating a large income tax debt. Because it was a no-load mutual fund firm that held the IRA, he saved money on this advice; it was free. But did he receive the best advice? No. In fact, his heirs paid dearly.

I found that the time and money spent planning can be one tenth the time and money spent later by heirs of a poorly planned estate. Mr. Berry should have transferred the IRA to a spousal rollover; then, because he had no children, he could have named his nieces and nephews or a trust as beneficiary. This arrangement would have allowed him to stretch out payments over a longer period of time and reduced his minimum distribution and his taxes. Heirs would have some control over the amount of income taxes to be paid on the remaining IRA after his death. The heirs could have saved hundreds of thousands by his proper planning, because their payments could have been stretched out over a longer life expectancy than the one he used. All of these other options were lost because he worked with a firm that did not have the know-how to know better. (In a later chapter I will help you evaluate firms, so that you will be able to hire the right one.)

After leading a seminar in 1999 with an estate attorney, it became even clearer to me that what was thought of a few years ago as a "penchant of the rich" is now for the masses. Many assumed that only rich people hired financial advisors for a fee. But with the booming 401(k)s, 403(b)s, and pensions, professional advice now is a necessity for the average retiree. Trusts were for rich people, I once thought. But today people live longer, and their retirement plans may be worth a thousand times what their parents saved. With such large estates, many modern families need a credit-sheltered trust (known by different names, such as a *family trust*) in order to smooth the transition of money to children and control both income and estate taxes.

A close friend went to an attorney to review her will and to create a trust for her disabled son. The cost shocked her. Then I explained that to settle (probate) the estate without a trust would actually be more expensive. Her son would have paid more in probate and administration expenses (about $3,000) than it cost to set up the trust ($2,000). Of course, depending on where you live and the complexity of your affairs, this expense could be higher, but in light of the savings and convenience a trust offers, most consider them worth every dime spent. Moreover, the trust provides for a guardian, a trustee to manage the money, and a plan to spend the funds in a proper way so as not to lose his Social Security disability check. What a feat! More for less—I like those numbers. When it comes to estate planning, attorneys can truthfully say, "Pay me now or pay me more later." There is no escaping the income and estate tax problem; even if the government lowers the taxes today, it may raise them again at any time. Even with recent estate tax changes that went into effect in 2001, the new tax rates will return to the old schedule in 2011.

In his book *Where Are the Customers' Yachts*, Fred Schwed Jr. implies that financial professionals earn substantially more from their clients than clients earn from receiving professional advice. Therefore, one might conclude professional advice is much too expensive and not worth paying for. But equating a client's investment performance to a professional's income

is like comparing apples to oranges. Because of articles and books that create negative perceptions of the financial industry, many people have become
distrustful of investment professionals. On the other hand, I do not trust people to know about matters in which they have little or no training. For too
many retirees, their only link to advice for most of their lives was to call a
toll-free number and get a different person on the line each time they called.
Worse still was to get different answers to the same question. In order to
keep the 401(k) plan or TSA costs down, employer-sponsored retirement
plans had to skimp on something. By meeting only the bare-bone, minimal
requirement for educating their employees, they saved a good deal of money.

Let's take a situation where one professional was of little assistance. Mr.
Applebee (again, a fictitious name) wanted to roll over his ripe retirement
plan. Following up on an advertisement from a local bank regarding a variable annuity (VA), he jumped at the offer of a monetary bonus if he signed
up and transferred his 401(k) to the insurance company annuity. It was not
clearly disclosed to him that if he withdrew all his money within a short
period, he would get hit with a back-end penalty, also known as a *surrender charge*. That is, taking all his funds out in the first year would cost him
almost 6 percent of his initial rollover. After nine months, he did not like
how the rollover was being managed and decided to transfer it. He was able
to take 10 percent without surrender charges, known as the *free balance*; to
remove the remaining 90 percent of the initial value cost him $26,000! A
few annuities have no immediate surrender charges, but even they have high
internal expenses and are not so simple to transfer. Fortunately, he learned
that he could transfer funds into a brokerage account and purchase with a
professional's assistance CDs, stocks, and bonds with no surrender charge.
If he did not like the service, he could move the account without any has-
sle or penalties. This mess could have been avoided if Mr. Applebee knew
which questions to ask up front, or if he had read the prospectus before
investing. How many people buy things without ever reading the fine print?
Most of us do at one time or another.

Look for the Appropriate Investments

Most annuities sold are commission-based products and are not a good alternative for someone who wants the flexibility to move funds elsewhere—
especially qualified (retirement plan) money. If Mr. Applebee had paid for

advice, most advisors would not have suggested a tax-sheltered annuity, because a rollover IRA is already a tax-sheltered account. As one financial advisor said to me, "Why pay for two umbrellas, when it's less expensive to have one?" Moreover, with the changing markets, you want an advisor who can change investments at any time. Within the variable annuity you have a limited number of investment choices, which restricts your portfolio. As well, the financial advisor is paid to sell a product rather than receiving an ongoing fee to invest and monitor your account. Variable annuities now include more choices, but I believe there are still too many restrictions within an annuity contract. On the other hand, it is possible to find more of a tailor-made plan for less cost than annuities offer. You will not be able to negotiate down the internal expenses of an annuity, which you can do with a fee-only investment service (more on this topic in Chapter 13).

I am not bemoaning insurance annuities. I have recommended them, especially to shelter nonretirement (nonqualified) money—that is, money in regular bank accounts, but not money in a 401(k) or 403(b). There are some terrific annuity investments, but those who buy them should understand all the conditions, and buy for the correct reasons. They may be used for retirement money, but full disclosure always should be made preceding the investment so that the client has complete understanding of the fee structure, investment limitations, and surrender charges. With annuity sales breaking record numbers, sooner or later you will probably be approached by your bank, insurance agent, or broker with annuities in their quiver.

When you are paying for advice, you are paying for an objective assessment of what is *best for you*. A "fee-only" advisor is not motivated by a commission on the sale of a product, and therefore is more apt to give you objective, disinterested guidance. Much like attorneys and accountants, who are your advocates, financial advisors who are paid a fee should work only for your welfare, because they are being paid by you to both make you money and save you money. I do not mean to suggest that financial advisors who work on commission are unethical or selfish. My claim here is that fee-only advice is preferable for large retirement accounts because the advisor is hired to seek the best investments and is not influenced by commissions. When the advisor is receiving a fee—a fixed percentage of the account—the more he makes you, the more he gets paid. The advisor gets paid less if he loses money. In a sense the advisor is being compensated not to transact a sale, but to grow your wealth. Whether you meet with a commission-compensated advisor or one who gets paid a fee for advice, remember, there are those who charge dearly but give poor advice, and there are those who charge far less and give great advice. In his book *The Right Way to Hire Financial Help*, Charles A. Jaffe writes, "Picking financial advisors, as I explained to a friend, is tricky, filled with subjective judgments that can affect a lifetime's worth of work and savings. It is not an exercise to be taken on with a cavalier attitude" (MIT Press, 1998, p. 3). By the end of this book you will know the terminology that will get you past the glossy corporate brochures. With a little effort you can learn to judge for yourself whether a firm has the credentials you are looking for.

Another real example (with a fictitious name), Mrs. Plum did not read the prospectus because "it was too technical." Therefore, although she was given the information in writing, she did not notice that her annuity had to be withdrawn when she turned seventy-five years old. This condition has left Mrs. Plum in a pickle. She is now approaching seventy-five, and she is in very good health. The entire principal in the annuity, she is told, must be taken out, causing her to have a tremendous income tax problem or forced annuitization (giving up her principal and taking a guaranteed annual income). Neither is a good choice for her. She will no longer be able to shelter her money from taxes. Many retirees will live into their nineties, and, because of contract age restrictions, their annuities will be paid out earlier than they want. Here again, payment features of an annuity contract must be understood; get a financial advisor to review and explain them. In Mrs. Plum's case, she may be able to transfer the annuity to another annuity with a longer payout date, but then certain restrictions on the money will begin again with the new contract. Some states have an age limit when annuities are *required* to be distributed—in New York it's ninety. Take such a distribution while in a high tax bracket and you can get whammed with taxes at the wrong time. This is one good reason why your advisor must know state regulations.

Investment Proverb 13

In general, use insurance annuities for nonqualified money, and use a self-directed, brokerage rollover IRA for qualified money.

The stories in this chapter are not meant to scare you, but to convince you that you should trust professionals only after you have learned how to discern the services you need. The stories demonstrate how financial decisions, when carelessly made, can exact a large toll. When attorneys are not called in until a person is on her deathbed, little can be done. Salespeople disclose information by handing out a prospectus: if clients never read them, who is to blame? Because people do not spend as much time shopping for advice as they spend shopping for a car, many wind up with a financial lemon. They do not want to put tough questions to their advisor, because the expert must know. There are no government standards for competence, and it takes little skill to open an account. With retirement money it is easy to make errors, but with a little preparation and patience you can become your own CFO, learning how to discern what is best for you and your family.

7

How to Make the Best Use of Your Retirement Distribution Options

"No one can build his security on the nobleness of another person."

—WILLA CATHER, *ALEXANDER'S BRIDGE*

In a *self-directed plan* you can run the show alone or, better yet, you can be the ringmaster and hire a financial advisor, consultant, or money manager to work with you. We cannot totally depend on others to make decisions that can determine a lifetime of our income. Just as we don't leave the raising of our children to teachers, so too we must recognize our own responsibility to provide ourselves with a sound retirement plan. On the other hand, the world of investments is complicated and can be better understood with professional assistance in both design and implementation. Qualified monies are those dollars that come from qualified retirement plans such as 401(k), 403(b), profit sharing, and pension lump sum. Nonqualified money is everything else that does not have the character to be rolled over into an IRA. Unless you are getting a monthly pension, these sources of income need your oversight.

Some of the Rules to Know

Before you go to a baseball game, it's wise to familiarize yourself with how the game is played so that you get the most out of it. Many companies give seminars to their employees on the rules that govern retirement plan distributions. These seminars are often complicated, and much of what you get still needs interpreting. I have both given and attended these talks, so I want to highlight some of the more important topics that many employees find confusing. In this technical area it is good to learn more. It is also good to have an advisor to discuss these topics as they apply to you. Remember, laws change. A strategy that works for you now may not work for you later. Your advisor can tell you which rules apply to your situation and how best to use them.

Normally, if you remove money from a retirement plan before you are fifty-nine and a half (exactly six months after your fifty-ninth birthday), you will pay a 10 percent penalty and might suffer an income tax consequence as well. Some advisors have gotten it wrong; it's a mistake to think that the year you turn fifty-nine and a half is the earliest you can take distributions. If your job is terminated or you retire between fifty-five and fifty-nine and a half, there is a carve-out rule that can help you if you need funds. Since you can carve out money from your fat 401(k), *but not an IRA*, you need to know how much you want before you transfer money into a rollover. With this loophole it will not cost you a 10 percent penalty for early withdrawal; however the carved-out dollars still will be subject to income taxes. Remember it this way: "Carve the turkey before you roll it."

So let's suppose that you need $100,000 to build a condo, and you are under fifty-nine and a half. *Before* you transfer your 401(k) plan to a rollover IRA, you can (if you're in the 31 percent tax bracket) pull out $131,000 and send $31,000 in for prepaid federal taxes, and then build your condo. If you make the mistake of rolling money first, then you will have a problem removing it because you are under fifty-nine and a half. You may owe less than 31 percent in taxes, but your accountant can make that calculation. I suggest that if you have other earned and unearned income, the accountant will need an accurate estimate of the taxes you should remit at the time you take your distribution. You do not want to trigger any penalty. Remember, *the IRS can charge penalties on penalties.*

I chose a 31 percent federal tax rate in the example for good reason. If you are like many early retirees who get another job after retiring or if your spouse is working and earning an income, *you must be careful.* See your accountant to get an estimate of the taxes to be withheld, because you may need to withhold more than you think. You do not want to be surprised and owe taxes when you do not have the money. Too many uninformed people wind up borrowing money to pay Uncle Sam taxes. This predicament does not occur when a good advisor is first sought out. With many early retirees going into their own start-up businesses, retirement money must be spent wisely and taxes accounted for. Start-up companies burn up cash, as we have seen with Internet companies in 2000. Also, you may (or may not) owe state income taxes, depending on the state laws. Different accountants can come up with different figures as to what you owe for taxes, depending on the complexity of your financial affairs. If you have a complex tax situation, you may need a second opinion. Like financial advisors, many accountants specialize in tax preparation. Here again, your financial advisor can recommend an accountant, an actuary, or an attorney who best suits your needs.

Substantially Equal Periodic Payment (SEPP)

For those people under fifty-nine and a half who may receive money from qualified retirement plans, there is a second way to avoid the 10 percent penalty, by using another rule called the *substantially equal periodic payment (SEPP) rule*, also known as *rule 72t*. I have used this rule to help a forty-five-year-old mother of four get extra income after her husband died. She took an SEPP from a 401(k) her husband had left her. I also helped a divorced woman get an income from her ex-husband's retirement account. After getting a *qualified domestic relations order (QUADRO)* from the court, she was able to request a lump sum of money be transferred from her husband's 401(k) to her rollover IRA. This arrangement created a vehicle for a monthly income using rule 72t.

It is quite common for retirees to supplement income by working at jobs that pay less than the one they left. One client went back to his former employer as a consultant under contract after retiring and after taking a lump sum from his pension plan and 401(k). To keep his standard of living, he rolled over the retirement money and had a monthly check sent to him. Although he was only fifty-five years old, he took the funds by way of SEPP and avoided the 10 percent penalty. Once again the rule allowed him to work the hours and job he wanted. Without SEPP he could not have done it. By withholding taxes at a high percentage from his monthly check, he still had the opportunity for more income at a later date. If he stopped working, we could cut the withholding tax rate and give him a larger monthly payout.

You have different methods of calculating the payout, and since your advisor can choose from a range of returns, you can create a withdrawal schedule that meets your needs. The following examples show a sample SEPP withdrawal under two popular methods, the amortization income option and the annuity (or level) income option.

In both illustrations the constants are (for example purposes only):

- Single life expectancy
- Age
- Interest rate
- Initial investment of $500,000
- Average annual return of 11 percent

Amortization Income Option

Age	Beginning amount	Annual distribution	15 percent tax	Net amount
56	$500,000	$35,573	$5,336	$30,237
57	$519,427	$35,573	$5,336	$30,237
58	$540,991	$35,573	$5,336	$30,237
59	$564,928	$35,573	$5,336	$30,237
60	$591,497	$35,573	$5,336	$30,237

Annuity (or Level) Income Option

Age	Beginning amount	Annual distribution	15 percent tax	Net amount
56	$500,000	$39,997	$6,000	$33,997
57	$515,003	$39,997	$6,000	$33,997
58	$531,656	$39,997	$6,000	$33,997
59	$550,141	$39,997	$6,000	$33,997
60	$570,660	$39,997	$6,000	$33,997

These examples assume the retiree withholds 15 percent for federal taxes and no state taxes. It is important to note that, if you earn additional income and have fewer deductions, your tax bracket can be much higher, and you will want more taxes withheld.

The interest rate used to compute the amortized annual distribution payment is 5.5 percent. The annuity (or level) distribution option is computed using the UP84 table 5.5 percent. For each method the payout will be stable for the next five years. With the help of software such as MoneyTree's Retirement Solutions, an advisor can play with the numbers to get the payout that best fits your personal goals.

If your advisor feels that a higher computed interest rate can be assumed, then the annual distributions can be increased, but this will leave less money to compound. Unless the markets can deliver greater than an 11 percent average return, it would not be wise to use more than a 6 percent computed interest. Since the projected average return, as I previously discussed, is not guaranteed, a lower payout is less threatening to the overall growth of the portfolio. You can set the computed interest rate lower and create an even safer withdrawal plan. There are a lot of arbitrary numbers that can be plugged into these computer programs, and advisors must be cautious as to what assumptions are made so as not to mislead the retiree. Once the payment schedule is set, the retiree will need to keep it per the SEPP rule: *for at least five years, or until the retiree hits fifty-nine and a half, or whichever comes later*. There is a third method to compute the payout, the life expectancy method, but it is seldom used because it leads to very low initial payments. If you have a spouse, there is another way to lower the payout; you can use a joint life expectancy in your calculations. Rarely is this done, because most early retirees are in need of more income, not less.

Let's Get Creative!

By applying the 72t rule (or rule 72q for TSAs and TDAs) one can come up with unusual strategies for removing money from a qualified IRA. For example, one of my clients needed money for a child's college education. He used the SEPP rule to take monthly payments without penalty from his IRA. Many 401(k) plans would not allow for such a payment, but here an IRA offered an alternative. Suppose you had a part-time job and you needed to draw only a small SEPP from your rollover IRA. Because the payment can be calculated using three different methods (and using your age and an expected federal rate), there is an income range from which you can choose. If the lowest income amount is more than you need, you can divide the rollover IRA or lump sum distribution into two rollovers, and then do a SEPP on one and not the other.

Example of Splitting the 401(k) or 403(b)

Note: This procedure should not be done without first checking with your advisor!

In this example you are rolling a lump sum of $300,000, and you need $6,000 in annual income. To achieve this goal, divide the plan into two accounts, as follows:

Rollover 1	Rollover 2
Principal: $100,000	Principal: $200,000
Withdrawal rate: 6 percent	Withdrawal rate: 0 percent
SEPP income: $6,000	Income: None taken
Objective: Conservative income	Objective: Aggressive growth

It gets more complex to manage money doing a SEPP on Rollover 1 while leaving the other (Rollover 2) to grow, but it can work well. You can have one rollover designed to provide income at low risk, and the second designed to provide aggressive growth of capital. If you need more income later, then the second portfolio can be tapped. Each account should have its own asset allocation model (or plan). As well, you can calculate the distribution based on the joint life expectancy of husband and wife, which would lower the minimum withdrawal. The reason the objectives of the rollovers differ is that the risk/reward profile of each portfolio differs, and this difference determines the percentage of money invested in each asset class, as was discussed earlier. Farther down the road, you can split the second rollover account into a third. You then SEPP the second plan, letting the third grow.

It is important to note that before you carve out or roll over money from your 401(k), you should pay off any loans made from the 401(k). A few employees at my company had loans against their 401(k) when we were merging. People who had borrowed funds from their plan had to pay back the loans or *be taxed on the entire unpaid debt!* One woman at another company had to put off retiring for two years in order to pay off her loan. These loans can cause big income tax problems if they are made just prior to retiring, or if you get stuck in a job termination. If you need funds, it is far bet-ter to use a home equity loan rather than 401(k) money; you can deduct the interest on a home equity loan. It is wise to pay off as soon as possible all loans made against retirement money. Not only do you want to get that money working for you again in a tax-sheltered account, but also you are protecting yourself against any unforeseen job termination.

Your Life Expectancy Is Not Your Own

When the calculations are made for an annuity payout from a pension or a withdrawal from a rollover (under the SEPP rule), the calculation takes into consideration your age. The IRS gives everyone a unisex life expectancy (see Table 7.1). Here is where women make out a little better than men. Although women usually live on average three to four years longer than men (which would reduce payouts for women) both sexes share the same life expectancy table.

Although this table may change with new longevity studies, you can see that the longer you live, the greater your life expectancy becomes. A forty-year-old has an actuarial life expectancy of eighty-two and a half years (40 + 42.5), while an eighty-year-old has an eighty-nine-and-a-half-year life expectancy. This table will also be used when you begin to calculate your minimum required distribution at age seventy and a half, which we will discuss later. For now I want to examine other areas of interest for those taking distributions prior to their required beginning date.

Table 7.1   IRS Life Expectancy Table

Your age (years)	Your actuarial life expectancy (years)
40	42.5
45	37.7
50	33.1
55	28.6
60	24.2
70	16.0
75	12.5
80	9.5

Source: *Internal Revenue Service*

If you begin withdrawing before fifty-nine and a half from a rollover IRA, you must continue until you reach fifty-nine and a half, or for five years, whichever comes later. A new IRS revenue ruling, 2002-62, allows you to lower the payout schedule once during this payout period without penalty. Those who had been taking too much from IRAs now have a way of getting some relief by changing to the life expectancy method, if they haven't already used it. However, if you change the payout schedule more than once in this period, you will face a 10 percent penalty on all withdrawals. If you are fifty years old, that means taking payments until fifty-nine and a half, at which time you can change your payment schedule. There are two problems I have encountered with using this special SEPP rule. First, if you are, for example, fifty-eight, you will need to take SEPP for five years, until you are sixty-three, before you can change your payout option. Waiting until age sixty-three may not be a desirable plan, because even if you need more or less by then, you are locked into the SEPP payout method. So if you are close to fifty-nine and a half, try getting money from other sources until you reach that age; by then you are past the early withdrawal penalty period. I have found that borrowing insurance cash value can be the ticket out of this problem.

A second problem can really haunt you. If you SEPP the money and your payout is (after a few years) *too low*, you cannot change it. If you try to take a greater amount, you will be penalized at a rate of 10 percent each year, going back to your first payout. Wow! That penalty can be stiff. If you took out $50,000 per year for six years, you would owe a whopping $30,000. The IRS has telescopic vision for these errors. Because you cannot raise the annual amount, it may be a good reason to take a little more than you need the first year. Better yet, do not retire until you are certain your income needs can be sustained. Another idea would be to set up a second rollover as a backup, and tap that one if you need more income. When taking a SEPP, it is good to have other sources to draw on, if you are five or six years away from fifty-nine and a half.

This work of analyzing your income needs, your SEPP calculation, and your other income options is the work of your financial advisor or accountant. Some of us will do this analysis for no cost to win over your business, but it should be part of the larger financial planning process. There are important steps you must consider when looking at retiring. One first step is to plan where your income will come from, and the second step is to assess how your investment will produce the income you need. People can hire a fee-only financial planner to do the first step and a fee-only investment management consultant to do the second step. Some firms have both professional disciplines on staff; it will become more common in years ahead that successful investment firms will have specialists in both fields. One will concentrate his or her efforts on the overall picture of life-income planning, which will include estate planning, and the second will implement the investment management decisions.

The Social Security Gap

People ask, "When should I plan on getting Social Security?" When full Social Security benefits begin depends on your birthdate, but I believe that the best recommendation is to take it as early as you can get it when you need the extra income. Retiring before you get to the earliest Social Security age can make planning a challenge. I call the time from retirement until your first S.S. check the *gap years*. A few companies fill the gap with what is known as a *Social Security bridge*, which usually is around $500 per month until you reach age sixty-two or sixty-three. If you are self-employed, you will not have this benefit. Without much income from the government or their company, early retirees must create an income that will sustain their lifestyle until the first S.S. check comes. Do not be a daredevil and attempt to jump too large a gap. It is safer to work another few years than to try to shoot for retirement too soon. We know that if you depend on a high withdrawal rate in the initial years of your retirement, much is left to chance—and chance has many mistresses. It would be just your luck that market returns come in poorly for five years, and you run your retirement account down 60 percent. Consider this example:

Initially your account is worth $1,000,000.
You remove $70,000 per year for five years.
Your investments in a bad market decline $250,000.
Your total account after five years is equal to $400,000.

If you stop taking withdrawals, you will need $600,000 to get back to $1,000,000. That is, you would have to wait until it grew 250 percent. At a 10 percent annual return you would wait over nine years. When you are living on a fixed budget, waiting for your money to grow without income can be brutal.

After you get Social Security started, you can reduce the demand on your investment portfolio. Taking S.S. and, at the same time, stopping (or reducing) your withdrawals may reduce your taxable income, because S.S. is not taxed at the same high rate as IRA withdrawals. Once you no longer need as high a cash flow from your rollover account, you may cut back your withdrawals and consider a more aggressive investment mix, even at an older age. Most important, all capital gains, interest, and dividends left in the IRA will go on compounding, tax free. If you intend to leave a good deal to someone much younger, such as your children, a more aggressive portfolio is appropriate. Often people will begin taking more IRA money during their early retirement years in order to bridge the gap to Social Security. As you can see, there are important decisions to be made, and some are irreversible. One of those important decisions is the choice to wait until full retirement age or to take S.S. income at age sixty-two. Someone at the highest benefit level retiring in 2002 at age sixty-five plus two months would receive $1,660 per month, while a person retiring at age sixty-two would receive $1,382 per month. The *average* monthly benefit for all retired workers as of 2002 is $874 per month.

For those concerned with living a long life, the following calculation may have an impact on the choice you make. Consider Jane, age sixty-two, who retired in 2002 and signed up for Social Security. Let's suppose that over the last thirty-five years she earned an income that qualifies her for the highest S.S. payout for her age. According to *current rates* provided by the Social Security Administration, if she had waited until age sixty-five and a half to get her traditional, full-income benefit, she would have received an estimated $1,744 per month (or $20,928 per year). By signing up for S.S. at sixty-two, she took a 22.1 percent cut to her full benefit. Thus, her income amounts to $16,583 per year (.779 × $1,774 × 12). The following calculations compare her income over a forty-year period under the two scenarios: taking money at sixty-two versus waiting three years and six months. (Because we do not know the rate of inflation, the amounts of income produced over the forty-year lifespan do not include a cost-of-living adjustment.)

Social Security Income Paid Over 10-, 20-, 30-, and 40-Year Periods

Jane's Age	10 years	20 years	30 years	40 years
62	$165,830	$331,660	$497,490	$663,320
65½	$209,280	$418,560	$627,840	$837,120

When to begin taking Social Security and when to remove money from your retirement account are part of this difficult balancing act we have been discussing. New financial calculators used by professionals can help you look at different scenarios or what-if situations. Your cash flow needs should be mapped out as clearly as possible, and income from your investments must be in accord with what the market can deliver. Your income stream can rise or fall dramatically if you work (more or less) after retiring from your primary job, which must be taken into account. Other sources of income can be your savings bank or real estate or business income, but the most reliable retirement check is your Social Security. For those who have been very thrifty, other income may come from nonqualified annuities or the cash value buildup in a life insurance policy. The selling of one's residential property has been, in the past decades, a source of a large lump sum, which then is reinvested. It is not uncommon to see retired people inherit money from older relatives or be given gifts of money or property or receive an insurance settlement. All these resources—big or small, near or distant—should be discussed with a financial advisor in the examination of the bigger picture. Once the gap is closed, then comes the check—but what will that amount to? You need to give your advisor your expected Social Security estimate, which you can get from the government if you do not know it already. For early retirees who are no longer working, a full S.S. benefit can be replaced by a partial one as described in Table 7.2.

Table 7.2   Full Social Security Benefit Versus Partial Benefit

Year of birth	Full benefit age	Partial benefit at 62, percentage of full benefit
1937	65	80.5 percent
1938	65 + 2 months	79.5 percent
1939	65 + 4 months	78.7 percent
1940	65 + 6 months	77.9 percent
1941	65 + 8 months	77.0 percent
1942	65 + 10 months	76.2 percent
1943–1954	66	75.4 percent
1955	66 + 2 months	74.5 percent
1956	66 + 4 months	73.7 percent
1957	66 + 6 months	72.9 percent
1958	66 + 8 months	72.0 percent
1959	66 + 10 months	71.1 percent
1960 and later	67	70.4 percent

Source: *Social Security Administration*

The calculation, for example, for a person retiring in 2003 at the age of sixty-two will have benefits reduced to 77 percent of full benefits. If full benefits at age sixty-five and eight months were to be $1,000, then the retiree would get $770 retiring at sixty-two. The longer you wait the more monthly income you can count on. A spouse also receives a benefit based on either his or her income or the retiree's income, but the spouse must be at least sixty years old. As well, there are several formulae used to calculate the living spouse's retirement benefit, depending on how much earned income the spouse had received during working years. Moreover, the calculations are more complex if one spouse dies leaving a widow or widower entitled to dual benefits based on his or her own as well as the spouse's income and when benefits first began to be paid. Your benefit and the amount your spouse may be entitled to will depend on the average of the highest thirty-five years of income earned. If you have no earned income for the last five years before you collect Social Security, SSA will count those years as zero-income years, bringing down your average income. For some it will be best to work until age sixty-two, at least, to bring up their average earnings. Regrettably, before sixty-five (plus any additional months), known as your *full retirement age*, any earnings you have above a certain limit will be costly. For example, in 2003 that limit is $11,520. If you earn $21,520, then here is the calculation:

$$\$21,520 \text{ earned income} - \$11,520 \text{ limit} = \$10,000$$

A Social Security check of $1,000 per month, or $12,000 per year would be reduced to:

$$\$12,000 - (50 \text{ percent} \times \$10,000) = \$7,000 \text{ per year}$$
$$\$7,000 \div 12 \text{ months} = \$583.33 \text{ per month}$$

As you can see, the $1,000 per month would be reduced to $583.33, because you continued to work and earn above the earnings limit. Things change after you reach full retirement age; at that time there are no limits on earned income and no reductions to Social Security income benefits.

If you decide not to retire at full retirement age and continue to work full time, you can increase S.S. benefits by waiting to collect. First, each additional year you work adds another year to your income records. Higher lifetime earnings may result in higher S.S. income. Second, your benefit increases a certain percentage if you choose to delay the benefits. For example, Joe Jefferson was born in 1943 and started saving late in life. Although his full retirement age is sixty-six, he waited until age sixty-nine to retire (see Table 7.2). By waiting three years, Joe added another 24 percent (8 percent × 3 years) to his benefit. (See Table 7.3 for increase for delayed retirement benefits.) If Joe had qualified for $1,000 per month at age sixty-six, at age sixty-nine he would receive a check for $1,240 per month. For late savers like Joe, working longer may be the only way to afford retirement.

The early retiree—any retiree, for that matter—will need to plan with greater care than the past generation. For the early out, the S.S. gap may be much wider than for someone retiring in the 1990s, because of an earlier retirement date. Moreover, the Social Security income will be less of a percentage of the full benefit, making it harder to sustain a livable income into later decades. Given that the ratio of workers versus retirees is decreasing, there is no certainty that Social Security income—either full or reduced—will be as high as Table 7.2 projects. In order to save the current system, keeping it from bankruptcy, a congressional committee is addressing the subject of solvency and has had discussions regarding reducing proposed benefits. Uncertainty about how we will pay for future benefits makes retirement income planning uncertain at best.

You can see the complexity of this problem called *life-income planning.* It all sounded so simple when you attended your older friend's retirement party. Everyone laughed and joked about how the new retiree now had the

Table 7.3   Increase for Delayed Retirement

Year of birth	Yearly rate increase
1917–1924	3.0 percent
1925–1926	3.5 percent
1927–1928	4.0 percent
1929–1930	4.5 percent
1931–1932	5.0 percent
1933–1934	5.5 percent
1935–1936	6.0 percent
1937–1938	6.5 percent
1939–1940	7.0 percent
1941–1942	7.5 percent
1943 or later	8.0 percent

Source: *Social Security Administration*

world by the tail. Oh, sure! Little did you know that the real concerns about money just begin at retirement, because if you have it, how will you invest it? Who will help you with the many choices you will face? The planning and investment management decisions you make at or just after retirement will significantly contribute to the success of your long-term financial health. It will be these choices that will influence your spending and saving habits for years to come. If you do not believe me, look at the extremely close correlation between consumer spending and the S&P 500 index. Which is the tail and which is the dog? As spending goes up, so do stocks, and as the market goes down so does spending. Harry Dent Jr., author of *The Roaring 2000*, has made a career out of charting the "spending wave" and how it is correlated to demographics and the stock market. Mr. Dent theorized that population trends can predict increases, as well as decreases, in stock market returns. Ex post facto, Harry could not forecast the destruction of the World Trade Center and the economic disruptions that followed. Welcome to the crazy world of finance!

The SEPP Spigot

There is another reason the SEPP rule is a valuable financial tool. If your rollover account does not need to be tapped as soon as you retire—that is, if your savings, vacation pay, or severance pay can get you by for a few years—then the rollover money can grow tax sheltered until the time you need it. The SEPP choice is always there waiting to be turned on like a spigot. The need for a steady income stream may not be only for living expenses, but for other purposes. Suppose you have a big college bill and you need a large sum. You can take a home equity loan (get a deduction for the interest payments) and pay the tuition bill. Then you can SEPP an IRA (income is taxable) and pay the loan on a monthly basis. With a large rollover and a little creative thinking you can become a financial whiz.

Another Use for the SEPP

We already know that the protection of your assets is as important as the management of them. How does a person pay the high cost of long-term care in a nursing home or home nursing care? The expense could range from

$50,000 to $90,000 per year, increasing with inflation. If your long-term care expenses exceed your income, then you may end up spending down your principal. Not a pretty picture! If you have a spouse or a child, there may not be much left to give them if you enter a nursing home. And as for your promised bequest to your favorite charities, they will come looking for the funds at your death and there will be only bills for your estate to pay.

With a SEPP many people are able to use a rollover IRA to pay insurance premiums on a long-term care policy that would protect the IRA as well as all other assets. An annuity payout also can be used to pay the premiums. If you decide that you should have this protection, be sure to buy a policy that can be used in any state you may move to. Many people relocate, and thus need portability of long-term care insurance and other financial instruments, such as trusts. Another use of the SEPP is to pay for an insurance policy in which the death benefit can be used to pay estate taxes and probate fees or fund a life insurance trust. If you have a large amount of property, which may be illiquid at death, you do not want your heirs to enter into an estate sale to come up with cash. One strategy is to purchase an insurance policy to create cash for your heirs. Let your retirement plan pay the premium, and your heirs will receive insurance that is free of income tax. With proper planning, you can have your cake and eat it too.

An insurance policy can also give your heirs money, replacing the funds that you gift to charity. If you place money into a charitable remainder trust or a charitable lead trust, then the death benefit from an insurance policy can be given to your heirs in place of the funds you gave away. What is productive about this idea is that the life insurance proceeds do not create an income tax problem for your heirs if you do it right, and you get a tax deduction while you are living for the charitable gift placed into the charitable trust. If you have the ability (the resources) to use a SEPP for insurance payments, then it may not sting as much to create such complex planning strategies. Be sure to speak to an attorney who is familiar with estate taxes and trusts to help you along. He or she can figure out the best method to use according to your personal goals and situation. Such attorneys hope for the invitation from clients to "save me taxes." Until recently, only wealthy families with over $100 million had the funds to hire a full-time staff of financial advisors to put in place their financial plans. Now, with the new wealth concentrated in retirement plans, most of us will need the same services that have been necessary for the rich for decades. If you know the criteria people with money use to look for the right firm to work with, then you too can find the same services that large institutions and consultants provide their blueblood clientele. As you can now gather, the search for the right advisor is part of a complicated planning process, and my research will help guide you through it.

Investment Proverb 14

An easy way to find creative solutions to your income needs is to understand your income options, like the SEPP.

When attorneys and accountants work to save you taxes they are not doing something to anger the IRS, but to use the laws in your best interest. The rulebook belongs to the IRS, so it can charge a penalty for both intentional and unintentional errors. There are exceptions to rules and penalties that financial planners love to point out. They read the rules, too. For example, an exception to the 10 percent penalty is a disability. One client retired before fifty-nine and a half and took a distribution from his 401(k) and transferred it to his rollover IRA, but did not do a SEPP. Before he took his first payment, he had to get a written statement from his doctor saying that he was disabled and could no longer work. Although this process took several months, during which he spent down his savings account, he was able to get a disability waiver to the under fifty-nine and a half early withdrawal penalty.

Working Part-Time and Taking SEPP

Another situation that is becoming more commonplace today arises when the employee does not retire but may be cutting back and working part-time. Suppose John Nicholas, who is under fifty-nine and a half, and his wife want to buy a condo and do some traveling before retirement. They want to use their 401(k) or profit sharing plan to pay for it, but they do not want to be penalized for early withdrawal. Unable to get at the cash, they go to an actuary, who calculates for them the amount of money they need to remove from the profit sharing plan. They transfer those funds to a rollover IRA, called an *in-service distribution* of retirement assets. Then, once the money is in the new account, they SEPP this account and get a monthly income to support their lifestyle. Even though Mr. Nicholas has not retired, he and Mrs. Nicholas can do all they want, because they have more time while supplementing their earned income with unearned SEPP checks. If you have a 403(b) plan, are over fifty-nine and a half, and are still working, you can transfer your current assets to a rollover and continue to contribute to the 403(b). Then you can SEPP the rollover funds to supplement your income, do some traveling, or follow whatever your dreams may be.

A distribution to beneficiaries made due to the death of any retirement plan participant is another exemption to the 10 percent penalty. Even if the person receiving the distribution is under fifty-nine and a half, there is no penalty, but the funds are taxable if they are taken. A good attorney or other financial advisor should make you aware of the choices heirs have and the tax implications of this event. One estate attorney tells clients to educate their children and spouse regarding the outcome of being a beneficiary. He warns clients that when adult children get the call asking them what they want done with Dad's retirement funds, most say the four magic words, "Send me the money." In the next chapter we will look at the reasons why this can be the *worst* thing to say.

Any time you begin taking income from an account, such as a rollover, you can see the need for a high level of confidence in your return expectations. Like an endowment fund, which must manage money for the good of both current and future students, you must find a way to endow your retirement income. The earlier you retire, the more difficult it is to manage this endowment plan. Over thirty years, you will experience vast changes in the marketplace. In the past thirty years alone, we have already seen four recessions: 73–74, 80–81, and 90–91, and 2000–2002. We have witnessed two industrial revolutions: first, the movement to incorporate computers into daily work, and second, the movement to use electronic networks to communicate personal and business transactions. To make an analogy, a woman does not easily become an opera star. She must first learn to sing and act congruently—to hold a note while dying or being ravished. If your financial plan is to have a successful performance, it must be versatile enough to sing congruently with economic slowdowns or inflation.

Since the economy is not growing at a static rate, but experiences both small and large cycles, the job of an investment consultant is to assist the investor in feeling confident that long-term goals can be met through all circumstances. The difficult times must be honestly dealt with when they arrive, but if you have not planned for these times, when they come you may feel like a victim and try to find someone to blame. The investment process you take to meet the multilevel demands of retirement must be chosen in a deliberate fashion. It must be well thought out and written down, so that if you become ill your appointed trustee or guardian knows how you have managed your money. If you pass on, your investment strategy can be handed down to someone who comes after you, such as your spouse or a trustee. Although the strategy may be changed, if an heir is not familiar with managing money, he or she will know how you went about investing your funds and what goals were important to you.

Personally Tailored Advice

A SEPP or a distribution from a qualified retirement plan should be viewed in the light of a total investment picture. When making major changes, such as retirement, you do not want just one piece of your financial affairs reviewed, because each piece makes a unique contribution to a complete plan. The goal of a financial review before you retire should not be to change anything immediately, but for you to understand where you have come from (financially and personally) and where you are going. Ask yourself questions such as, Whom do I admire in my community, and why? What not-for-profit organizations in my community are important to me? Where would I like to live and why? These kinds of questions will help you see how you may want to live in retirement. By knowing how to get the income you need to maintain your lifestyle, you will have freedom to do what you want for your family and community. One retiree said it clearly: "Retirement is not an event." In planning a retirement each of us must expect to have a challenging and changing life ahead.

Lack of Advice Can Cost Plenty

Many painful mistakes can be avoided by planning, especially mistakes made after the sudden death of a spouse. If you have an advisor to help make rational judgments and find the right people in different disciplines, you will not regret the advice. Recently, a forty-year-old woman spoke to me about needing a CPA to review her tax return, because she had neglected her finances and had created a mess. Her husband had died the year before in his early forties. She had quit her job and taken her lump sum from a retirement plan, as she put it, "to get her by." Her husband had managed the money in both retirement accounts and was successful at it, and now she was lost. With major income tax problems, distrust for the investment person who would not return her phone calls, a large mortgage payment, and IRS penalties facing her, she was ready to spend thousands of dollars in legal and accounting fees to get out of a bad situation. If she had gone to an estate attorney as soon as her husband had died, she would have avoided much emotional and financial anguish.

When money in a retirement plan grows to become a person's major asset, as we see now in the United States, it is paramount that one find good tax advice, life-income planning advice, and investment management advice. To find the needed assistance one must seek out experts who specialize in personal finance, accounting, and estate law and money management that render individual and personal advice. The first interview with these professionals is usually conducted on a no-fee basis so that you (the potential client) can get a feel for what services she can perform for you. If you do not feel all your questions are being answered, you are free to look elsewhere. In Chapter 8, I will help you with the discernment process so that you can become your own chief financial officer, finding a financial advisor to assist you in your duties. Hawaiians call their chief wise person *kabuka*. If you already have a financial advisor, I will give you a way to evaluate your relationship with that person at the end of Chapter 13. If you will be searching for your own kabuka, you can use the same list of questions to ask. Whether you have an advisor or not, by reading the remaining chapters you will learn how to better measure the quality of financial services you should expect to receive. While most personal finance books offer investment strategies and stock picks with the promise to make you millions, in this book I offer you a sound investment process and how to implement that process to produce a worry-free life income.

8

How You Can Provide Added Income for You and Your Heirs

"It is a bad plan that admits of no modification."

—PUBLIUS SYRUS

It's common to confuse *income* with *assets*. Some assets may not produce any income yet may be converted to income, such as an insurance policy, non-dividend-paying stocks, or stock options. And some income is not derived from assets—for example, Social Security. Because we do not see the bigger picture, most preretirees put off reviewing how their assets are structured and thus do not realize their estate plan has already begun to take shape. For example, you may have already elected a beneficiary of your retirement plan. On the other hand, if you have no beneficiary for your assets named in a will, the state you reside in will name one for you. While you may want all your property to go to your wife, New York, for example, provides that *without a will* your probated property would be divided among your children and your spouse.

There are questions all retirees and preretirees ask themselves that can substantially affect estate planning. Are there enough resources to plan an estate for your spouse or heirs? If you are given a choice among different pension (monthly) annuity payouts from your employer, do you know which option is best for you? How much does your spouse need if you die first? Is this amount enough for your spouse to live on for thirty or forty years from now? If your company offered a cash balance option, how do you know it was a fair and reasonable amount compared with an annuity? Some people have no choice but to take a cash balance payout because many new retirement plans are cash balance plans. For others, there is no choice but an annuity. Confusing? With a cash balance option people can receive a lump sum of money instead of an annuity and transfer it to a rollover IRA in order to avoid immediate taxation. Many people who are offered the cash balance option take it rather than a pension annuity.

Choosing an Employee Retirement Pension Option

If you are fortunate enough to have a pension plan retirement benefit, you will need to decide how you want that benefit calculated. Producing a steady retirement income may not be as simple as you think. Before retiring, most employees will be asked to elect a payout option from their employer's pension plan. Taking an annuity pension income on your life alone is called *lifetime benefit*. You cannot outlive an annuity income, and it will pay you the largest annual amount versus all other annuity choices. If you live longer than your life expectancy, this choice would be good, but if you die the day after retirement, your spouse would get no money. The income continues only while you live; all is lost upon death. Although it is the highest payout, unless you have a strategy to help a surviving spouse, such as a large insurance policy, it is not recommended. You can leave your spouse penniless. Also, a divorced spouse can sue for a portion of this benefit.

If you take a pension annuity on the *joint life expectancy* of you and your spouse, your check is less than the payments made on your single life alone, because the life expectancy (LE) of two people is greater than one person's LE. This benefit paid equally to you or your surviving spouse is known as a 100 percent payout of the *reduced lifetime benefit*; it is the most often chosen annuity option. Another choice will give your spouse 50 percent of the reduced lifetime benefit after your death, and another choice, 25 percent of the reduced benefit. Each time you give your spouse less lifetime benefit, you get more income at the beginning of retirement. This scenario makes choosing an annuity income both an income planning and an estate planning problem, and until recently an annuity income was all most retirees had to work with. Growing each year is the new retirement option to take a cash balance distribution versus the annuity. According to the General Accounting Office, as of March 2001 about 20 percent of the top 1,000 companies offer a lump sum distribution of pension benefits, or a cash balance plan. This new retirement plan gives younger employees significant benefits after a few years of service, but it has not been favorably received by senior workers. (If you are not allowed a cash balance payout, you may want to skip to the section on life settlement transactions later in this chapter.)

"Retirement is a welcomed event for many individuals"—so say the pension plan brochures. But as you can see, with the annuity income option, if you and your spouse died in the same auto accident after your retirement, your entire life income would end, leaving none of the remaining income for your heirs. If you were a single person and retired, nothing of the annuity would remain for heirs upon your death. If you are offered a cash balance, and it is a lowball figure, your company may be cheating you out of benefits. How would you know? Although the Civil Rights Act of 1991 and the Older Workers Benefit Protection Act gave retiring people greater power to file lawsuits against employers, many employees are not aware of their rights. Corporations are now requesting that people give up their rights to sue for wrongful discharge or discrimination in exchange for larger severance packages. I wonder how much good will come of this practice. As more companies switch to 401(k) plans and away from a guaranteed pension, people will find there is less government protection of income. An ex-employee of Enron lost over $700,000 of her 401(k) plan invested in company stock and is now left with a small Social Security income check. Defined contribution plans, such as 401(k)s, are not protected under the government's Pension Benefit Guaranty Corporation. Retirement is not such a welcome event if you begin to agonize over your many choices and worry that you are being treated unfairly.

The Cash Balance Election

On the advice of retirement planners, many people are opting for the cash balance payout rather than an annuity income. A cash balance allows you to take a lump sum of money and roll it over into a personal account. When rolling a 403(b) or 401(k), you can set up a rollover IRA with a custodian firm. Your spouse must sign off, stating that it is OK for you to take the funds and place them into an individual retirement account. (A spouse may have reasons, such as a pending divorce, not to allow you to take 401(k) assets and place them in an IRA.)

The same goes for the cash balance option. The calculation of the cash balance is made by company actuaries and is so difficult to understand that I have never seen a pension administrator or human resources professional give a clear explanation of it. For the preretiree, the cash amount is usually based on the four-year average of the U.S. treasury bond rate, your age, your income level, and your length of service. *Your employer does not owe you a lump sum conversion of your pension annuity payment; therefore, the cash balance calculation can vary widely from firm to firm and from time to time.* As of yet, and quite surprisingly, there is no set standard that guides employers in the calculation of the cash balance. While some companies are more generous than other companies, some employees and unions have sued employers for allegedly attempting to undercut retirement benefits.

A pension plan offers you "financial security during retirement," says the benefits brochure, but I have seen too many people speculating with their benefits. An investment advisor I know told me a story about her son, who took his 401(k) plan and put it into a day trading account. He bragged when he got his $40,000 up to $110,000, but he later admitted that he lost all but $10,000. "When Fortune flatters, she does it to betray," said Publius Syrus. The lessons we learn are often bitter. If this man had spoken to an advisor, he might have gotten a better perspective on the value of losses incurred with retirement money: there is no deduction for realized losses, and they last a lifetime.

In Germany there is a saying: "The way you speak into the forest is the echo you get back." I feel that retirees and advisors should share a relationship based on listening, understanding, and mutual respect. I call it *client-driven consultative planning.* While the process takes a lot of time— more than one meeting—the retiree will gain confidence that his financial security has been taken into account when he does business with an advisor. With the large cash balances and 401(k) plans being distributed, the modern retiree must communicate to the financial advisor not to take undue risk with funds that the retiree needs to last a lifetime. During the initial process the risk/reward problem must be resolved, so all know what can be expected. Because your retirement will last many years longer than your parents' did, you must work together with your financial advisor to find out whether the amount you have saved is enough. If you are a spendthrift, your advisor should point out your weakness. He or she may even advise you to choose an annuity option over a cash balance for your own good. An honest advisor may lose you as a client, but I would rather give up income than do the unethical—further deceive you into thinking you are not a squanderer. In our business the Securities Exchange Commission takes the "know-your-client" rule quite seriously. Mindful of the rule, an advisor should work in your best interest.

A Simple Case Study

Let's look at an example of pension payout and how choices can affect your income and the total assets in your estate. Tony is sixty and a widower with two adult children. The maximum retirement benefit offered by his company on his life alone is $4,000 per month ($48,000 annually). He can never outlive this payout, nor will he see a decrease in this amount. (A few plans offer a cost-of-living increase.) But if he takes this option he will not leave any inheritance to his children, because his payments end at his demise. There is nothing for his children.

On the other hand, suppose Tony is given a cash balance option. Instead of an annuity, he is allowed a generous lump sum of $564,700. He then can roll over this amount and make annual 6.5 percent withdrawals from his account. His house is paid for, and his needs can be met with $3,058 per month ($36,705 per year). This arrangement allows him to address several retirement and estate planning concerns.

First, taking the cash balance frees him from taking the fixed pension and allows him the use of a rollover IRA. He gives up a guaranteed $4,000 monthly income, some of which he does not need, in order to gain access to $564,700 plus the income this money can produce.

Second, since he now has the principal in his account, he can name his two children as beneficiaries of his rollover. If he dies, they can divide the lump sum, whereas they would get *nothing* if he took the monthly life annuity plan. The children will appreciate Dad a little more for making the right choice.

Third, if this account grows as expected, Tony could later shave off more funds for other purposes or increase income each year that his account rises. In the short term, because of market volatility he may see his principal dip below his initial investment, but over the long run, his account should be able to maintain his life-income needs, while still being accessible for extraordinary expenses.

Moreover, he has a great probability of financially doing better than with the fixed-income annuity choice. (Some advisors may encourage a small portion—say, 20 percent—of his total assets to be annuitized immediately to guarantee *base* income for life.) He may start out with less income than the pension annuity, but eventually the income and principal can outperform the fixed-income option. Earlier we showed that the long-term ownership of equities could increase income by increasing principal. Unlike the annuity, the rollover has no guarantee of a lifetime income; on the other hand, the lifetime annuity guarantees nothing for his children and gives him no access to investment opportunities, such as bonds or equities.

Now, if the investment decisions are not wisely made in the rollover, he could *outlive* this account, and then he would have been better off with the annuity he was first offered. Other than for the risk of owning bad investments, the lump sum is superior to the annuity when it grapples with the problem of inflation. I have seen teachers who have annuitized their 403(b) (TSA) plans at retirement. After twenty years on a fixed monthly income, they wished they had rolled over the funds and taken out money as they needed it. (A 403(b) plan can be rolled into a rollover IRA, but unique rules govern TSA distributions.) These teachers gave up growth of income, growth of principal, and the chance to leave heirs a sizable inheritance, all for a "secure" monthly income. Compounding the mistake, over twenty-five years the buying power of the monthly income was cut by 66 percent.

In Tony's case, if he stays within a budget, he has a better chance of being a good steward of his assets by taking the lump sum and having it properly managed. Whether he dies in a few years or many years from now, his total return on the portfolio could easily be greater than the annuity income, and he would have something to leave to heirs. If the cash balance is large enough, and he manages it properly, he gets to meet his income goals and have money to bequeath.

Remember that the decision to take the annuity income is an irrevocable one, unlike the decision as to *how* money is to be managed. Once you take an annuity, you gain income but lose a valuable resource. How well Tony manages the funds will determine whether he made the right choice. With proper return expectations given to the portfolio, with the investments balanced so that the rewards are sought at the lowest risk, and with the portfolio continuously monitored, Tony should be able to accomplish more with the rollover than with any annuity choice. If Tony is a spender, all bets are off. Those who squander their wealth will take more from their account than it can reasonably produce, and then ask, "Where did it all go?" In that case,

Tony is better off with the fixed annuity, and the money manager or advisor would be smart to refuse Tony's account.

Some employees who take the cash balance option say that this money is to be invested for the long term, that they want to live on the income alone and grow the principal and income. But do they? A few clients will call and say, "I cannot believe my account is so far down." Then I add up the extraordinary withdrawals they have taken, and they cannot believe how much they have removed in one year. I have learned to warn people that they need to keep to a budget. Before taking on clients who I sense are capable of spending more than they should, I use a computer program to show how quickly their account could fall to zero. If they do not stick to a spending discipline, they will become their own nightmare. I have concluded that when taking the cash balance and placing it into a rollover, two disciplines must coexist. If either one is violated, the account is doomed.

Investment Proverb 15

*Most retirees must have both a spending
discipline and an investment discipline.*

Unlike the previous generation, today's retirees are not spending much less than they did before retirement. Although retirement planning programs, such as those found on the Internet, assume everyone will reduce spending 25 percent at retirement. I do not see this happening. Although it is important that preretirees find their after-tax income need before retiring, people seem never to find the time to do the work. If you skipped over the list of expenses at the end of Chapter 2, go back and find the total. Remember, you are looking to answer the question, What is the cost of my lifestyle? A good budget and control over your monetary habits are as important as how much money you make. Many wealthy people have died bankrupt for not balancing their checkbooks.

Using Life Insurance to Create Income

There is one trick that allows retirees a way of taking a pension annuity and protecting their estate from an early death. Going back to Tony's case, suppose he decides to take the $4,000 per month on his life alone. If he qualifies for ten-year term insurance, and is a nonsmoker, he can then purchase an insurance policy with a face value of $500,000 for an annual cost of approximately $2,500. Assuming he can get along on $3,000 a month from the annuity (rather than $4,000), he can spend money on the insurance premiums *and* gift money to his children each year as well. The beauty of this strategy is that when he dies, a $500,000 insurance payout is income tax free to his children. If he holds the policy only ten years and then drops it, he has already gotten $480,000 in total payments ($48,000 per year × 10 years). If he wanted to continue the term insurance policy, he may (depending on the policy's options) be able to convert to permanent insurance. With such a conversion, he could then buy a whole life or universal life policy that will not end, giving him insurance protection until his death. Although he may have to give up some face amount or pay higher premiums, he will be able to leave a legacy without worry. (The choice of insurance and its conversion properties must be discussed prior to purchase.)

Remember that the rollover income paid to heirs is 100 percent taxable as ordinary income. Although the Economic Growth and Tax Relief Reconciliation Act (EGTRRA) of 2001 lowered estate taxes in most cases, income tax on retirement assets remains a problem. Tony's heirs can lose 30 percent to 40 percent of the retirement plan to income taxes alone. The $500,000 insurance death benefit is tax-free income to his heirs; therefore, it becomes the preferable payoff to his children. This technique is called *pension maximization*. Note: *It does not work at all for the uninsurable or those who cannot afford the premiums.* If Tony had a spouse, and he wanted to take the single-life pension annuity plan, he could purchase the insurance and name his wife as beneficiary instead of his children. His children could be named contingent beneficiaries. When he died and the pension stopped, his wife would get the insurance payout free of an income tax liability. When she died, if she had not spent the funds their children would inherit this portion of her estate income tax free.

Life Settlement Transactions

The sale of an insurance policy is known as a *life settlement transaction*. For Tony, a ten-year term insurance policy would cost more in the eleventh year (when he turned seventy) to keep the insurance in force, but he could save some funds for that purpose. As well, if his wife dies first, he could cancel or even sell the policy! You read that correctly. The owner of an insurance policy (in this case, Tony) receives cash for his term or whole life insurance when the ownership of the policy is sold (transferred) to the purchasing company. What wonders there are in the financial world—*people pay you to die.* Perfectly legitimate! Just do not sell the contract to somebody who has no scruples and then invite that person to join you on a deep-sea scuba dive.

"In this transaction the remaining future premiums are paid by the insurance company," writes one financial advisor. The *settlement company,* which is the buyer, would probably have you convert term insurance to whole life (permanent) insurance, then reimburse you for the cost. If you are terminally ill and have a short time to live, you can get a large cash settlement for your insurance policy, known as a *viatical settlement.* That is why the settlement company will usually want to know about your health. Firms and people invest in your death, and you get cash in return while you live and use the funds as you please. Remember: your advisor will have access to a stable of insurance providers and settlement companies. She could shop the street for the most competitive rates or find a company that can do the shopping for you. Some viatical companies will create a loan against the death benefit of the policy, which may be even more favorable than the selling of the death benefit. In either case, as I warned in the beginning of this book, you must look closely at the reputation and experience of the companies you deal with. If you have old insurance policies that have not been cashed in and you become terminally ill, you may consider a viatical settlement or loan to generate needed funds. A local bank or insurance company can also make loans to you. You can use the death benefit as the collateral for the loan.

Purchasing a Viatical as an Investment

Buyer beware! Do not purchase a viatical with the promise of making money. First, the contracts are not saleable; and second, they can be offered easily by scam artists, because as of this writing most states do not consider viaticals securities and therefore do not regulate them. Let the viatical settlement companies take that risk. Many advocates for the retired have warned us that older people are targets for shady viatical sales. On the other hand, large companies have the wherewithal to wait out the poor investment returns that are highly possible. Peter C. Katt, CFP, writes, "My conclusion is that the viatical market is so inherently appalling that no respectable financial planner should ever participate in the solicitation of terminally ill persons or investors for viatical firms" (*Journal of Financial Planning*, April 2001, p. 36). A client of mine bought a contract hoping for a promised 10 percent per year. He has been sorely disappointed. After speaking to him, I found that he really had poor knowledge of how the contract was structured and how the person who sold the contract to him got paid. Good advisors stay on top of the investment world, as well as the underworld, and can guide you to those investments that make sense for your unique situation.

"Mathematics is the science that draws necessary conclusions," says Benjamin Peirce. And he would know. He authored *Linear Associative Algebra* in 1870. As you can see, the calculations to be made combine the client's needs, goals, and temperament with what the law allows and what the financial world has to offer. What amazes me is how rapidly laws change, and how investment products and services evolve so quickly that the average person finds it impossible to keep up with the blizzard of options. As we speak, the insurance annuity industry is coming out with more payment options and more investment options as one company tries to win market share over another. Money managers are finding new inefficiencies in the market to exploit in order to outperform each other. Nothing stodgy remains in business. As a matter of interest, I tend to believe that pride is the coffin of progress, because in pride you begin to lose the desire to improve.

The best of financial advisors are always taking financial courses, researching trends, and reading trade publications to better serve their clients. Since there is so much to learn and to apply, different disciplines— such as risk analysis, financial planning, asset management, and estate planning—are becoming more specialized. Advisors cannot wear all the hats they once did, but can do a better job for clients by focusing on specific areas of expertise. Finding the right advisors is a lot like finding the right friends; they are there when you need them.

Investment Proverb 16

The jack of all trades may become
the master of none.

When you are seeking advice, the fees you spend should be explained in terms of value received and money saved. Many advisors act as though they're so intelligent and skilled that you, the lowly client, should not question their fees. Simply ask questions, no matter how foolish they seem to be. It is your money. You are justified in finding out what you are paying for and how the person you have hired will earn his money. Many insurance and financial companies have learned to take an amoral attitude toward how advisors are compensated, assuming that what the client doesn't know won't hurt her. In her book *Smart Questions to Ask Your Financial Advisers*, Lynn Brenner writes, "In personal finance one thing separates smart consumers from confused consumers: knowing what to ask."

As a final example of being poorly educated: the AARP found that 50 percent of people buying mutual funds at banks *thought* they were FDIC insured! In a later chapter I will show how just a few questions can reveal the capabilities of a financial advisor, and in the last chapter I will help you evaluate financial advisory services. For now you are beginning to see how an advisor can unravel the complex issues surrounding retirement options and help you leave more for your heirs.

Company Stock in 401(k) or Shares in Employee Stock Ownership Plans

Being up on the tax code certainly can save you a bundle in retirement. Let's take an example that I have come across more frequently today than in the past. I was able to apply IRS Code 402(a) to company stock I received when my firm merged with another firm. It allows the distribution of company stock from a retirement account to go directly to the retiree as a lump sum of stock. Although it can go into a rollover IRA as well, the rule allows for an unusual tax break. This stock must come from a 401(k) or an ESOP plan purchased by the employer or employee in the plan while working. The difference in value between what the company paid (or what you paid) for the stock and what it is worth when you get it is called *net unrealized appreciation (NUA)*. Tens of thousands of dollars in taxes can be saved when the rule is applied correctly. Few people know this legal loophole to reduce taxes. Here is an example of how it would work.

Suppose you retired from Blue Electric Company (BEC) and you had a choice to roll over 1,000 shares of the stock from your 401(k) to a rollover. The stock cost the company $10 per share, and now it is worth $100 per share. Your net unrealized appreciation is as follows:

BEC stock cost: $10,000 (1,000 shares × $10 per share)

BEC stock value: $100,000 (1,000 shares × $100 per share)

$$\$100,000 - \$10,000 = \$90,000 \text{ NUA}$$

If you take the stock in a lump sum when you retire, then you will include on your tax return only $10,000 in taxable income (that portion the company contributed) while the NUA of $90,000 goes to you *untaxed*. (You must take all the stock from the retirement plan for this arrangement to work, but you can roll over some and take some shares.) An important thing to know is when you sell the stock, whether immediately or twelve months later, the gain is taxable at the more favorable long-term gain rate of 20 percent. On the other hand, if you roll over any of the stock to a rollover IRA, it would be taxed as ordinary income when you take it out. You would lose the favorable long-term gains tax rate. Going through the math in the following example, which demonstrates what would happen if you transferred 1,000 shares of BEC stock to a rollover IRA, will help you see why a consultant can save you money. It works especially well for those who are in a high tax bracket during retirement years, because it converts ordinary, taxable income into long-term gains.

Roll over BEC stock worth $100,000.

Five years later it is worth $150,000.

Take funds out of IRA: At 28 percent tax rate, paid $42,000 (plus state taxes, too).

Total tax paid: $42,000-plus.

Value you received: $108,000.

Consider now taking 1,000 shares of the stock at retirement using NUA.

Take BEC stock worth $100,000.

Cost basis of stock: $10,000 × 28 percent tax = $2,800 out of pocket.

Five years later, sell stock for $150,000.

Minus cost basis: −$10,000.

NUA is $140,000.

Long-term gains tax at a 20 percent federal rate is $28,000, plus state capital gains tax.

Total tax paid: $30,800.

Value you received: $114,200.

In this example it would cost you at least $6,200 more to roll over the stock, versus not rolling it. If the stock were not rolled over and you sold it immediately you could use the NUA rule on the sale. In summary, with this strategy there is a good chance you would have less tax to pay over the long run, and you would free up more money immediately upon retirement.

Investment Proverb 17

*Creating and then spending low taxable
dollars is always preferable to spending high
taxable dollars.*

The NUA rule is tricky. It must be executed by the book. If you have company stock in any retirement plan, then your accountant, attorney, or advisor should be quizzed to see whether she has information on the rule. If she cannot find an answer, find one who can. Your company must provide you with the cost basis of the stock. If you placed some of your own money into it, the company will tell you how much. If you contributed after-tax dollars toward the stock, then there is no income tax due on these dollars, but your contribution needs to go into the tax calculation too. *Here, all calculation should be made before execution of the strategy.* In that way, you are given a choice.

Many retirees looking to spend money immediately after retirement and not wanting to tap their rollover would be wise to check out the NUA rule. Those *posttax* contributions you made to your retirement will be sent to you at retirement and should give you some money to spend until you need your rollover funds. If you are under fifty-nine and a half, you may not want to take distributions from the ESOP that are taxable, but instead roll over the stock. There are different interpretations of the IRS code for those who are under fifty-nine and a half and receiving company stock, so you must get dependable advice. If you get different interpretations of the code, *pick the most conservative advice.* You do not want to be haunted by the IRS if they begin to crack down on how the ESOP shares and employer contributions should be taxed.

Private letter rulings (PLRs) are rulings made by the IRS on specific cases that help guide lawyers and accountants as they study the thinking of the IRS. Much about the way advice is given regarding NUA and retirement distributions is taken from these rulings. A Danish proverb says, "Lawyers and painters can soon change white to black." And so can the IRS. You should see an attorney or an accountant regarding any tax laws that apply to your specific situation. If your tax advisor cannot answer your questions, find one who can.

What Is Income in Respect of a Decedent?

There is another reason for using the NUA rule in estate planning. If you roll your company stock into an IRA and your heirs inherit the stock, they will pay tax on the full value at their income tax rate. Retirement plan income passed on to heirs is called *income in respect of a decedent (IRD)*, and it may be included in the gross income of the person who acquires the IRA, TSA, or 401(k). That is, if your son or daughter is in the 28 percent (or possibly 31 percent) federal tax bracket, then he or she will be taxed at these high levels when receiving the income. Wow! What a tax! I recall a recent heir to her dad's General Motors 401(k). She was given two choices: take all the cash immediately or over five years. There was no other option allowed by General Motors. If her dad had rolled the money to a rollover IRA, with proper planning she would have had other options. You would think that a large company could offer more options to an heir, but it did not. Most companies will not allow any advanced estate planning strategies written into their 401(k) plan document. And it is probably too complex for them to do so.

In our earlier example, if you take the BEC stock and pay tax on the cost basis, you then can gift the stock to your heirs. They can hold the stock, and they will have no taxes to pay until they sell it. When they sell the shares, they are taxed on the NUA at the favorable 20 percent long-term gains rate. In the years ahead, the rate may go down, increasing the value of the NUA. As you are given the NUA tax break, you can pass the break on to your children. You may also gift these shares to a charity directly or to a charitable trust and get a tax writeoff and pay no capital gains tax. Gifting highly appreciated stock to charity is one of the best financial planning moves, because both you and the charity gain. For many retirees who leave a large estate, it will be a matter of choosing Uncle Sam or their favorite charity.

Who Are the Heirs to Your Retirement Money?

Death benefits of all qualified accounts, such as an IRA, 401(k), or 403(b), are subject to both estate taxes and income taxes, but good planning can reduce both of these taxes. In the BEC example, the gift of stock (rather than rolling into an IRA) wields a swift blow to the tax bill. By getting the stock out of a retirement plan, income tax owed on IRD disappears. Thousands can be saved. By gifting the stock, estate taxes on the stock disappear, too, because the estate is reduced by the gifts. Amazing how few people actually understand these concepts, yet if you do not know them you may never get to use them. Many retirees, upon leaving a firm that offers a retirement plan with a no-load fund, bank, or brokerage firm, simply convert the account to a rollover IRA without first asking for financial or estate planning advice. A big error! They lose (without knowing it) all the NUA benefits for themselves, and they may leave their heirs with lots of income and estate tax liability mounting into the hundreds of thousands of dollars. When it comes to income tax and estate planning, free advice can turn into costly advice.

On the basis of this example alone, you should be encouraged to seek advice *before* retiring. Because there are so many convoluted paths to take, when planning for retirement and for the distribution of your estate you need a firm understanding of IRS code and deft mathematical skill to help you choose which path may be best. When going to an advisor before retiring, you should seek answers to the following questions:

- What is the least expensive estate tax plan for me? Is it the best plan?
- What is the most advantageous income tax plan for me?
- Where should my qualified (401(k), 403(b), 457, and so on) retirement plan assets be moved?
- How should my retirement assets be invested?
- How should my retirement assets be monitored?
- When should I gift my assets to heirs and to charity?
- What should I expect in the form of current income?
- Should I pay off or refinance my mortgage?
- Which investments should I spend first at retirement?
- What should I do with ESOP stock in my retirement account?
- How and when should I exercise incentive or nonqualified stock options?
- What should I do with my company insurance policies?

- Do I need more life insurance to cover estate fees and taxes?
- What should I do to protect my estate from long-term care expenses?
- What should be done with nonqualified deferred compensation, like severance?
- Do I need a life insurance trust, living trust, or other trust work?
- In the unfortunate case of a divorce, how will assets be fairly divided?

These questions are part of my own preretirement concerns. If you have retired and are not satisfied with the answers you get, when you finish this book you will know how to find the help you need. I have gone to an attorney to redraw my will and to be sure my estate has enough cash to pay taxes, administration, and probate fees. My estate plan should have enough design to it that my wife and children need not panic seeking advice because the advisors are already lined up. I have given them more than one choice of advisors. If both my wife and I die, a trustee and guardian has been selected to watch over the estate for our children's benefit and manage our trust. Much of this arrangement is not for the sake of self-interest, but out of love for my family. I said to my wife, "There are two things that motivate us most: money and love, and love is the most preferred motivation."

Many of the choices you face at retirement depend on what your employer has to offer, how long you think you may live, how much you want to leave to heirs, and how well you manage your money. Working closely with an advisor can create the plan that meets your needs and your personal and family goals.

9

How to Use a Rollover IRA to Leave More to Your Heirs

"There is never an instant's truce between virtue and vice. Goodness is the only investment that never fails."

—HENRY DAVID THOREAU

It's best that you understand all your company benefits and know all the personal investments and insurance policies you have outside the company. Many times, these contracts were purchased over thirty or forty years ago and are lost, sitting in the attic somewhere accumulating dust. I recall one client coming into our firm with a mildewed bag full of money—a foul smell permeated the office. Another client who would not have us hold his U.S. treasury bonds found he had lost them—years ago these bonds were in bearer form with no name on them. He had to get congressional approval, actually attaching a request to a bill in Congress, to replace the U.S. debt owed to him. (Today these bonds are not issued in bearer form.) Another client discovered some old stock he had been sitting on worth $25,000 that was not paying him income and had little growth potential, yet he had a $26,000 credit card debt that was costing him $4,600 per year in interest. His excuse for not selling the stock and paying off the debt was that he had forgotten about the stock! He is the kind of person who never saw the value of a financial review until after he retired, and even then it took a call from me to get him to consider it.

It is far easier for *you* to locate securities and important documents (and to replace lost ones) than it would be for your heirs. For documents you do not have, such as insurance policies and annuity contracts, you should find proof of their existence and store them in a place easily accessible to heirs until you get new documents. Do not put them in a safety deposit box with your name on it, because your heirs will not be able to enter it until official representatives are present to witness what's inside (and that can take months), tying up the use of those documents. When they are already grieving your death, heirs should not grieve about the grave you dug.

Do not overdo it with the stuff you save. Keep only what is really important. A client's wife complained to me in tears that her husband saved every paper he received from his former brokerage firm, insurance company, and banks. She told me, "There are boxes in the basement stacked to the ceiling, and I know they are a fire hazard." Her husband saved these items for fear that he would be lost without the information that reached back more than fifteen years. Who is right? In this case, the wife felt she would be inundated with work if he were to die. Now in their seventies, they wanted to sell the house and move into an apartment. What would they do with all these files he claimed were "important"? After a long conversation with both of them, I convinced her that we would have much of the necessary data stored and that most of what was in the basement was garbage. When we finished our meeting, he was convinced that he had neglected the most important paperwork of all: *he had no will nor trust*. That was another mess that had to be cleaned up.

Before retiring, you need to make an inventory of all your assets and insurance polices, letting your spouse in on this work and showing him or her where your important papers are stored. One of my clients had his entire financial plan laid out in a binder with specific instructions to his wife on how he managed their money, and how I would assist her in keeping to his investment philosophy. He had created a financial roadmap for her, and I would be her navigator. People with investments should have a written *investment policy statement (IPS)*, which summarizes the goals and methods by which money has been managed and directs how funds should be managed once they are deceased. (I will describe in a later chapter what an IPS contains.)

Five-Year Rule and Postdeath Distributions of 401(k)s

"The 401(k) is an estate planning killer," says a friend and estate planning attorney. There is a rule that most 401(k) administrators follow regarding the death of an employee. If you have a 401(k) or 403(b), and you name your estate, a nonqualified trust, a charity, or a non-spouse as a beneficiary, your 401(k) will be paid out immediately or over five years ending on December 31 of the fifth year after the day you passed away. Known as the *five-year rule*, it can dump a lot of taxable income into your heirs' hands when they may least want or need it. James Lange writes, "Many existing 401(k) plans will not allow a stretch IRA for non-spouse beneficiaries but will require the entire plan proceeds be distributed the year after the IRA owner dies" (*Financial Planning*, March 2001, p. 92). Most 401(k) plans cannot handle distributions upon death to anyone but a spouse—as I showed in the example of GM's 401(k) in the previous chapter. Sad, but true. For many retirees, rolling a 401(k) into a rollover IRA will allow you to name your spouse as primary beneficiary, and he or she can roll the funds into a rollover in his or her own name when you pass on. So an exception to the five-year rule is the *spousal rollover*. Only a spouse can roll over 401(k) money into his or her account and *not* comply with the five-year rule. The spouse can then name the children as beneficiaries. Isn't this all terribly confusing? Tell the IRS.

A Five-Year Rule for Rollovers with More Flexibility for Heirs

If your children inherit your rollover, then they will need to retitle your account. An example of a retitled account: Brokerage Firm Name, Custodian, Joe Jefferson FBO Joe Jefferson Deceased IRA, Marge Jefferson. With this account, Joe's child named Marge can (upon Joe's death) leave money in a tax-sheltered account. She can then stretch the IRD taxable income over her own life expectancy. Yes, yes, yes! As long as you name a human being as your beneficiary, your rollover can be stretched out. If you fail to designate a beneficiary and you are under seventy and a half when you die, then naming a charity or your "estate" causes the five-year rule to come into play. On the other hand, if you leave your funds in a 401(k) and do not roll it, on your death (if you did not name a spouse) your children *would not* be able to stretch out payments, and that is an estate planning killer.

Remember: what the law allows, your 401(k) provider may not allow. For a variety of reasons most 401(k) plans today do not allow a stretch-out benefit for non-spouse beneficiaries. The consequence: your children will receive money from your 401(k) plan over five years, or worse yet, some plans will distribute all funds in the year the employee dies. In either case, the non-spouse beneficiaries will lose the stretch-out privilege that could have given them a tax-sheltered account for many more years! So be sure to name a human being as your primary beneficiary; it may be one of the easiest things to do while providing you with many benefits. In addition, if you have a non-spouse beneficiary in mind, an IRA rollover will give them the unique opportunity to get the maximum tax savings with a stretch-out.

Advantage of the Rollover Stretch-Out (or Stretch IRA)

Imagine that Joe Jefferson has one child, Marge, age forty, who is employed and earns $60,000 per year. He leaves this child his 401(k) plan worth $500,000 upon his death. The money is IRD and so is taxable income when she takes it. The forty-year-old woman has a life expectancy of forty-two and a half years. In our example, Marge, rather than taking $128,546 per year for five years and paying taxes at a 36 percent tax rate, defers the taxes by taking much less per year from the deceased rollover IRA. For example, instead of getting $128,546, she takes $11,765 the first year, putting her in a 31 percent tax bracket. The way we get that amount is to divide life expectancy into the total IRA. It looks like this:

$$\$500,000 \div 42.5 = \$11,765$$

Marge will remove $116,781 less than under the five-year rule. A big difference? You bet—and a much smaller tax consequence. Many preretirees will inherit IRAs from parents and will need to see an accountant or advisor to be sure these calculations are correct, because they change each year. Using Table 9.1, you can estimate the additional years you may live. You can withdraw funds each year from an inherited IRA over that period. Thirty or forty years seem like forever when you're young, but if you ask a seventy-year-old he'll say, "Forever comes soon enough."

The fixed life expectancy is reduced by one for each subsequent year. For example, at age 55 life expectancy is 28.6 years. The required minimum distribution for a 55-year-old is 1/28.6 of the IRA in year one, 1/27.6 in year two, 1/26.6 in year three, and so on for a maximum of 28 years, when the account is depleted.

This way of withdrawing funds is called the *installments over life expectancy* method. Each year that you can get payments that go beyond the five-year rule that governs most 401(k) plan distributions, you get an income tax deferral. Your children can make money on the taxes they owe to the government by deferring taxes. Since the choice of stretching out payments over a child's life expectancy is allowed by the IRS when removing funds from an IRA, the IRA is the preferable place to hold retirement funds. Thank Dad for being so wise as to name Marge! Unlike the IRA, the 401(k) could not have accommodated Mr. Jefferson's request to pay out money to his daughter over a forty-two-year period. To clarify the rule for you: if you intend to give money to a person(s) upon your death, be sure to name the person(s) as the beneficiary of your rollover. If you name your estate and not a person, then your heir may not be able to stretch out payments, but

Table 9.1   Fixed-Period Single-Life Expectancy (Ages 40 through 59)

Starting age	Life expectancy	Starting age	Life expectancy
40	42.5	50	33.1
41	41.5	51	32.2
42	40.6	52	31.3
43	39.6	53	30.4
44	38.7	54	29.5
45	37.7	55	28.6
46	36.8	56	27.7
47	35.9	57	26.8
48	34.9	58	25.9
49	34.0	59	25.0

Source: *Internal Revenue Service*

would either take them over five years or over your life expectancy (if your death came after your required beginning date). Either way, the beneficiary would lose some flexibility.

Using the Installment Over Life Expectancy Method

In order to show me the difference between the installment method stretch-out plan and the five-year rule, Wil Heupel with Accredited Investors created for me a sixteen-page spreadsheet that I can only summarize below. Needing to make assumptions, such as tax bracket and rate of return, in order to create an illustration, Mr. Heupel and his colleague Mr. Snow plugged into their computer a return of 9 percent on the funds invested in the rollover. The after-tax withdrawals also were reinvested at 9 percent. Although I am sure Marge would have spent some of the funds, we needed to hold certain variables constant to prove this amazing point—that *tax deferral* is the cat's meow. Assuming the initial $500,000 rollover is stretched out over forty-two and a half years, the following figures show its superior value:

Marge's Balance Sheet Using Stretch-Out Versus Five-Year Rule

After year	Value of rollover plus funds outside of IRA	Value of five-year payout with funds reinvested at 9 percent
14	$1,589,491	$874,054
24	$3,160,844	$1,573,206
34	$5,402,325	$2,378,975
44	$8,442,610	$3,844,262

After forty-four years the difference is $4,598,348 more, or 119 percent better.

Even after subtracting the taxes, the income from the forty-two installments will last longer than a five-year payout, and both income and principal is tax sheltered while held in the rollover IRA. With the lengthened payout period, it is possible that Marge could wind up with 119 percent more in funds. If Marge has a child, she can leave her child as beneficiary of the

IRA funds. (Allow me to note that if you leave a minor as a beneficiary, it would be wise to check with an attorney to create a trust. If you entered into a second marriage and you have children from a first marriage, a trust can bring relief, knowing your children will have rights to your money under the trust arrangement.)

Letting Marge take money out over her life expectancy is called a stretch-out because the payments made to her are lengthened from a five-year period to a longer "life expectancy period." Thus, by creating a smaller payout schedule in the early years, the inheritance has more time to grow. So what do children do when they get the call from the 401(k) department (or IRA custodian) regarding Dad's retirement? They foolishly say, "Send me the money." They might have done just the opposite if they had received tax-saving advice about the five-year rule or a stretch-out. If Dad's money is in a rollover, they should tell the rollover custodian to put the funds into a deceased IRA, leaving it in Dad's name but paid out to them.

In the example we've used so far, a further twist in planning can take place. If Marge left her dad's remaining rollover to her own son before removing it all, then her son could stretch out that money over his lifetime. This second stretch-out could turn a $100,000 rollover account into millions of dollars. Amazing! Until 1999 this second stretch-out was not even thought of, but the IRS allowed it to happen, setting a precedent.

Investment Proverb 18

*Getting retirement money can give you a
headache; an estate attorney should be consulted
regarding any retirement distributions
you may inherit.*

What Are Required Lifetime Distributions?

Things get even more complicated when the retiree reaches seventy and a half. At this juncture the IRS says that the retirement account must begin to pay the retiree a required minimum distribution (RMD). Estate attorney Natalie B. Choate wrote in *Life and Death Planning for Retirement Bene-*

fits, "The minimum distribution rules of IRS 401(a)(9) dictate how quickly (or slowly) benefits come out of retirement plans. Understanding these rules is the key to successful tax planning for retirement benefits."

She continues, "There are many 'gray areas' in the tax treatment of retirement benefits—questions that the regulations simply do not answer; points of law subject to different interpretations; or regulatory positions that seem contrary to law or for some other reason likely to be changed in the future" (*Life and Death Planning for Retirement Benefits*, 3rd edition, 1999, p. 5, self-published and found on www.ataxplan.com). *Complicated . . . gray . . . changing . . .* those words should be enough to encourage any retiree into seeking estate planning advice. Although the new IRS rules approved on January 11, 2001, have simplified distribution calculations and requirements, they did not simplify how you deal with designations of beneficiaries. As well, the IRS added some requirements that will make it easier to monitor your account and to penalize you. Your advisor's acumen regarding these rules will determine how well your estate is prepared to deal with distributions.

An attorney who wants to remain anonymous gave me an interesting story to tell financial advisors. A client approached him to review his estate plan. He gave the attorney his old will, and at a follow-up meeting he brought along his highly regarded financial advisor. It seems the advisor had made the client a great deal of money in his rollover IRA, and the client wanted to include him in the estate planning process. After reading the will, soon to be replaced, the attorney found that the current will named a bank as executor of the client's estate. "Did you know," said the attorney, "that if you die with the bank as the executor, the bank will take the money—successfully managed by your advisor—and place it in the control of the bank's investment department? The bank will transfer your rollover, and your advisor will lose the account." Since it had been years since the will had been drawn, the client had forgotten what was written there and was quite struck by the thought that another firm might take over the management of his account. To the relief of the financial advisor, the client immediately had his will redrawn naming a new executor.

This story makes an important point that I cannot overemphasize: you need an estate planning (elder law) attorney on your team of financial professionals. This person can be of great value many years prior to your retirement and then review your estate plan in a follow-up meeting when you get there.

Let's consider an example of the retiree with money invested in a rollover IRA at age seventy and a half. Suppose Mary (whose husband is the same age) taught high school and built up a 403(b) account, and then went to work in industry and accumulated a 401(k). The required beginning date (RBD) for the minimum distribution is April 1 of the year following the year a person turns seventy and a half. If Mary waited till the last minute, then she would have to take two distributions in that year. Since she does not need the extra money, it is best that she take out the first distribution in the year she turns seventy and a half so she does not get taxed heavily in any one year.

Let's suppose Mary combined her 403(b) and 401(k) into one rollover account. Doing so would more than likely save on fees and expenses and make money management easier. (I find that retirees usually like to consolidate their accounts with one custodian.) Mary then begins taking out funds at seventy and a half. New IRS rules, effective January 1, 2001, allow her to take distributions over a joint life expectancy no matter whom she named as her beneficiary. She can always take out more than the RMD, but she cannot take out less than the minimum. *Warning: Removing less than the required minimum distribution triggers a 50 percent penalty on the distribution that should have been taken.* Ouch! To reiterate: for most people, the required beginning date for taking distributions from an IRA is April 1 following the year the person turns seventy and a half. Usually people begin taking funds out the year they turn seventy and a half, so that they are not forced to take two minimum withdrawals the following year. (There is an exception to this rule: if you are still working after you turn seventy and a half, you are not required to remove the RMD.)

As of December 31, 2003, Mary's combined 403(b) plan and 401(k) plan become one rollover worth $500,000. To find the RMD, Mary looks at Table 9.2 and finds a factor of 27.4 for a person age 70. Next, she divides $500,000 by the factor of 27.4, which equals $18,248.17. This becomes her minimum distribution in 2003.

Old rules would have you zero out your rollover by age 89. Under new rules you can still have funds at age 115; the divisor would be 1.9, leaving 47 percent of the account intact.

Those retirees already over seventy and a half can now change their IRA distribution method to meet the new minimum distributions required. No longer is the designated beneficiary irrevocable, but you can change your beneficiaries back and forth. Many retirees who have wanted to lower their distributions because they had made calculations based on old methods may now use the new table. Older retirees can now stretch payments over a longer period than they previously had planned on, making it possible to leave more money to future generations.

Table 9.2   Lifetime Required Minimum Distributions Uniform Table*

70	27.4	93	9.6
71	26.5	94	9.1
72	25.6	95	8.6
73	24.7	96	8.1
74	23.8	97	7.6
75	22.9	98	7.1
76	22.0	99	6.7
77	21.2	100	6.3
78	20.3	101	5.9
79	19.5	102	5.5
80	18.7	103	5.2
81	17.9	104	4.9
82	17.1	105	4.5
83	16.3	106	4.2
84	15.5	107	3.9
85	14.8	108	3.7
86	14.1	109	3.4
87	13.4	110	3.1
88	12.7	111	2.9
89	12.0	112	2.6
90	11.4	113	2.4
91	10.8	114	2.1
92	10.2	115 and over	1.9

*The numbers in this table reflect the IRS Regulations 1.401(a)(9)–9 revisions as of April 17, 2002.

Under the new rules, the designated beneficiary can be changed prior to the owner's death but *not afterward*. More specifically, the rule says that the designated beneficiary (DB) is determined from the list of beneficiaries after the owner's death. Moreover, the new rule allows the primary beneficiary to disclaim ownership of part or all IRA assets for the benefit of another person(s) or charity after the owner's death.

Here is how it works. Suppose Jim (fifty-five) and Sal (fifty-one) each inherit half of their mother's $50,000 rollover IRA, which she had inherited from her husband. Let's also suppose that Jim has a high-paying job and a small family, and Sal has a moderate income and six children. Not wanting the extra money or the tax burden, Jim decides to disclaim his inheritance. To do this, the new rule allows Jim the right to leave his portion, $25,000, in the IRA for his brother to claim. Sal now has $50,000 and *must* take out funds over his own life expectancy, which is 32.2 years. By using new stretch-out provisions, Sal can slowly withdraw money and control taxes on the IRA distributions. According to Table 9.1, the first year Sal must remove a minimum of $1,552.80 ($50,000 ÷ 32.2). He can pay for his child's education—or spend it however he likes, but he cannot put it back into another IRA or retirement plan. (Note: Sal *cannot* use Table 9.2. That table is only for the IRA owner, and Sal is a beneficiary.) Although simplification of the IRS rules regarding the RMD calculations and the new ability to disclaim assets have given investors and estate planners more planning flexibility, they have not altered the need for wise legal counsel.

No longer is a retiree over age seventy and a half faced with irrevocable RMDs based on short life expectancies. On the other hand, the wealthier a retiree is, the more planning is necessary in order to properly transfer assets to the next generation. As Natalie Choate states, "The option to defer taxes can be extremely valuable. The financial effect on the family of taking out all benefits within five years after the participant's death, versus being permitted to take them out gradually over the life expectancy of a designated beneficiary, is dramatic" (*Life and Death Planning for Retirement Benefits*, 3rd edition, 1999, p. 13). This option is allowed by the IRS when your money is in a rollover, but it is not allowed by many 401(k) plan documents. "Qualified [such as 401(k)] plan participants cannot use the new rules until the plan is amended" (*Journal of Financial Planning*, March 2001, p. 85). And those favorable changes can take years, if they happen at all.

After much research, I found that the one advantage the 401(k) has over an IRA is federal creditor protection, which extends to all ERISA-qualified retirement plans. Under ERISA, retirement money in qualified plans is protected from personal bankruptcy and lawsuits. While IRAs are not qualified plans, states have been enacting laws to protect these precious assets from creditors. Before moving money to an IRA you should be sure to check with a financial advisor or attorney to see what protection is offered to you in your state. The positive side to these laws is that the exemption from creditors makes all retirement plans ideal for accumulating wealth. For more information on state statutes regarding IRAs, go to www.mosessinger .com/search and search for "protecting retirement plans."

Once you know the protection afforded you, the rollover is the superior choice, especially if you want to attach additional bequests to your IRA. Some estate lawyers call it an *IRA will*, which is a legal document giving your IRA direction beyond what most IRA beneficiary forms allow. Some custodians of IRAs will not accept the IRA will, and you need to find out whether yours does if you decide to use such a legal instrument. If you want your grandchildren to receive some of your IRA, you need to say that on your IRA beneficiary designation form. A beneficiary designation such as *My children equally, per stirpes*, advises James Lange, "protects the interest of the third-generation child or children (i.e., owner's grandchild) of a predeceased second-generation child" (p. 92). Without the proper advice your money could wind up in the pocket of someone you never intended to give it to. We call that a *failed estate plan*.

Summary of the New Required Minimum Distribution Rules

- A new calculation method simplifies and lowers the required minimum distribution for most IRA owners; even those who already turned seventy and a half can use the new method. This will allow more money to accumulate for decades to come.
- After the owner's death, multiple beneficiaries can buy out each other's portion, or each can disclaim his or her portion, giving it to another beneficiary.
- Beginning in 2002, custodians and trustees of IRAs will be required to calculate the RMD, informing the owner and the IRS of that amount.
- If you do not name a person as a beneficiary, the five-year payout rule for IRAs applies in most cases. With an estate or a charity as named beneficiary, the old rules would have forced a payout of all assets within one year of the owner's death.
- You can have multiple beneficiaries of one account, and (after death) your heirs can separate your IRA into multiple IRA accounts. This arrangement allows each beneficiary to make his or her own stretch-out plan based on his or her personal life expectancy.
- Be aware! To enforce compliance with the minimum distribution rules, the IRS now requires the custodians and the trustees for your IRA—and all IRAs—report the "prior year" December 31 balances of the accounts.

When I weigh the advantages and disadvantages (illustrated in Table 9.3) from an estate planning perspective, I would *not* leave my retirement money in my 401(k) or 403(b) plan. You must weigh these choices as well, given the investments in your plan, the advice you need to manage them, and the distribution options. Most investment books do not do justice to the complexities of retirement, estate planning, and money management. And the entertainment media does not have the time to get into the deeper affairs of personal finance and macroeconomic issues. Even the new websites that promise a high level of investment expertise cannot give a high level of *personal advice*, because they are marketing advice to the masses. As well, technology cannot dig deep into a person's private psyche, whereas probing discussions on issues such as family loyalties can reveal why a person may or may not want to leave money to a child or sibling. You cannot afford

Table 9.3   Summary of Options for 401(k) Plans and Some 403(b)s Versus Rollover IRAs

Option	Advantages	Disadvantages
Take cash distribution	Cash in hand	Up to 45 percent in taxes due Possible 10 percent penalty
Keep assets in 401(k) or 403(b)	Tax-deferred growth May have low annual expenses Creditor protection under ERISA	Limited withdrawal options Limited investment options Limited estate planning options May have to manage it yourself
Roll over assets to IRA	Tax-deferred growth Larger number of investments More estate-planning options Consolidation of retirement assets More money-management choices May leave more money for heirs Check state statutes for creditor protection	May have higher fees

to be wrong when you ask, Is this advice going to create the best plan given my personal situation? Although the new rules require your rollover custodian to make the calculations of your RMD, you are still responsible for making sure you take out your required minimum distributions. You must be sure to add up your distributions, checking the total against the RMD. The new rules allow the IRS to easily catch any mistake you make and penalize you.

With the new rules, which allow for greater flexibility, you can remove rollover IRA money at a slower rate, and thus pay yourself over many more years. With one exception, as long as the participant of the rollover is alive, the minimum withdrawal is the same for everyone who is the same age, regardless of who is the beneficiary. The exception is for those who have a spouse who is more than ten years younger—then a different table can be used. With smart planning you can reduce taxes and avoid stiff penalties. You can develop a high level of confidence in your advisor if you get your questions answered. Your understanding of the planning process, as outlined in this book, will guarantee that you have done an adequate job in preparing for retirement and the transferring of assets to your heirs.

PART THREE

MANAGING YOUR NEST EGG

"I remember my father telling me the story of the preacher delivering an exhortation to his flock, and as he reached the climax of his exhortation, a man in the front row got up and said, 'O Lord, use me. Use me, O Lord—in an advisory capacity!'"

—ADLAI STEVENSON

10

The Advisor Advantage

"I pass with relief from the tossing sea of Cause and Theory to the firm ground of Result and Fact."

—Sir Winston Churchill

According to the Employee Research Benefits Institute (ERBI), the primary reason small business employers are motivated to sponsor a retirement plan is "to increase business profits." Whether you are employed by a small or large business, there is a powerful movement among investors to take more responsibility over their financial future. Government is creating more ways for people to individually save for retirement; for example, it is expanding contribution limits to 401(k)s and IRAs, and adding catch-up provisions and more IRA choices. Corporations, as well, are creating self-directed 401(k)s, and are encouraging lump sum distributions of pension benefits, known as the cash balance plan. With the increased freedom to manage our own retirement money we are assuming a much higher responsibility over our future welfare. Because workers change jobs more often today, the way pension benefits are offered has changed too. I have known many people who have rolled over several IRAs, 401(k)s, and pension distributions, creating a sizable personal account. Sounds all well and good, until they face the burden of making long-term investment decisions on such a large portion of their wealth.

Paternalistic Big Blue has 110,000 retirees drawing a monthly pension benefit, and they use their 401(k) money just as an extra kicker to their real income. Workers employed by younger or less fortuitous companies are not so lucky. According to the Employee Benefits Research Institute, only *22 percent* of all people with 401(k)s are offered a pension plan benefit too. That number is falling. The major shift in retirement planning brings new challenges. Mainstream workers and retirees can use their own contributions (some companies offer a match) and their own talents to grow and manage their 401(k)s—and similar defined contribution plans such as a 403(b)—in order to fund long retirements.

On the other hand, how many people are qualified to handle the management of vast amounts of money without a relationship with a person who knows the investment backroads? With the movement to put more pension and retirement assets in the management hands of the retiree comes the seedy side of the picture. As companies develop retirement plans that either force or entice people into taking their cash balance, new millennium retirees are left holding a bag of responsibility they never thought they would have to hold. As 401(k)s and 403(b)s grow to be a major source of assets and income, these plans will affect lifestyles for decades to come. Unless the cash-rich retirees feel confident in handling alone the vagaries of investing, they will most likely seek a long-term relationship with one or more professionals. If people will need income thirty, forty, or fifty years after retiring, then much will be demanded of those who hold themselves out as advisors.

Can advisors who do an excellent job in giving "planning advice" also manage money? Can insurance agents licensed to sell mutual funds and annuities offer a plan that will produce a sound retirement income for their clients? Does the retiree have a way of knowing what advice is best for his or her personal situation? Do advisors who hold themselves out to be experts in building a college education fund need different skills in managing retirement funds? Must financial advisors also learn to be financial educators? You can learn how to differentiate the kind of advice you should expect. Although I know there are good and helpful people giving investment advice, there are those who may better meet the needs of the retiree—someone especially attuned to *your* perspective.

The Gramm-Leach-Bliley Financial Services Modernization Act of 1999 *repealed* laws set up in the 1930s to prohibit and restrict affiliations among banks, insurance firms, and securities firms. This far-reaching act of Congress has created confusion among investors as each of these industries enters into the other's territory, blurring the kinds of services and products they offer. Across states and even countries, banks are buying mutual fund companies, insurance companies are purchasing broker/ dealers, and broker/dealers are buying banks. In 2000 Unicredito Italiano, a large European bank, purchased Pioneer Mutual Funds of Boston. Insurer MONY Group bought Advest, a Wall Street firm, and soon after the Charles Schwab Corporation bought U.S. Trust, a bank. And the list will go on. Still, there are tens of thousands of independent financial planning and consulting firms that have alliances with broker/dealers, and money-management firms that compete with the large firms, like Merrill Lynch, in offering fee-only advice. No matter what kind of firm or professional you will be speaking with or now have, it will help you to know what types of services different advisors offer and how to rate them.

If you know a person (or firm) carrying a designation or title I describe in this chapter, it is still up to you to determine whether their services live up to your expectations. My descriptions should give you a reference point, but what kind of relationship—based on a joint responsibility—you create with your advisor is a matter you need to review with the professional you're hiring. Some advisors wear many hats, especially in small towns where there is less likelihood of specialization. Yet in small towns, because people know each other well, it may be easier to find a trusted professional.

Wherever you live, finding a good advisor, even a general practitioner, is better than going it alone. Even Tiger Woods has a coach. When you read the seven standards for picking a money manager in Chapter 11, you will see why professionals earn their keep, whether you are paying fees or commissions. Employing the services of a counselor or school psychologist for your child does not diminish your responsibility or workload as a parent, but rather *augments* your parental skills. The same goes for working with a financial advisor (FA) or consultant; the relationship is meant to increase your investment wisdom. Moreover, FAs know other resourceful professionals who add to the advisor's knowledge and may serve you via referral for specific work in areas where your FA lacks expertise.

Types of Advisors

Financial advice, in its broadest definition, is offered by people who carry any one or more of the following designations and may work for different kinds of employers:

- Usually employed by insurance companies: Personal financial representative, insurance agent, life underwriter
- Most often employed by brokerage firms: Investment executive, registered representative, stockbroker or bondbroker, financial analyst, financial consultant
- Most often employed by independent firms or self-employed: Financial consultant, financial planner, investment counselor, investment advisor, investment management consultant, money manager, senior advisor
- Employed by corporations: Benefits consultant, retirement specialist
- Employed by banks: Trust officer, financial analyst
- Employed by accounting firms or independent firms: Financial specialist

An American Century survey found that "76 percent of investors do not have a financial consultant they can trust" (*Journal for Financial Planning*, July 2000, p. 27). What you need is a way of finding an advisor you *can* trust—not for one-time advice, but for advice that could last a lifetime. Just as you would spend time finding a spouse, a house, or a doctor, you must take time and care in hiring an advisor or building a proper relationship with the one you have.

There are well over 800,000 people who call themselves financial advisors in the United States. Most provide advice on a commission basis only, while others do it on a fee-or-commission basis; some are employed by large firms, while others are sole practitioners who have their own money-management and financial planning practices. One company may allow two different ways of paying for services. Another may have a fee-only business model. Many advisors in business for over twenty years have had nothing but commission products to offer until recently. Many of these advisors have been moving their business to a fee-only service, because they found they attract a higher-net-worth clientele willing to pay a fee. Other FAs who work with accounts less than $50,000 may not get paid enough to offer fee-only service, so they remain with commission products.

Investment executives, also known as *registered representatives* or *stockbrokers*, may have some access to money managers or mutual funds on a fee-only basis, but they work on a commission basis also. They are employed by firms that clear trades through a network or use other firms called *broker/dealers* that trade stocks or bonds and thus incur a trading cost. Those working for larger firms may have access to more services and money managers, but I find the smaller firms are catching up quickly with the technology available and may give you more personal advice.

Financial representatives, financial planners, and *insurance agents* are all licensed to sell investment products, such as mutual funds and variable annuities, but they may not have much training in investment management of large portfolios. These are just general titles; you need to look closely at what services they offer and at their experience. Generally they earn a commission for products sold. They may be at the beginning stages of their career and have little or no experience in managing money or giving securities advice. Their value to you may be in how well they communicate the services and skills of others within their organization. Rather than developing their own skills, they have others in the organization do the more complex work. In general, financial planners and insurance agents take in the largest group of advisors.

Investigating Designations

You will find highly qualified people who go by the titles I've just listed; as well, you will find many poorly qualified people. You need to get to know their services and how they are compensated. Ask for references to check. Certified professionals are often required to take continuing education courses to remain in good standing, and you can check to see whether they have kept up with their educational requirements.

Some are *chartered life underwriters (CLUs)*, who specialize in solving insurance and estate problems. *Chartered financial consultants (ChFC)* are proficient in investments and real estate and can manage retirement portfolios. You can find them in the Society of Financial Service Professionals (www.financialpro.org).

Certified fund specialists (CFS) have completed a high level of training in mutual funds. CFS designation is provided by the Institute of Business & Finance (www.icfs.com). *Registered financial consultants (RFC)* must meet the stringent requirements of the International Association for Registered Financial Consultants (www.iarfc.org). Well-rounded *estate advisors* can be found by contacting the National Association of Estate Planners and Councils (www.naepc.org). The National Association of Insurance and Financial Advisors is another well-run educational organization (www.naifa.org).

The certification *certified senior advisor (CSA)* is granted by the Society of Certified Senior Advisors (www.society-csa.com). There are many other professionals, including CPAs, who give personal financial planning advice and go by the title *personal financial specialist (PFS)*. In the next chapter I give special attention to the *certified financial planner (CFP)* and *certified investment management consultant (CIMC)* designations.

Many associations have a code of ethics that is meant to serve the client well, but remember that a code is only as good as the person who upholds it. Abraham Lincoln once said, "I judge a man's religion on how well he treats his dog."

Financial analysts, retirement specialists, and *benefits consultants* usually work with large corporations but are beginning to work for individuals and small companies as well. They do specialty work in giving investment or legal information to those in charge of retirement plans. These people do not often work directly for an individual. If you are told someone goes by one of these titles, you may want to find out where the person was trained and see whether he or she has a certification. Such titles as a *charter financial analyst (CFA), master of science in financial services (MSFS), registered employee benefits consultant (REBC),* or *chartered retirement planning consultant (CRPC)* are most common. These professionals need many years of experience, as well as training from accredited colleges or institutes, to be certified.

These titles and designations do not say much about the individuals' abilities or capabilities to assist you in managing money, and often are confusing. If one adds the word *registered* or *certified* or *chartered* before a title, then this means an organization has awarded a professional designation to the person, and some of these designations are more difficult to obtain than others. For example, Allstate Life, a major insurance company, has changed its name to Allstate Financial. A lifelong friend, an insurance agent with Allstate for some twenty-five years, has been told his new title is Personal Financial Representative. He now is inundated with selling investments, rather than selling insurance, and he admits to not having the training or the time to commit to this new corporate makeover. He feels his title does not truly represent the work he does best—selling insurance and servicing insured clients. No matter what title a person has or the "brand name" the firm carries, a major breakthrough for the retiree is working with a person (or firm) who will take you through a valid *investment process*— not to be confused with a *sales process*. Keep in mind that the process must take time; if it does not, then you must question whether you are receiving truly personal advice. Your "special" FA should be able to clarify what your working relationship with her entails. As your investment knowledge and relationship with your FA grow, you will be less likely to be impressed by the company logo, and more likely to rely on your own communication and discernment skills. A legitimate investment process should give you a sense of confidence that your relationship will be fruitful—for many, this relationship will someday become a friendship.

But always be cautious. I know one client who finally ended a relationship with a well-known insurance firm. He told me, "I went with the *firm*, because it is one of the oldest companies in the country and I thought my money would be safe there. Little did I know that the new *agents* were not acting in my best interest, but just wanted to churn my account for added commission." Something smelled funny when an agent approached the retiree to exchange his old annuity (TSA) for another TSA without seeing any additional investment opportunity. The surrender charges on the new TSA would begin over, and this got the client thinking. At sixty-eight, he did not want to wait another seven years to get rid of the surrender expenses. The relationship never blossomed into a trusted friendship. In the end, because agents had been involved in such poor business practices throughout the town, it became the major reason the firm had to close its local office.

If you have an FA, you must ask yourself, How has my relationship with this person developed? Was the introduction through a cold call, a friend, a seminar, or a professional referral? Each may be a legitimate source, but some may be better than others. How thorough was your initial financial interview or review? How did you come to trust this person? In response to my recommendation of a law firm to create a trust for a client, the client asked, "How do I know whether they will charge me for work I do not need done?" "Well, you do not know about anything for sure," I said, "but if I advise a client to see an attorney for a trust, I have already concluded that a trust is most likely needed and the job will be done correctly." If I recommend that a person get a financial plan drawn up, I help that person find a planner who fits the bill at a reasonable cost. A professional's reputation is at stake in any referral, and the referral process among professionals is considered an honorable way to facilitate the client's overall life plan. You have to count on someone to guide you regarding professionals such as accountants, attorneys, or possibly financial advisors—and better another professional than a neighbor. When it comes to your wealth, it does not pay to be cheap.

Locating Planning Help

In communities of all sizes, accountants, attorneys, and FAs who have been in business for many years come to know each other, especially if they belong to the same associations. If you are searching for an FA, a local estate planning council and financial planning council are excellent organizations to call on for professional referrals. Some advisors belong to the National Association of Estate Planners & Councils. Professionals involved in local councils learn who is dependable and what they charge for services. Also, the board of directors of local charities have FAs, attorneys, and other professionals as members, and the board members can usually be relied on as a resource. Over time, an advisor's *character* begins to build a business.

You can further check on people by asking for references and calling the associations professionals belong to. At www.nasd.com, you can see whether a financial advisor has received any customer complaints or if judgments have been awarded; just ask your advisor for his or her CRD number. As well, at nasd.com you can find out how long a person has been in the business and which states he or she is registered in. *Do not be afraid to discuss with an advisor what you find*; some complaints are not as serious as others are, and some may be frivolous. Remember that learning about the differences among the people who are advisors will help you better discern who will work best for you.

Ultimately, a good advisor is a coach who will help you understand the markets. With the coaching you receive from your personal financial advisor, you will become comfortable looking at your investments through the eyes of a good steward rather than a shy gopher or a stargazer. The difference between a relationship and a friendship is a matter of equality. In a relationship one person has authority over another; in a friendship people share ideas and decisions, and they come to mutual conclusions. Shared concerns and thoughtful discussion appeal to more retired people, I believe, than investment advice based simply on knowledge of the market.

With the Aid of an Advisor Your Behavior Improves

Dr. Jeremy Siegel, professor of finance at the Wharton School of the University of Pennsylvania, did a remarkable study. He found that from 1984 to 1996 the S&P 500 had a total return of 314 percent. When he looked at the return of the average investor, he found it to be 103 percent. One can conclude that the average person made more wrong decisions than right ones.

Behavioral finance looks at how markets gyrate and how they can trick investors, including professionals, into making the wrong investment decisions when they are most certain they are the right ones. I believe that with the aid of qualified advisors, the financial behavior of the individual can be vastly improved and confidence strengthened. In his book *Emotional Intelligence*, Daniel Goleman argues that a person's social success depends less on IQ than what he calls *emotional intelligence (EQ)*. Children with high EQ can delay gratification to meet long-term goals and become more successful. Behavior finance studies EQ as it pertains to investors. The professional you are working with must be someone who can help raise your EQ, or you may wind up with the inferior returns of the average investor found in Dr. Siegel's studies.

Even though there is no such thing as the foreseeable future, there is good reason to believe that if you have a trusted personal advisor—together with a *personal investment policy*—your long-term goals will be achieved with consistent returns. While individual stocks seem to move more erratically these days than in the past twenty years, researchers have found the overall market is as volatile as always. The variability of investment returns alone is a formidable reason to enter into a continual relationship with a level-headed advisor. If we are going to invest large sums into stocks and bonds and still remain calm, we need to get used to our portfolio's swinging tens of thousands of dollars. In order to see our securities produce above inflationary returns, we must invest in things that fluctuate in price, and yet we must not let our emotions get the better of us. Volatility is not the cause of poor returns; investor behavior is. Without a friendly advisor, you may be tempted to lose confidence in your portfolio and sell at the wrong time, or you may remain stymied by the market altogether and never make the riskier investments.

Especially interesting to all of us—investors and advisors alike—is that the volatility differential among individual securities and the S&P 500 has increased during the past decade. Because individual stock prices have become more erratic, the public's *perception* of volatility has changed, leaving many fearful of entering the market. With the advance in computer-aided trading strategies among institutions and individuals, with a greater number of companies specializing in narrow lines of products or services, such as those related to the Internet, and with the new "hedge funds" placing huge bets on borrowed money, conditions in the market have changed. For many of the sophisticated investors with these new technologies and strategies, one unexpected movement in a sector of the market can create large losses. In 1998, Long-Term Capital Management, an investment firm run by several brilliant economists (including a Nobel Prize winner), nearly went into bankruptcy due to large bets on a risky investment strategy that utterly failed.

(It cost players \$3.65 billion to bail out the company.) As well, with mass media able to disseminate bad news (or the hint of it) so quickly to a huge audience, an immediate negative reaction causes a stock's price to fall dramatically. Consider how Procter & Gamble fell *more than 30 percent* on a bad day in March of 2000! If we are going to be investing for decades, we must become used to the way the markets behave in the extremes. An African saying goes, "When elephants fight it is the grass that suffers." You do not want to be trampled on when the bulls and the bears do battle.

Experienced Professionals Have Dealt with Market Swings

Studies done by John Campbell of Harvard and Burton Mialkiel of Princeton concluded that today's investors perceive the stock market as becoming ever more volatile. They found that individual stocks are swinging up and down to a greater degree, so that it is becoming more important that portfolio managers diversify to reduce risk. Of course, individuals must do the same. On the other hand, they found that the volatility of overall market-index returns "show no systematic tendency to increase," as reported by *Bloomberg Wealth Manager (BWM)* in its July/August 2000 edition (p. 38). Dramatic swings from day to day and month to month still are and always will be the norm for the market. While volatility remains with us, it is also important to note that the returns over long periods (ten and twenty years) should come in close to normal returns we have seen over the past seventy years. One of my clients has said, "But I don't have twenty years—I need money now."

So what's the fuss? The action of the market is not what advisors worry about; it is the *action of the client*. FAs are aware that there are decades when the stock market booms, like the 1980s. There are decades when bonds outperform most stocks, like the 1970s. There are periods when real estate loses ground, like in the early 1990s, and when real estate does well, like in the 1970s. What remains is the question: How can anyone maintain consistent returns with inconsistent and unpredictable annual results while withdrawing money for many years? The uncertainty alone could wreak havoc in the mind of any sensible retiree; without an advisor to turn to in time of doubt, that person might never learn to feel comfortable owning securities.

Long-term studies prove stock ownership is profitable, but this assessment will not matter when your stock portfolio is down 25 percent. What will matter is how well you have prepared for a potentially large decline in the market or when it is caught in the doldrums for several years. In the 1970s the number of stockbrokers shrank in half. If people were consistent, then why the shocking decline in the brokerage business? Many people just stopped buying. During the sharp decline in October of 1987, why did Fidelity Direct Funds get over a million phone calls? People panic, especially those with lots of money in retirement plans. Lynn Brenner writes in an article titled "Storm Warnings" that the money invested by retirees and managed by financial advisors will be "the problem that's likely to dominate 21st century [financial planning] practice" (*Bloomberg Wealth Manager*, July 2000, p. 50). Already we are seeing real concern in the ranks of the retirees themselves. One of their major complaints is that they have received little investment guidance from former employers as they moved out the door of the human resources department, separation-of-service envelope in hand. Besides the financial issues, few companies help retirees come to terms with the nonfinancial issues. Michael Stein, author of the book *The Prosperous Retirement*, mentions that there are eight spokes to a person's "lifestyle planning": physical health, mental health, diet, exercise, social relations, personal relations, intellectual stimulation, and spiritual balance. He feels these points can be addressed with an advisor, along with investment returns—some have called it life planning rather than financial planning.

How Will Your Portfolio Behave?

Behavioral finance tries to understand volatility and poor returns from the point of view of the investor as well as the investment. Good advisors must listen closely to the client's psychological needs, as well as financial needs, to develop a financial plan that will give the person a good night's sleep. Good FAs do not simplify the investment process just to get the account open. Their standard for making investment recommendations is not dependent on a glowing Morningstar ranking of a mutual fund. Even Morningstar admits that their "star ranking system" is descriptive rather than predictive. They recommend that people use their "star" ranking service to evaluate and compare the past performance of the funds and as one of many tools of evaluation. We, like many advisors, use Morningstar data daily to evaluate and compare thousands of funds. So why do I hear, "Morningstar *only* ranks this fund a three-star" to imply that a fund is undesirable, at best, a has-been, without considering contributing factors such as size of companies in the fund or its beta—the fund's sensitivity to a benchmark. In this business you need to look inside the book rather than judging it by its cover.

When I called Morningstar and asked an analyst there what he would buy, he said, "A three-star fund on the way to becoming a five-star fund." Most investors would not understand his logic, nor mine. Yet, it is a logic that investment professionals use to better balance portfolios. The data that Morningstar and like firms collect (some firms evaluate the data, too) is invaluable to those who know *how to interpret* those numbers and monitor their changes. One study done by Financial Research Corporation (FRC) of Boston, which studied 766 portfolios from 1988 to 1998, found that one-star (lowest) and two-star funds tended to underperform universal averages in the year subsequent to the rating. On the other hand, FRC concluded that there was *no discernable difference* in the *future performance* of a three-, four-, or five-star fund. As well, the researchers concluded that, on average, small funds (ones with less money rather than more) outperformed large funds in thirty-two of forty measured periods. To the uninitiated, ranking systems and portfolio size are very deceptive. One of the essential investment advisory services a firm can offer is to take the significant and important data provided by Morningstar and other firms and do their own in-house analysis to decide for themselves what are the investments best suited to build a client's portfolio. Investment firms spend hundreds of hours collecting and measuring raw performance data to come up with their best ideas. They then monitor that data for positive or negative changes. These firms can do what average individual cannot do—that is, call and speak to the lead portfolio managers. They do not rely on popularity of the managers, because managers can leave the firm without an investor's say-so. For example, Thomas Marsico, an eleven-year veteran manager at Janus Funds, left to start up his own company in 1997. A loss of a manager can dramatically change how a portfolio behaves.

Some investment advisors, including banks, brokerage firms, and insurance companies, are not as thorough in their detective work, and they sell funds based solely on Morningstar ratings. One bank I know of recommends *one fund family only*, because it is highly ranked. But what happened to the other great funds ranked at the top? If a firm has only one growth fund to offer a retiree, where do you go when it begins to lag behind its peers? What happens if it loses its management team? What happens if the team's style drifts? For the average investors, the trust departments of most banks offer few choices and nearly no relationship-building process and lack lifestyle planning skills. Since they are trustees of much larger funds—high-net-worth investors preferred—they often frown on having you enter into a personal investment process that gives you the power to ask questions and discuss how you want to see your money invested. You may be lucky enough to find a trust officer who takes a personal interest in your life, but many do not have the time, nor are they encouraged to do so by the firm. They often prepackage investment products, charge higher fees, and offer less face-to-face service than an individual financial advisor. The financial magazines are even less personal, because the mass media has its own restrictions and limitations on disseminating information. If you look closely at advice magazines you may often find that their best buys were last year's winners, without much attention given to discipline or style of management. Where is the due diligence? As well, nearly ignored by many magazines are a large number of mutual funds that do not spend advertising dollars or are too small to advertise. Not much press is given to those funds, which are not paying the fiddler. On the other hand, when their *preferred* funds fail to perform, you will not find a sell recommendation on them. Getting out is left up to you and only you. Without an advisor you may be left hanging.

Beware of Other Biases

A similar bias in the selection of stocks occurs at large brokerage firms. The SEC has been investigating many complaints on this issue, and more regulations may be forthcoming. Did you ever notice that analysts seldom put a sell recommendation on a stock? It may be for fear of losing underwriting business. Studies have shown that for every one hundred "buy" recommendations put out by brokerage firms, on average there are fewer than two "sell" recommendations. It is tough for someone to stay objective after learning in childhood, "Don't bite the hand that feeds you." Analysts fear that if they give a sell recommendation on a stock, they will get a wrist slap, a pay cut, or, worse, may be fired. Many spurned corporations are vengeful, putting underwriting pressure on any firm whose analyst publicly does them in. One might conclude that there is a conflict of interest that is embedded in the capitalistic system; if so, *it is not going to go away.* One also can conclude that as competition heats up for advertising and underwriting dollars, biases may become more prominent. Ethics classes aren't a rage in business schools, philosophy is no longer required at most colleges, and even many private colleges have rid themselves of talking about moral issues. Capitalism is not democratic in nature, nor is it fair. Webster's dictionary says it is an "economic system in which the means of production and distribution are privately owned." Thus, capitalism could never be a self-governing system, because at its core it can be indifferent to larger local and national issues.

What We Learn from the Study of Behavioral Finance

I believe that many investors and financial professionals have not examined behavioral finance; if they had, the Internet debacle might have been avoided. That kind of speculation brought capitalism to nearly its worst moment. If investors would take behavioral finance seriously, they would not ask why booms and busts happen. The same people who say they want to "buy low and sell high" become angry when their darling stocks come down. After the top of the market passes they say, "I can't understand it; everything looked terrific." At the bottom of the market they move money to CDs, arguing, "I could at least get 6 percent guaranteed there." When you are saving money while working, it does not matter much if the markets sell off one or two years, but retirees have a much more complex set of needs, emotions, and expectations. As a group they behave differently than the person still accumulating wealth—or, at least, they *should* behave differently. One new retiree admitted that he lost his entire 401(k) by day trading. When it came to investing, he had an immature behavior. He was on a high before the high-tech bubble burst, feeling confident enough to quit his job. His high-tech bias did him in, another casualty of poor planning and neglect of professional advice.

The study of behavioral finance is a must for any investor (courses can be found in major business colleges and institutes). The randomness and volatility of the markets provide grounds for uncertainty among a majority of people who least desire it or can least handle it—the retired. Managing a retirement account, where the retiree is withdrawing funds and, at the same time, needs to grow the account to keep up with inflation, is one of the most difficult balancing acts in money management. And what we do is art rather than science, but good science helps. Lynn Brenner writes, "But designing a portfolio for a 21st-century retirement is no cinch even for a retiree with substantial assets and a modest lifestyle. . . . Perhaps the thorniest issue for advisors going forward will be determining a prudent spending rate for their clients. It is going to be a shock to many clients how little they can safely withdraw every year from a portfolio that must last for two to three decades" (*Bloomberg Wealth Manager*, July 2000, p. 49).

According to John Nofsinger, a finance professor at Washington State University, the cause of some of the worst investment behavior that lost a lot of people money in 2000 and 2001 was overconfidence. In an article by Laura Bruce, Nofsinger said, "People feel that because there's so much information available that it leads to good decision-making" ("Does the Stock Rule the Mind or Does the Mind Rule the Stock," Bankrate.com, August 22, 2001). Overconfidence and quantity and ease of information are often cited as the top reasons why so many people failed to diversify. He goes on in the article: "Believe it or not, when it comes to making the right decisions, whether in investing or anything in life, our brain isn't always our best friend." And when we make a bad decision, he says, "We feel bad about it and it's hard to have a good self-image of ourselves" ("Does the Stock Rule the Mind or Does the Mind Rule the Stock," Bankrate.com, August 22, 2001). It takes humility to admit one made an error, and I found that to be the reason many people have a hard time selling losers in order to cut losses and move to better investments. Human emotions, such as pride, fear, and greed, come into play when making investment decisions; an investment process that takes this into account can help mitigate the potential negative effects of these emotions.

There are investment firms that (with good intentions) say, "No one shoe size fits all." They say that you need a portfolio that fits your personal goals, then they give you three options to choose from: conservative, medium, and aggressive. What they are actually saying is, "One of three shoe sizes fits all." I believe there is an investment process to finding the shoe that fits you. It is a challenge for the financial advisors to create a trustworthy investment process that can be applied to each retiree in order to come up with the unique recommendations tailored to that individual—specifically, the least risky plan to meet his or her income needs for life.

Unforeseen Issues Can Surface

Throughout the planning process, clients and advisors discuss the *expectations* that clients bring to the table. People come from a wide variety of personal experiences that form their worldviews. A retiree whose parents grew up in the Depression or one who lost money running her own business will have a set of expectations that will differ from one with neither of these experiences. Added to this element, when working with couples, an FA must try to understand a combination of backgrounds and viewpoints. The complexities grow when couples have not personally worked out other problems in their marriage or have different views about leaving money to children or charity. They may even have odd ways of communicating with each other that the advisor is not used to.

I recall one couple who began yapping at each other when I asked for answers to some risk tolerance questions. One spouse was open to taking greater risk, while the other could not understand that in a down market their stocks or bonds could be below water. My frantic answering of multiple questions and concerns, having to repeat myself by rephrasing sentences in order to add to their understanding, frustrated all of us. The unsettling conversation got to the point where the wife began thwacking her husband on the shoulder and yelling at him, "You're not listening to what Frank is telling you." He shrank into the safe corner of his chair each time she raised her hand, but then he bombarded me with more unanswerable questions beginning with "What about . . ." or "What if . . ." He would say, "Tell me if I'm I asking you a stupid question. I've got to know what the market could do to my money," and this kind of comment further agitated his wife. The poor listening skills the husband exhibited were signs of immature behavior when dealing with large sums of money, and this kind of verbal and nonverbal exchange happened in several sessions with them. Although I knew they cared deeply for each other, it was always exhausting to meet with this couple, because they had such poor communication skills.

On the other end of the investor "expectation" spectrum is the more knowledgeable client who has seen terrific returns during the 1990s. These retirees want to live off returns that lately have exceeded the norm. A recent article, "A Report on the March 2001 Investor Sentiment Survey," stated that 42.5 percent of mutual fund investors expected returns of 10 percent to 20 percent over the next year; 8 percent of investors expected returns greater than 20 percent. Quoting the article: "The returns of 12 percent or more anticipated by over half of the respondents are above the average 10.5 percent return on equities calculated by Ibbotson & Sinquefeld (2001) for the seventy-five years to the end of 2000" (*The Journal of Psychology and Financial Markets*, 2001, vol. 2, no. 3, p. 128). This kind of false expectation can really make planning a nightmare for advisors. I am sure I have lost more than one client to FAs who have bragged about past returns, having set in the mind of a client that these same returns are as certain as the sunrise. If this behavior spreads, it will someday become the nemesis of Gotham. Some firms will suffer lawsuits from those who will claim they were poorly informed regarding the risks they were taking and the returns they expected to get. Many of these suits will be dismissed if the advisor can show proof that the client realized that the risk she took was appropriate for her financial situation and goals. If there is one answer to disappointment, it is to have a well-stated strategy honestly fleshed out and written down before investments are made and after the retiree understands that his or her behavior matters.

11

Creating a Financial Planning Review

"These unhappy times call for the building of plans
. . . that build from the bottom up and not from the
top down, that put their faith once more in the
forgotten man at the bottom of the economic
pyramid."

—FRANKLIN DELANO ROOSEVELT

Each of us is given something wonderful to do on this good earth. Usually that means to serve others in some way or to build something from a heap of material; to bring something special—healing, order, or beauty—to the world. I tend to believe we all have a calling to be a good steward of our assets and the resources around us. Your own stewardship can begin here with the question, Do I need a financial planning review? A review is not a recommendation as to what stock or fund to own or to sell. It begins with an analysis of all your assets and investment goals. If you are retiring, you may already have planned years ago how much to save. A review within a couple of years of retiring can help a preretiree determine whether he or she is on target. The time and money spent can clarify more than financial goals.

I live in an area where people are fee sensitive, so I believe it is best to start here explaining how people in my business earn their income. Some planners do comprehensive reviews charging only a fee, some a fee and commission, and some commission only. Other planners charge a fee, but they will subtract the fee from commissions if you wind up doing business with them. Some advisors work on a retainer basis. If you are dealing with a planner, find out upfront how she will earn her money. In finance, *nothing good is free*. Anyone who says his service is free is most likely on the road to selling you something. One poorly informed retiree with $200,000 told me, "My planner said it would cost me nothing for a review and only $25 per year to have him manage my money." "Nonsense," I told her. "No one can keep an office open and spend hours with you only to earn $25 per account." Obviously, the advisor's commissions are hidden well enough so as not to make her feel the desire to explain them. Only a foolish investor would not look more closely at this situation and try to figure out how expenses are calculated. I do not want to make a case against commissions, but rather to inform you that you need to know what and how you will pay for services—commissions are justified if the quality of advice is excellent, and fees are unjustified if the advice is poor.

Some fee-only planners will charge by the hour, a retainer fee, or a percentage of your total assets. Hourly fees range between $125 and $300, but more often they charge a flat fee that depends on the complexity and size of your assets. Financial columnist Charles A. Jaffe writes, "[D]etermining what a financial advisor's services cost and what you can afford to pay, what their services are, and whether they have the ability to deliver on their promises, simply requires that you think of financial services like every other good or service you buy, no different from hiring a plumber or a television repair man except you feel a bit out of your league" (*The Right Way to Hire Financial Help*, 1998, p. 10). Whichever way you pay an advisor, what you need to do is build a relationship as you have with other service providers. A retainer arrangement allows you to work closely with an advisor on many issues. This kind of fee structure is not found at large brokerage firms, but is offered by some independent advisors. For clients with $2 million or more, the retainer may be more appropriate. A registered investment advisor's ADV form will spell out fees and services. A fee for a comprehensive financial review where the client's assets are less than $1.5 million and there are no complex issues to deal with falls between $300 and $1,500. If assets are between $1.5 and $2 million, fees can range between $1,000 and $2,500. If the review includes reading of insurance policies, wills, trusts, or benefit statements from your employer, or if it includes tax-planning issues, investment recommendations, retirement planning, college planning, or business planning, then you are looking at more time, which may include an attorney in the process. The bill then can range from $2,500 to $3,000. For very complex planning, the bill can go as high as $10,000. To build a trusted relationship you need to figure out how you are going to work with your advisor and how you will appropriately compensate her for the kind of relationship you want.

What Type of Financial Advisors Offer Financial Planning Reviews?

Although many FAs call themselves financial planners, a general term too easily used in our industry, there are planners who are board certified and need continuing education to remain a standing member. In our nation there are over 36,000 certified financial planners (CFPs). While most have their own firms, larger firms are encouraging the designation. To acquire the CFP designation, one has to take five investment courses, and the certification process can take about two years. Like a CFP, a personal financial specialist (PFS) is a designation offered to certified public accounts who want to work within the financial planning field. Over 30,000 planners belong to the Financial Planning Association (FPA). Some are new to the business or may be either in training or working with CFPs. Of those in the FPA, there are more than 17,000 CFPs. They can be found at www.fpanet.org. Information on the standards and licensing for the CFP are found at www.cfp-board.org. There is also a fee-only organization known as the National Association of Personal Financial Advisors (NAPFA, www.napfa.org), which believes that the only acceptable method of compensation is fees only (no commissions). Although NAPFA has only 690 members, they are making good gains in the planning field with their fee-only (or fee-for-advice) approach. None of the members charges commission on products, so they have quite an objective agenda. Many professionals belong to several organizations for educational purposes so that they may better serve clients. Continuing education requirements are the great value that these organizations bring to their members. It is not difficult to pass an exam to get a certification, but to keep up with changes in areas of law, insurance, accounting, and investments, it helps to belong to an organization that requires members to grow professionally and guides them in that process, helping to maintain high standards. Remember that passing an exam and getting a designation is not the same as giving you excellent service. In the end, you will make your assessment on a did-I-get-my-money's-worth basis.

Although the CFP designation is an excellent beginning point for a retiree seeking advice, many CFPs run a commission-based business. Any planner you work with should disclose how he gets paid for a plan, but you may have to ask. If he charges little or no fee to do a plan (or review), then he will charge a commission on the sale of products suggested at the end of the review session. The plan may become a selling tool rather than an objective opinion. You can see how easily a plan can lead to a sale. James Wilson, past president of NAPFA, states, "There are pretenders and providers in this business" (*Financial Planning*, June 2000, p. 72). He believes that one should provide advice only for a fee and should not sell financial products. However, until there are more FAs willing to move to fee-only structures for the middle-class investor, the largely commission-based business model will not disappear. And it should not. There are investors who prefer paying commissions when the services they receive justify them.

You may be surprised that most financial advisors will tell you they get paid by the company, or that they get paid a *finder's fee*. If this arrangement is so, then they are getting paid a commission by the company, but you are being charged an annual fee tacked onto your mutual funds and/or annuities. So if you need a plan or review it *should not* be one that is "free," because you will be steered to what the planner sells as his or her way to get paid. On a fee and commission basis, planners will charge a fee for planning, but often cut that fee if you decide to take their investment recommendations, because they will earn a commission. Every worker must earn a wage, but it helps you to know how you are paying for that advice. Keeping in control of the financial process means not being afraid to ask questions—believe me, you will not be putting a *reasonable* professional on the spot.

When a planner is paid a commission or a fee, the way it is expensed to your account should be revealed to you. A confident planner should not be afraid to tell you how he or she is compensated, even if it means the loss of your business. That person will earn your trust by being honest, and thus earn your business, too. Before buying anything, you can review all charges by asking the planner to list the annual fees, costs for a planning review, and costs for managing your money. Also, the person should make you aware of the 12b(1) fees, any mortality and expense fees, administrative fees, and any CDSC (contingent deferred sales charges or back-end load) on any products he or she suggests. If the planner does not tell you about fees and expenses, then ask. If the FA balks at these questions, walk away. When you are given a prospectus, read the expenses reported therein. Have someone read it for you if you do not trust yourself with the math. If you have a fee-only planner this will make it easier to know what you are being charged, and you need not worry about being sold a product. If you invest funds with a fee-only planner and you do not like the investments, or your relationship sours, you can sell the investments at no commission cost and close the account. With commission-based plans you may be stuck with charges to exit funds that are not performing—the aforementioned contingent deferred sales charge. You may suffer twice: a broken relationship with someone you once trusted, and the cost to unwind your investment position.

Asking the Right Questions

Many investment executives and financial consultants working for banks, brokerage firms, and insurance companies have access to financial planners (including CFPs) within their firm. Here you need to be careful, because you want an unbiased view from an expert regarding your financial affairs; at times these planners can be motivated to sell you products rather than giving you personal objective advice. The telltale question you can ask is, How will the firm get paid for the plan? If they charge only a fee and you can walk away and put that plan (or review) to work at another firm, then it is objective advice. If you cannot pay a fee and go elsewhere, then there may be some hidden agenda behind the advice. Again, it may be good advice, but you will not be certain what the motives are for the recommendations. Whomever you choose, you must ascertain whether this review was developed purely for your benefit or for the benefit of the broker or agent in order to make a sale. You want to develop a relationship with a professional with high ethical standards, whether he or she is paid a commission or a fee. If you have an advisor, the following chapters will improve your skills in communicating your personal concerns during a retirement planning review.

Some people who know how to crunch numbers, having followed a strict plan all their lives until retirement, may not feel that they need a formal financial review. On the other hand, I ask you, without a professional opinion, how certain are you of knowing that your car is tuned up or that your computer is running efficiently? You do not wait for a breakdown to find out—or do you? Your financial planner can help you get your investment picture formalized. On Normandy beaches during World War II, on the day after D-Day, lots of the men and arms were dangerously spread out on different beaches and ridges; unlinked, they could be slaughtered. Victory hung on a pendulum. A timely German counterattack could easily have penetrated and destroyed them. Allied General Montgomery, knowing the immediate challenge, purportedly said that it was necessary to get the whole organization sorted out and working smoothly. Financial planners recognize that although most retirees have gotten to the point of acquiring enough assets to no longer need to work, their situation is a serious one that needs to be directed carefully from this point on. Your soldiers are on the beach, the pendulum of victory is swinging—and the FA is the general of your plan.

A plan review, then, will identify goals and better organize your affairs, even investigate your hobbies and nonfinancial goals. It will help you answer many of the what-if questions planners are familiar with: What if I die early in retirement? If I become disabled, who will be able to transact my account? What if I want to volunteer; can I afford not to work again? And they will help answer the what-about questions, such as What about the jewelry I own—is it worth naming a beneficiary? What about my named beneficiaries of my retirement plans? They work to answer the how-can questions, such as How can I save income taxes and estate taxes? How can I transfer money to my heirs without going to court over the matter? How can I give to charity and still leave something for children? Knowing many more legal loopholes, tax strategies, and possible investment scenarios than the average investor, the planner is trained to get the whole thing organized and running smoothly.

Some fee-only planners will not offer you specific stock or bond investment advice, because they feel that their work is best done in developing a plan rather than managing money. There are planners who will have on staff investment professionals to manage money for you on a fee or commission basis. Note here that in small financial planning firms, planners may be forced to wear several hats. They may be working on financial plans, trying to keep up with changing tax laws and IRS rulings, and also implementing plans with investment advice and management. To many independent planners working in one- or two-person shops, it is becoming apparent that they need to direct business to other professional consultants who will make the money-management decisions for them. John Reken-thaler, director of research for Morningstar, addressed this issue. His concern is that today, "Planners are dealing with insurance and tax issues, estate planning and client relationships. They don't have the time and energy to create, test, and monitor a mutual fund-selection system" (*Bloomberg Wealth Manager*, July 2000, p. 21). You need to find where the planner (or advisor) spends most of his or her professional time. Some advisors study the markets and make investments decisions and do little actual planning work, while others are essentially insurance sales oriented and do little of the management of investments. Even if you have a financial advisor, you may have a person who understands planning but does not have the skills to manage *retirement* money. The first step, before making investments, would be to enter into a process that includes a comprehensive financial plan (or review). The review should include (or do) the following:

- Organize a personal balance sheet that shows what you have done to this point
- List your investments that support (or do not support) your investment goals
- Examine your tax liabilities and suggest ways of controlling or reducing them
- Review your cash flow (sources of income and cash needs), and how they change
- Consider how and when your options to buy company stock should be exercised
- Make calculations regarding the surviving spouse's income goals
- Suggest trusts and other legal instruments and strategies to benefit your estate
- Review your risk exposure, especially your medical and long-term care coverage
- Outline steps to take to reach your goals, including writing wills or trusts

If you have not done any estate planning, you can also include this area in your review. Questions you want answered are:

- Which pension income option do I choose, so that if I die my spouse has enough to live on, even if he or she lives to 120? Can there be some remaining for other beneficiaries?

- Which insurance option would be best to take: do I convert from term to permanent insurance? And do I need more or less insurance protection?
- What is the best estate planning strategy for my children and/or charity?
- How can I save my heirs a lot of headaches when I die or if I become disabled?

Keeping You out of Trouble

It is during the comprehensive review that a planner looks for minefields in your asset allocation mix. Many cases come to mind where this review would have kept people out of trouble. Allow me to share an example close to home. A local electric utility company retired thousands of employees in the late 1980s and early 1990s. Many of these "company" men and women held large blocks of company stock in their 401(k) plans. Thinking that a utility stock is a dependable investment, they held on to their shares while enjoying a high-dividend income. At the height of the market for this stock in 1994, it traded at $25 per share. In 1995 it paid a dividend of $1.12 per share. A few years later the stock went to $6 per share, and the dividend was cut to *zero*. Unfortunately, there are plenty of other examples, too. At stockholder meetings for Daimler Chrysler, an auto company, we find many disappointed retirees. Until 1997 they got a dividend income hike each year from Chrysler, but they are not seeing that success with their new stock. Moreover, the price of Daimler stock has fallen more than 65 percent from its high in January 1999, and the company refuses to raise dividends in the near future. One may find that a few companies were worth holding for many years, but if you want to lower your risk, asset allocation prevents overweighting a portfolio in any one company.

Many retirees who remain equity owners in their former companies have been severely disappointed because they hung on to too much company stock. Now, I ask you, would this have happened if they had gotten professional advice? Financial advisors see this problem often, and most know that when a client has nearly all his or her retirement funds in one stock it's time to diversify. If you have all your assets in one basket, as Mark Twain said, *"watch that basket."* I have learned it is easier to watch a number of baskets than it is to keep my eye on one. Sentimental bias can severely hamper an employee's decision-making process. Yes, too often people fall in love with their company stock, but the stock does not love them back. An objective FA can help you sort out how these shares should be treated in the overall scheme of your plan and help you deal with your feelings about these shares. In addition, many stock option holders often exercise options and then make the mistake of holding too much company stock in their retirement years. With a growing number of companies offering stock options, retirees need guidance in selling stock and diversifying.

How Can Investment Management Expertise Add Value?

Although many firms combine the two, financial planning is one service and investment management is another. Once you have a good handle on your total financial picture, after a financial advisor completes a comprehensive review or financial plan, the question you should ask next is, How will my retirement money be managed? The answer to this question is better put to a trained investment management consultant or a registered investment advisor (or a person who is dedicated to managing money) and not to a financial planner, unless the planner has a person or department dedicated to money management as an additional service. Here is where many retirees fail to see the difference between planning and investing. If they have found good advice regarding what to do, they assume that the same person can give the best advice on how to do it. Many financial planners, who spend most of their time reviewing cases, often do not have the investigative tools and skills needed to manage large sums of money. To be fair to planners who do make a living managing money, my suggestion is to apply to them the same high standards that I would to investment consultants as set out later in this chapter. You can ask your business acquaintances, retired friends, and family to offer a few names of people who manage money for retirees. You should seek advisors who can give you references from people like you—retired people whom they have served for at least three years. Endowment funds do not use general financial planners, but use people with investment management skills to prepare an investment policy and help choose securities and money managers and then monitor them to meet their long-term goals and return targets.

In the near future, fee-only investment management firms (whose skills have been used mostly by wealthy institutions) will see their growth come from the new retirees with large sums of money to invest—those retirees will come from middle-class America. Why will management firms attract retirement money?

First, I believe the need for specialized investment skills to manage sizable amounts of serious money for a long period of time (as many as forty to fifty years) is becoming more obvious. Already many firms are hiring financial analysts and spending millions of dollars on technology to create endowment-type asset allocation programs for affluent retirees. Their portfolio recommendations go beyond using index funds, so commonly in vogue with many individual investors, 401(k)s, and even many planners. These firms are targeting the retirement market, because they know the wealth that is being unleashed.

Second, the quantity and quality of investment data needed to manage retirement funds is now available from more sources, such as Morningstar and Lipper. This makes unbiased analyses possible for those who want to spend the time and money doing the research. Most retirees do not want to commit the time and money to do this work themselves and will seek out those who do it as a profession.

Third, when markets enter difficult periods, most people desire a relationship with an advisor who will help to keep them on track and review their strategy with them. Retirees will hold their FAs to higher standards and will demand fiduciary-like responsibilities over their retirement accounts. FAs will hold mutual funds and RIAs accountable for their part in managing money.

Fourth, a corporate trend has begun. Companies realize that it is less expensive to give employees a lump sum of money, than to pay them an annuity for the rest of their lives. Younger employees are attracted to companies offering cash balance plans, because they can take their pension money with them if they leave the firm. For older workers with life expectancies far beyond their parents', the cash balance looks attractive, too. Who knows how long our lives will be? Certainly longer than they have been, and corporate America may not want to foot the bill. As well, the movement of retirement money out of pension plans and 401(k)s being paid to the retiree will grow more popular as a way of corporate "rightsizing." Notwithstanding the corporate motives, professionals strongly feel many investment and estate planning opportunities are available when retirees roll 401(k) money into their own individual retirement accounts.

But, you may wonder, how do management consultants add value? Certainly they will need to be paid as well as the actual money managers. The money manager—who makes the *investment decision*—gets a fee for doing the stock or bond analysis and then picking the best investments for the portfolio. The management consultant—who makes the *investment management decision*—gets a fee to find the right managers or mutual funds. His or her work answers the important questions:

- What asset classes should I own?
- What firms do I hire to manage each asset class?
- How do I take advantage of different investment styles to reduce portfolio risk?
- How are these firms to be monitored?
- By what standards are we to measure success?
- How is the overall portfolio doing relative to my investment policy and goals?

It has been documented that these management decisions are as important as the stock-picking decisions, possibly more important. Investment management consultants are the *due diligence detectives* and, as Cervantes said, "Diligence is the mother of good fortune." These professionals are looking for what is behind the numbers the money managers show as returns. Their work protects you from falling into many investment traps. To give you an idea of the detective work they do, I will list some of the duties of the investment management consultant or the team of professionals who specialize in this area of finance.

The Process of Deciding

"It takes more than a hood and eyes to make a monk," goes the Albanian proverb. All money managers who offer their security advisory services to the public are registered with state and/or federal authorities. Let me warn you, *it takes no investment experience and a two-hour test to become a registered investment advisor (RIA)*. The state and federal governments regulate the RIA, but the RIA may have no training in security selection in order to qualify. RIA is one of the easiest designations to obtain. On the other hand, the ADV forms filed by the RIA disclose to the public specific business matters requested by the government. Although the RIA does take on fiduciary responsibilities, a trained investment management consultant wants more than a title before sending an RIA money to be managed; that is, she wants hard evidence of a firm's *ability* to manage funds. Due diligence seeks this evidence of capability. Under current regulations, CFPs can automatically qualify for an RIA designation, but many do not go through the paperwork to register. The U.S. government does not have the manpower to closely supervise all those who hold themselves out as giving advice. *It is up to you to ascertain the quality of the money manager (RIA) you are going to work with.* Titles do not count as much as the investment process the RIA has established. Your financial advisor should be your agent in establishing an account with an RIA, because he or she has the knowledge and experience to determine which firms are competent. For example, the Investment Counsel Association of America (ICAA, www.icaa.org), offers a designation known as *chartered investment counselor (CIC)* that promotes high standards and ability among its 270 members.

Donald Trone, director of the Center for Fiduciary Studies at the University of Pittsburgh's Katz Graduate School of Business (www.cfstudies .com), developed a due diligence process for evaluating both mutual funds and money managers (RIAs). In the July 2000 *Bloomberg Wealth Manager*, Mr. Trone outlined specific standards that advisors and trustees should consider before making investments. I want to use his points as a guide to show you what value there is in having a financial advisor as your investment management consultant. Pension plans and endowments must take similar diligent steps to meet requirements as requested by government regulators. By learning more about the process, you will be a more intelligent investor. If you do not understand the investment process, then find an advisor who can teach you what he or she does before you place your money in his or her hands. This kind of teaching can also make you much better friends.

Seven Standards for Choosing Money Managers

Like the carpenter picking the right lumber for the house to be built, the Center for Fiduciary Standards sets guidelines by which investment professionals pick the right investments managers for a portfolio. It may seem confusing, but the benchmarks against which we compare each of the manager's (or fund's) performance are not the same as the benchmark for the total portfolio. The total portfolio and targeted dollar return is what the client sees as the bottom line—the completed house. I have obtained permission from Mr. Trone to summarize the standards and benchmarks that can be set for each individual manager (or fund), which is the lumber we use to build with. Since this process is the work of the professional, I have paraphrased (Mr. Trone's eight due diligence criteria are included in my seven standards) below the research involved.

Correlation to Peer Group

This standard means that a fund must show that the style it has chosen looks and smells like those that claim to be using the same style. A fund (or money manager) claiming a "value" style must then be analyzed to see if it is keeping to the kind of investment style it claims to be. There is a statistic that assists investors in measuring how closely the fund compares to an important benchmark, and this correlation helps in the analysis of performance. The word "fit" refers to a statistical measure known as *R-squared*. An R-squared of 1.0 represents perfect correlation between, for example, an equity mutual fund and an equity index. An R-squared of zero means there is no correlation between the two. This statistic and others, such as beta, have sprung out of the application of modern portfolio theory. Many funds claim one thing, but soon drift away from their original style. A small company fund can slowly become a large company fund, and you no longer own what you once thought you owned. If this happens, the R-squared of the fund would show this drift. The management consultant learns to keep the fund honest—selling it if the style drifts outside an acceptable parameter. When looking for apples you do not want to buy oranges.

Performance Relative to Peer Group

This is a common standard, because you want to see if a fund has been managed well and is being managed well against other funds that claim the same style. Many management consultants may give weights to the different rolling-period returns, so that they can better compare funds against one another in the same style class, while others may compare returns to benchmarks for ranking purposes. When a fund or manager begins not to fit the criteria established, then the consultant may contact the manager to find out what is happening or may sell the fund. As Mr. Trone states, "An analysis done by the Center for Fiduciary Studies found that of 4,621 stock funds, *less than two percent* performed in the top 25 percent during the past three years through 1999" (*Bloomberg Wealth Manager*, July 2000, p. 22). Too many FAs (and investors) think they can (and must) pick the top funds every year and need to do so in order to succeed. Not true. They will be seriously let down and disappoint their clients, because their expectations are foolish. Even the best funds in the top 25 percent range in a three-year period have a great probability of falling to below average after a few years of success. Reasons: economic trends change what goes in and out of favor, there is overconcentration in a sector that goes out of favor, managers try to time the markets, or managers quit and need to be replaced. What we want is an investment discipline and consistency of performance.

Performance Relative to Assumed Risk

The ratio of performace to risk might be measured in a different way among different advisors, but the statistical data an advisor is looking for is meant to help answer the risk/reward question. This is the major question for the management of any large sum of money. The FA can compare funds to other funds in the same asset class and style by using statistical data such as alpha and Sharpe ratios calculated on each fund. Mr. Trone writes, "Alpha measures the amount of return a manager earns in excess of market returns, adjusted for the risk taken. A Sharpe ratio is a measure of return gained per unit of risk taken" (*Bloomberg Wealth Manager*, July 2000, p. 22). If a fund manager is "adding alpha"—that is, adding managerial value—we stand up and listen. The measurements of reward (the study of the volatility of investment return) are still evolving and are not the only ingredient in solving the risk/reward question. They are powerful statistical tools commonly used by consultants who have set high standards for their detective work.

Minimum Track Record

You would think this is a simple standard, yet how many retirees invest money in funds that have been around for fewer than three years? Too many! We have seen, lately, the advertising blitz from funds with one or two years of performance bring in billions of retirement dollars. The minimum should be a three-year track record; for conservative money, five years. You do not want to buy into an asset-management program that has been simply lucky. It is well known among advisors that as portfolios grow, the managers are less likely to find one or two big winners that create abnormal returns. Napoleon said that he would rather have a general who is more lucky than smart, but in money management you will do best to look for a firm that uses brains rather than chance to pick stocks.

Size of Assets Under Management

This is important in order to keep expenses down. An investment management consultant working on a fee-only basis is hired to examine fees charged by the manager. By studying the expense ratios and the size of the money being run, the consultant can determine whether the expense is too high and, if it is, can recommend you go elsewhere. If you pick expensive funds, then you must have good reason for doing so. Another important factor pertains more to large accounts than to small ones. As a general rule, writes Mr. Trone, "an amount an advisor gives to a money manager should never exceed 10 percent of the manager's total assets" (*Bloomberg Wealth Manager*, July 2000, p. 22). This factor may not be a problem for retirees, but the corollary is that you must check to see how much of a fund's portfolio is invested in any one stock or sector. When examining assets under management the advisor does not want a poorly diversified portfolio. I recall finding as much as 14 percent of an entire fund invested in one hot stock. Then that one stock plunged over 77 percent, and the entire fund dropped 37 percent in four months (from March 8, 2000, to June 30, 2000).

Holdings Consistent with Style

This standard pertains to the investment philosophy that each manager selects. Managers may choose earnings growth, financial strength, value investing in domestic stocks, or capital appreciation across international boundaries. You do not want to buy a domestic growth fund that ends up holding 20 percent in foreign stocks. It does happen that some managers say one thing and do another. Your advisor should be monitoring the funds for the stock or bond holdings so as to keep you in those securities that meet your objectives. Many a fund manager has been sued after drifting into derivatives that were not stated in the prospectus. It is better to have a monitoring system in place to evaluate what is known as style drift. After buying and owning apples you do not want to be eating prunes. Sure, it is not easy to get this information by the moment, but funds must report holdings on a semiannual basis. Most funds and managers will report at least quarterly, and the SEC may soon require funds to report holdings more often.

Stability of the Management Team

It is important to know whether the method of picking investments will be used by the new people who may replace old management. As people change, methods may change, affecting the long-term performance. We especially are concerned when a highly favored money manager leaves and the nest is watched by less experienced people, or when a committee approach replaces a single-person management style. When Peter Lynch left Fidelity Magellan, their track record changed. Although this knowledge is hindsight, consultants keep much closer to the fund management team than does the average investor. Most of the time, an individual investor will not know about management changes until many months after the fact, and often when it is too late.

This leads me to another bit of wisdom from the Old Testament regarding this process.

Investment Proverb 19

The plans of the diligent lead surely to advantage, but everyone who is hasty comes surely to poverty.
(PROVERBS 21:5, NEW AMERICAN STANDARD BIBLE)

After years of investment success and failures, as I look back I find that little Bible quote ringing true for my own actions. When I have done the research and the proper due diligence for myself and my clients, the chance of failure has been substantially reduced. When my clients or I acted on one piece of good information or a flashy advertisement, without knowing more about the firm and its business acumen, then we paid the price of speculation. The research standards I've listed are both sensible and responsible, and to meet these standards a consulting firm must invest a lot of time, money, and reasoning. Monitoring the investments after they are purchased takes even more effort. The standards are in continuous use once your investments are made in order to keep the asset manager and the portfolio honest. There is a sense of accountability once standards are established.

Although fees charged by the investment management consultant can be negotiated, Table 11.1 gives an approximate expense schedule; this does not include money-management fees for mutual funds, which would be less than 1 percent, falling between .4 percent and .9 percent. Although the average fund-management fees are higher, management consultants will seek out funds with below-average expenses—our *duty first* to the client—as part

Table 11.1   Fees for Investment Management Services Using No-Load Funds

Fee breakpoint	Annual fee
$50,000–$249,999	1.5 percent of assets
$250,000–$499,999	1.25 percent of assets
$500,000–$999,999	1.1 percent of assets
$1,000,000 and above	Negotiable

of our services. You can check the prospectus to see exactly what are the charges for managing the funds. This fund's "expenses ratio" is taken out of your return by the fund, so that fund returns are after fees have been subtracted, known as *returns net fees.*

If the management consultant hires a money manager to invest your funds in a *segregated (or separate) managed account* rather than a mutual fund, the fees can be structured to include the manager's expense, all commissions, and investment management fees. It is also known as a *wrap fee account.* Table 11.2 shows the fees charged by most financial advisors for segregated accounts. You may wind up spending more under this arrangement than you would by going the mutual fund route. In addition, I find it much easier to diversify with mutual funds than with the segregated accounts. Because of the high minimum required to open a segregated account, it keeps the average investor from investing in many asset classes. These fees may be negotiated downward. In a segregated account you will own individual stocks and/or bonds, and you will see these on your statement. Many of these asset managers cannot be accessed by the middle class directly, because often investment counseling (money-management) firms have minimum account sizes of five to ten million dollars. Besides, the consultant will work to keep your fees down and monitor the performance of the managers, doing the due diligence you hired him or her to do.

Table 11.2   Fees for Segregated (or Separate) Managed Account Services*

Fee breakpoint	Annual fee
$100,000	3 percent of assets
Next $750,000	2.5 percent of assets
Excess $1,000,000	2 percent of assets

*These fees are often negotiable.

A portfolio manager, an investment counselor, a money manager, and a registered investment advisor (RIA) are usually registered with the SEC as people (or firms) who will be making investment decisions for you. They must be trained well in the picking of stocks or funds, because they hold themselves out as giving advice for a fee. Because they need to show little experience to acquire these titles, you must examine their track record and background and read their ADV reporting forms closely. Many comply with Association for Investment Management and Research (AIMR, www.aimr .org) reporting standards and/or state or federal regulations, and if they do, they can show you proof of their abilities. They also must have on file ADV Part II (or equivalent) to show compensation and any regulatory problems. Many of the best money managers are not accessible to the average retiree, unless you go through a firm that has an "agreement" with the manager. I would recommend that you use an investment management consultant to help pick the money manager and/or mutual fund. There should be a good amount of due diligence whenever you give money to the firms, because they will often request that you give them discretion over your account. That is, they will ask you to sign a *discretionary agreement* (as required by law) giving them the right to buy and sell securities for your account without calling you or getting your preapproval.

Investment management consultants are people (or firms) who specialize in helping clients choose investment managers or mutual funds. They may first help a client with the process of finding the best asset allocation program to meet their goals. There are many investment management consultants, and over 3,000 who are certified (as I am). One group of advisors who offer investment consulting services is the Investment Management Consultants Association (IMCA, www.imca.org). They offer a certified investment management analyst (CIMA) designation. This organization sets high ethical standards for its members and offers conferences and courses to remain current in a quickly changing world.

With the financial planner reviewing your overall plan and giving it sound general direction, the investment management consultant steps in to help you manage the funds. Most medium to large securities firms have both of these professionals on staff. As well, both can and will help you establish a personal investment policy that will be designed around your risk tolerance and return objectives; they will help answer the retiree's risk/reward questions. Certified investment management analysts and certified investment management consultants have a mandatory requirement of experience before getting certified, and, as with many designations, are required to complete a number of hours of study per year. As well, they are trained in important areas that are particularly applicable to the unique needs of a person retiring with a large sum of money; most offer a fee-only investment program. Whether you hire a consultant with a designation or not, you must find out whether the professional (or firm) does the following work in order to earn the fee you are paying. If the professional (or firm) does not provide this level of service, whether they have it in house or they purchase it, then you should begin to look elsewhere. Good financial advisors do the following:

- Weigh economic data and forecast long-term returns for asset classes
- Offer money manager search (including mutual funds) and due diligence
- Assess your risk tolerance, time horizon, and other qualitative data
- Help develop a strategic asset allocation that can meet your goals
- Monitor investments and report performance to you

A client of mine once asked, "What is the difference between Merrill Lynch and Equitable-now-Axa Advisors, and between what your firm does and what they do? You all claim that you can manage my retirement." It is not an easy question to answer, but you can categorize firms into banks, independent financial planning firms, money-management firms, insurance companies, and brokerage firms. Small financial planning firms run their transactions through independent broker/dealer firms. So you are dealing with two companies, not one. The firm you are investing with is generally owned by an advisor who feels that to run his own business is better than taking directions from others, especially if those directions are rooted in a different investment philosophy. Most of these firms have well-trained people, but you need to find a firm that works especially with retirees. On the other hand, brokerage firms usually have a large corporate culture and often are more product oriented rather than planning oriented. The large brokerage firms like to do in-depth financial planning geared toward the high-net-worth client (someone with over $1 million in total equity or fixed-income assets, or $2 million with at least $500,000 in equity or fixed-income assets) rather than the middle-class client, which means smaller clients may find a lack of attention to their needs. In a large firm, try to find a person who has lots of experience working with retirees, or you may be sidestepped.

It can be confusing to try to understand the philosophy of the business you are dealing with, but things are made easier if you concentrate on learning about your advisor rather than about the firm. I believe the firm provides the product and the person provides the advice. No matter what the firm's makeup, you must find out how qualified the person you're working with is, how you will be treated when you have questions, and how you will pay for the treatment. As noted, there are good people everywhere, and whether you are dealing with a sole practitioner or a large bank or broker-age firm, you have a right to good answers to all your questions. If you get these answers, you should feel like the advisor is worthwhile, and that you are a valued client.

Smaller firms have tended to give their clients a much-desired personal touch. Although I work for a large firm, I still like to give people all the time they need. As the sole practitioner grows older, there are business suc-cession issues and client size limitations. Large securities firms that attract the most investment dollars can add clients more easily, because their busi-ness model allows it, but they may have a more difficult time in giving the average retiree "high-touch" service. If you find large firms unwilling to give you lots of attention, then you might consider one of the "ensemble" financial planning and asset-management firms that are moving to become larger and more comprehensive, yet trying not to lose the personal com-mitment required by most retirees. You must find the person and the serv-ices within a firm that best suit you. After the first interview you should have the answers to the following questions:

- Do you feel comfortable regarding the services you are going to pay for?
- When you have questions, will you get friendly and quick answers?
- Are statements understandable? Ask for a sample.
- How often will your portfolio be reviewed?
- Do you understand how the commissions or fees are calculated?
- Did the person take the time to get to know you?
- Did you check references from other retirees who have invested money with the financial advisor and firm?

In the 1980s, Sylvia Porter wrote books about finance; they included no mention of careers in personal finance. Now there are hundreds of thou-sands of brilliant, honest, hardworking people who are financial advisors, and it has become a highly regarded profession. You do not need to find someone who is certified to get terrific advice, nor must you use a fee-only advisor. Certification helps credibility but does not guarantee quality. Fee-only helps to put your best interest first but does not mean the person is a good steward of assets. Today, only about 18 percent of all revenues taken in by FAs come from fees; therefore, the rest is commission based. These statistics prove that the majority of advisors are finding it difficult to give up their commission-based business for fees only.

Whether you know a financial advisor or not, my suggestion is that you shop around and interview at least two FAs in order to get a better understanding of the various services they offer retirees. You must look past the hype and focus on the investment process they use to give you advice and manage your retirement money, being sure there is no conflict of interest. Check out a professional's experience (at least three years), as well as his or her references and credentials. It is also important to ask how many investment choices there are in the advisor's quiver. Does he offer thousands of funds, or just a narrow few? "In a calm sea every man is a pilot," wrote John Ray three centuries ago. Because bad weather will threaten to throw you off course more than once, you want a person (a comanager to whom you delegate some responsibility) who can help you sail safely toward your portfolio's objective. And finally, you want someone (and a firm) you feel has listened to you and is willing to work with you to meet your personal long-term goals.

Investment Proverb 20

*Patience and perseverance in discerning whom
to work with will not fail you.*

12

The Importance
of a Personal
Investment Policy

"For age is opportunity no less
Than youth itself, though in another dress."

—HENRY WADSWORTH LONGFELLOW

I met William (not his real name) at a seminar I conducted on managing retirement funds. Since he had done well in managing his 401(k) and now rollover IRA, he needed someone to place trades for what he wanted to buy. Before I had met him, he knew what he liked and he already had a personal investment policy (PIP) in his head that had worked well for him for several years during retirement. He had calculated the risk he was willing to take, and the return he needed to feel successful. He had a payout schedule that would not deplete all his retirement money, but leave a majority of it to his wife and after her, their daughter. As well, he explained his plan clearly. I asked him why he wanted me. And I wondered to myself what value I could give him. Having well-thought-out, conservative objectives and a sound means of obtaining them, William could manage his money fairly well without an advisor. He told me, "I need you to help me find and buy the securities that fit my portfolio, and then when I die, to work with my wife and to do the same."

I would like to share with you William's PIP, because few people have one. One major reason to hire a FA is to help you develop a formal written investment policy that will bring you even greater serenity than William had with his unwritten and rather informal investment policy. The problem I find in the financial industry is that too many FAs make recommendations without adopting a process that includes the development of a client's personal investment policy. As Jeffery Rattiner writes, "These planners shoot themselves in the hip; they recommend investments based upon current returns rather than adhering to a diligent system" (*Financial Planning*, February 2001, p. 119).

Every PIP is unique and tailored to your own personality and goals to meet long-term investment objectives. The PIP that William created and followed gave him a certain peace of mind rarely seen. I could tell that this portfolio was his own way of finding financial security—a life income for himself and his wife. He did need me to explain the market and to find what he wanted, but I did not need to ask a lot of questions. He knew where I stood in his plan, but I needed only to learn about him to serve him the best I could. Although I found him to be ultraconservative, I came to appreciate his ideas and investment method. I disagreed with him on asset allocation issues, but he listened well and took his own approach, which I honored. It is his money. What William constructed, he felt, was a simple (not simplistic) method to manage his money. He told me he did not want to see his account fall more than 10 percent in any one year, since he was nearing seventy and his wife was two years older and even more conservative. He did not need income, but would be comfortable with a total nominal return of 7 percent, because soon he would have to remove the required minimum distribution. He believed inflation would be about 3 percent to 4 percent per year and only needed to beat it by 3 percent to 4 percent to feel successful.

Risk Tolerance and Time Horizon

One must be open-minded for sensible investing to take shape. You are entering into a long process, not a quick purchase. Moreover, I hope that retirees who come to an advisor first understand the complexities of personal money management and retirement planning. Second, they should understand that a plan is the beginning of a working relationship with an advisor. And third, in the sense that the retiree has the power to hire or fire, the advisor should always work for the client's best interests, knowing that there is accountability to the relationship.

Advisors should understand that each person has carried a good share of troubles to get this far and does not want more. Retirees need to feel secure, and to know the risks they take on are managed ones. What they value should be understood and reflected in the goals set for the portfolio, which becomes your personal investment policy. Financial advice is about people, not money. When retirees say, "I do not want to touch the principal," it usually means they fear taking money from their original investment in order to live. That may be hard to do when the market goes into a tumble, and that risk should be discussed. There may be some coaching done by the advisor when stocks decline, and retirees should expect advisors to take a proactive approach to discussions during poor markets. Most of my retired clients expect income that can be counted on without undue pressure to spend principal. Investors of all kinds should expect an advisor to be an optimist in a bad market, a pessimist in a good market, and an opportunist in all markets. If I were retired, I would want somebody to be a good steward over my assets, whether I go on vacation, get sick, volunteer, babysit the grandkids, or play golf in the retirement league for the next forty years. Money management is not a job for those who have thin skins or for part-timers.

Mr. Rattiner writes, "Clients should assert their authority and fulfill their responsibility by developing investment objectives, establishing sound policies and holding portfolio managers accountable for implementing the Investment Policy Statement" (*Financial Planning*, February 2001, p. 119).

My client William had been the only investor I could remember who had come close to what Mr. Rattiner suggests. An investment policy should include a benchmark return that is somewhere above inflation projections, and William had taken that factor into account. That is, every investor's portfolio should beat inflation by a specific amount, or it will have failed to manage money well. Inflation is a long-term risk, and to not beat it means a loss of buying power over time. As well, William had answered an important risk tolerance question: How much can my portfolio decline in a year's time before I feel uncomfortable? His answer was 10 percent. Rarely have I found someone offering me this information before I ask the question. "No one cares to talk about risk," opined one retiree to me. "Aha!" was my negative-positive response, knowing that the topic has much greater meaning to investors than they are willing to admit.

The volatility of security prices is what advisors call *market risk*. If the market causes your account to fall 30 percent over a period of a year or two, could you wait it out before resuming an upward return? Behavior finance gurus say that the market's volatility causes people to sell low and buy high, to chase last year's winners and this year's media hype. William seemed above it all. He knew a 30 percent decline was too much. Even after a long-term fall there are usually large rebounds, but he just did not need the pain, and it is the pain that people cannot handle. He felt that for his wife's and his combined time horizon—maybe twenty years, although I thought differently—they did not need to invest in common stocks or equity funds. He told me everything was paid for, his only daughter was well off, and he had more income than he needed now. Although he had an unusually high net worth, he still bothered to have a firm personal investment policy. Even high-net-worth people can lose more than they would like and make large errors, selling on emotions rather than staying the course.

The target rate of nominal return (7 percent) that William picked could be reached with the asset allocation plan he had set up. It was not what I would call an *efficient portfolio*, which, according to my analysis, would include stocks or equity mutual funds. Although a low return target could be better met with some equity investments, I gave in to his investment strategy, because he had a moderate expected rate of return that he was capable of getting with a high level of confidence. His portfolio ideas were in the rough, and he needed me to cocreate the final product. The points that an advisor looks for in a PIP can be turned into an investment policy statement. Those important elements are the following:

- Time horizon
- Target rate of return to accomplish a specific goal
- Risk tolerance of the investor, both short- and long-term
- Efficient portfolio: assets are combined to produce the lowest risk to hit the target income and growth of principal

William lacked an efficient portfolio and could have improved his potential return, but he did have a personal investment policy. While some retired investors cannot pull away from cable financial news shows long enough to have a bite to eat, William could leave the country for a yearlong vacation. In the interim I could invest his funds just the way he would if he were here with me. He could become ill or leave the money to his wife, and she could carry on what he had begun if she wanted the same objectives. This is known as *ease of succession*; that is, the investment regimen could be passed to another investor in a simple, understandable format. Although I feel my job is finding investments that best suit his policy, what he felt good about was that I understood his thinking process. We had connected on a far deeper level than the person who just says, "Make me lots of money." He and I are partners in producing a life income. As Ross Levin, CFP of Accredited Investors, writes, "I work best with clients who are most willing to spend time trying to understand their ultimate purpose for their money" (*Journal of Financial Planning*, February 2000, p. 32).

Your FA can help you with the risk/reward question, and how to resolve it. The better an advisor's understanding of the financial markets and of you, the better he or she can then gauge how much risk you can take in order to meet your goals. Remember that the issue is not the market. The market and its returns are highly unpredictable in any short period of time. Statistically, you have a 50 percent chance in any one year of doing less than the expected average rate of return predicted in the market for the next twenty years. Knowing this risk can make you feel quite uncomfortable when you wish to be at a confidence level of better than 50 percent. Unless you become aware of how a good advisor can add real value, you may procrastinate— leave money in cash—and lose much of the opportunity the market offers. Many retirees want a return projection based on forty-year historical data, but want it delivered over the next ten years. The question your advisor can help you answer is how to pick an average return number with higher confidence than 50 percent that will be deliverable over the next ten to twenty years—your time horizon. The effort of this most difficult work, done well, will be to deliver retirees greater peace of mind.

William's confidence level is now quite high, because he set his benchmark rate of return much lower than stock market averages and chose securities, which have proved to be less volatile, giving up returns the stock market could deliver. His portfolio's downside risk is less than half of the risk of an all-stock portfolio. If a bad stock market came along, William would probably answer the question "How are you doing?" with "Fine." If the bond market went down he would answer "Fine," because he would know that the income from the bond securities would eventually make up for losses on bonds, and that the securities had a high chance of coming back up as they approached maturity. He did well, because he knew his risk tolerance, and where the money was invested matched his objective. He had an income expectation that matched his portfolio's design. Because many people do not understand the marketplace and are not developing investment policies that suit them personally, they do not feel confident or comfortable. Eventually, deeply rooted uncertainties will cause them despair when markets behave in a way they have not experienced or expected. Like many financial advisors, I believe in keeping people at peace with what they own.

The Importance of the Process

The time spent by an FA to develop a process and to educate the retiree will be fruitful for the retiree and family and will assist the FA in creating a longer-lasting, more manageable relationship. I believe that it takes patience to become a long-term investor; even if you never make any market decisions, you still need to create a relationship. In William's case, I could improve on his chance of investment success without increasing his long-term risk, but he does not want that service from me just yet. If he wanted my advice, I would change a few things, without changing his overall objective. "How would an investment management consultant improve on his personal investment policy?" you might ask. I will answer the question, so you will see that the investment process, I believe, is the most important step to take in order for a retiree to successfully manage a large sum of money over a long period of time. William is fine for now, but since markets and people are dynamic in nature, I believe there will be some future improvements made to his portfolio.

Investment Proverb 21

In the process, we will discover the investment policy.

Investment Process Step 1

During the initial interview we discuss the return that the retiree (client) needs in order to meet an investment objective, the time horizon during which the money needs to be working, and the downside risk that the client can handle over a twelve- to eighteen-month period. When designing a portfolio the FA will explain to the client the potential volatility, measured by the standard deviation (variability of return) of the aggregate portfolio. That is, the variability of the range of returns is discussed, so that the client knows that the advisor knows the risk factor of owning securities is being highly considered as part of the process. This is no time for false confidence. You want to know your FA will take only the additional risk that is necessary to obtain a higher level of return. Another way of stating it is that the FA will help you develop a portfolio that will meet your investment goal by taking the lowest investment risk possible, giving you a higher confidence level than with an FA who rashly shoots from the hip.

Important as it may seem, many advisors are unwilling to talk about possible loss for fear of upsetting the client. A good investment process should at the planning stage define some potential numerical loss the portfolio can experience. For example, the portfolio has a 95 percent chance of falling within a band of probable rates of return—that is, from negative returns to positive returns. We use a graphic representation of this range of returns, which helps us show the worst, best, and expected average return over one-, five-, ten-, and twenty-year periods. It helps to know that, in general, one can gain returns only at the expense of stability and certainty. It is best in the planning stage, when the client is in an unemotional state (rather than in the heat of the battle), that the client agrees to the portfolio's downside risk. In a way, the investment policy will act like a "governor" on an engine to regulate emotions, whether they be panic or greed. When markets are hot and we are tempted to chase the hot stocks or funds, the investment policy will demand that we do not, unless we rewrite the policy in such a way to accept more downside risk. When the markets are heading south, then the limits of loss (well defined in the beginning) will reiterate to us that, "Oh, yes, we have already taken that into consideration; there it is in writing. Nothing to be upset about." This big-picture long-range consideration should give us enough hesitation so as not to sell in times when it is best to stay invested. It does not prevent us from changing investments, only changing them for the wrong reasons.

The suggestion here is a strong one for those who are retiring: Do not think you can time the market. A client came in and asked, "What happens if you think interest rates are going to rise? Will you change the portfolio?" My standard answer: "How do we know for certain interest rates are going to rise? How far will they go if they do, and how long will the high rates last?" He started to see my point. The issue he brought up is called *timing the market*. In effect he was saying, "If you think rates are going up, are you not going to sell stocks and put the money into short-term bonds?" My response is always "No. Because in doing that we would give up the opportunity of owning stocks if we are wrong."

To make my point clearer I will use a common illustration found in most journals read by advisors. From 1989 to 1994 the average stock mutual fund earned a 12.5 percent return. During the same period the average investor earned 2.2 percent return. How come? *Timing the market, the average investor more often was wrong than right.* So if the client thinks that the market is about to fall, and expects me to call the date and hour, well then, maybe I am not the one he should hire. My bet is that by staying fully invested I will outperform anyone who claims to be able to time the market over a long period. Statistically the bet favors my method, and saves the client money to boot. Sure you can favor one asset class over another as economic data changes—that is called *dynamic rebalancing*—but I do not believe in swerving far from the path that the investment policy has laid out.

We now know that some risk is acceptable to meet an investment goal: the target rate of return. We know that we are not going to time the market; we are going to invest over a specified number of years, and we are going to refer back to these objectives and goals when we need to confirm or measure our progress.

Investment Process Step 2

"Well, what about those international stocks?" asked a client, and then she added, "I just do not like them." In this part of the discussion an advisor needs to understand the client's limitations—or educate a client to accept a broader view. There are many limits you can set right from the beginning rather than being surprised when you find in your portfolio something that does not suit you. Like an endowment, you have a right to choose what not to own. Remember back in the 1970s when the major universities dumped their holdings of African companies that practiced apartheid?

You also may have some important beliefs based on politics or morals, and your advisor should be sensitive to them; it is your money. One client mentioned that she did not want to own stocks of companies that experimented on animals in their drug research and development program, and she mentioned a particular company as an example. Although I liked the company, I had to honor her request. It took some looking to find a mutual fund that had a *socially conscious investment* objective. Other clients do not want to own tobacco companies or firms making money on casino gambling. Whatever may strike you as objectionable can, in most cases, be avoided in your investment policy. When you hire money managers, you often can dictate some guidelines, while others—mutual funds managers especially—may not have the ability to meet particular client demands.

What will be included in our search for investments is one of the most important decisions. That is, what asset classes should be considered as possible portfolio holdings? The strategic asset allocation model, which I suggested in the beginning of the book, takes shape here. The advisor begins the model portfolio by deciding what percentage of the portfolio should be allotted to cash, bonds, and stocks. Further, he or she breaks down how much within the stock (equity) portion is to be allotted to small, medium, and/or large companies. Further, he or she breaks those asset classes down into how much is to be allotted to value and/or growth styles of investing. This is diversification with a heightened sense of awareness that the right combination of asset classes can create less risky portfolios for the acceptable rate of return. If you can excuse the pun, it is diversification with class.

By using proprietary computer software, the advisor will create an optimal portfolio mix for you that becomes part of the investment policy you both work out. Here you are deciding to accept the important investment requirement that you *diversify*. In so doing, you know that you will give up trying to guess the one asset class that is going to outperform all the others. A reality check! You become certain that your diversified portfolio will stay within the boundaries of prudence. You may be investing in risky securities, but with the proper portion allotted to taking risk. One client said it succinctly: "You mean I can take a little bit of money and roll the dice?" Shoot the moon. Go for it. If the policy allows for risk, then you may own higher-risk stocks, because they are balanced with other, less volatile ones. This is prudent investing. Prudence is a virtue, described as "right reason in action." Prudence is not taught; it is learned.

If you are working with an individual money manager with whom you can see the stocks you own, you may be able to tell the manager that you want to be more aggressive or that you do not like a particular industry, like tobacco. If you are aggressive and you are working with growth mutual funds, then the portfolio mix will favor small, medium, and large companies that are considered growth stocks. It is good to read the prospectus to clarify what are the fund's objectives. As you can see, taking risk becomes a matter of choice. Thus, the investment policy should contain your limitations and, most important, the percentages to be invested in each asset class. Any other prohibitions or guidelines can be spelled out here as well.

Investment Process Step 3

Included in the basket of services, which will sustain your confidence in your advisor, is a performance review. You will want to know how the advisor will illustrate portfolio performance. You need to be able to answer the following: Has the overall portfolio performance met the investment goals set out in the beginning? Has each investment, within the portfolio, met the standards set up for the asset class it is supposed to represent? Here we can go back to Chapter 11 to see the investment standards needed to first choose the managers. When monitoring the portfolio, we can use the same benchmarks to see whether the investments still fit well. The evaluation process should continue on a quarterly, or at least an annual, basis. Reasonable standards should be set when monitoring each fund or money manager. Too many portfolios are set up well in the beginning but, as time passes, events and people change the way money is managed. Mutual funds and managers are notorious for "window dressing." Just before they are to report holdings to stockholders, they often load up on currently hot stocks in order to show the management bought them in order to make themselves look smart. They then dump these stocks a few days later as the values come down. It makes for a super-looking shareholder report, and it is known as *portfolio manipulation*. Closely monitoring the manager and portfolio may uncover some of these poor decisions as well as others, and possibly prevent these abuses at a later date.

Another trick we watch for is *style manipulation*. For example, a fund makes money with a big weighting in growth stocks. But, as a *Journal of Financial Planning* article in October 2000 asserted, "Funds routinely describe themselves as investing according to a particular style, while secretly making outside investments in order to improve performance relative to their peer group" (p. 131). Quoting from the same page, "Fund managers have a strong incentive to make bets not authorized under their fund's investment guidelines on investments that are outside of their style disciplines." Notwithstanding the loud cry by professionals for more disclosure of fund holdings and better SEC oversight of fund practices, the mutual fund industry has been resistant to change. The same article cited another study that proved that in 1999 more than half the funds under consideration had drifted significantly in style. Thus in a growth stock market, a value manager pumping some growth stocks into the portfolio will seem to be the smartest value manager on the street. However, this practice can get investors into deep trouble if they think they are buying a value fund, when in fact they are not. If advisors see unacceptable investment practices going on, they need to protect the integrity of the client's account and take action. On the other hand, it is not prudent to sell just because of an underperforming quarter or a few stock purchases that seem not to fit a fund style. What the advisor or investor needs to know is the reason why a portfolio holds certain stocks and not others, and if these stocks continue to meet the standards set by the manager's style and investment philosophy in the beginning. We simply want to own what we think we own.

Rebalancing the portfolio is another service that must be provided if you have a truly strategic asset allocation model. If any one asset class gets to be overweighted (because of strong performance relative to other assets), how often will your portfolio be placed back into balance? "You mean to tell me," a client asked, "you are selling my winner and buying the loser?" In a negative sense, yes. The truth is that the strategic allocation method attempts to keep the portfolio honest. That is, we know that we want to buy low and sell high, right? We can do that by selling high and buying low. In rebalancing, we will often sell what has been hot in order to buy what has been out of favor. Explained in that way, the retiree begins to see that we are taking money off the table, only to put it to work in another investment opportunity.

Asset rebalancing should *not* be done on a monthly basis. Studies have shown rebalancing works best annually; rebalancing too often does not allow an asset class to run its course. As part of the investment policy, we can choose the percentage trigger when the rebalancing should take place. For example, if any asset class gets to be more than 30 percent overweighted, then a portion should be sold in order to place it back into proper weight.

Let's suppose you had a million-dollar portfolio that owned $100,000 worth of a small company growth fund, equaling 10 percent of the portfolio. If the remaining funds did not change in value, and the small company growth fund rose in value to $200,000, the total portfolio would be worth $1,200,000. Since the fund is above the trigger point—it now makes up 16 percent of the portfolio rather than 10 percent—you would consider selling off some shares and reallocating the cash to the other funds.

If we multiply 10 percent times $1,200,000, we find that $120,000 is all we should have in this asset class. Subtracting $120,000 from $200,000 we get $80,000. We will sell $80,000 of the small company fund and reallocate the cash to other investments, bringing the portfolio back into proper balance. This discipline will cause you to sell high and buy low—one of the difficult things for investors to do.

Monitoring both the investment performance and the portfolio balance are reasons why we do not call this a purely passive portfolio method. Over the long term this strategy is superior to buying the S&P 500 (passive investing) and doing nothing more. In strategic asset allocation, you have asset classes that can outperform the index, and together the asset classes can have a lower standard deviation (volatility) than the index. When growth is in favor, you can own growth funds that outperform the index, and when value is in favor you can own value stocks that outperform the index. When you own both of them, your mix should have less downside risk, and yet can produce equal or better long-term results.

Remember, in any given year or two the S&P 500 index can outperform your portfolio, because the index is a handpicked index of 500 companies and overweighted toward large company growth equities. In 1999, ten stocks in the index made up 66 percent of the return, which came in at 21.05 percent. These ten stocks go in and out of favor just like other stocks do; as well, they can go to overevaluations—which is not explained by modern portfolio theory, but is explained by behavioral finance. These same ten stocks caused the major damage to the index in 2000 and 2001. The strategic asset allocation method works better with active management of the individual components of the portfolio, because active managers can better balance their sector allocations. On the other hand, advisors will recommend an index fund—other than S&P, such as small-cap, mid-cap, growth, foreign, or bond—if they fail to find a managed fund with consistent performance and low expenses and that makes a good fit within the portfolio.

Ian Hurwitz, CIMA with Wachovia Securities in Houston, examined active management over a long period of time—from 1971 to 1991. In his book, *Stop Playing the Market—Make It Work for You*, he writes, "Overall, 'value' funds have had slightly higher returns and lower volatility than the S&P 500 Index. . . . The 'earnings growth' style (managers) achieved higher returns than the S&P 500, but with greater volatility" (p. 175). With active management one can favor value-style over growth-style to lower volatility of the portfolio, yet not give up the upside potential of both.

One of many proofs that people misjudge potential performance is given in a study done by Francis Nicholson in 1963. As reported in the *Journal of Financial Analysts*, he took data from trust-quality stocks trading during the years 1937 to 1962. He showed that high price-to-earnings stocks under-performed the less appealing low price-to-earnings stocks. One might say, "with glamour issues, one pays a price." Paul Miller of Drexel Harrimann in 1966 found similar results by studying 1,800 company stocks from the period 1948 to 1964. More on this theme can be found in David Dreman's book *Contrarian Investment Strategies*. Whether you agree that value invest-ing outperforms growth, both styles can be blended into one portfolio.

During the latter half of the 1990s the S&P 500 index has been a more difficult benchmark to beat. Its popularity has become its success. There-fore, some advisors have recommended more exposure to index funds. As well, index funds expenses come in under 1 percent, costing between .25 percent and .75 percent less to run than an actively managed account. The average mutual fund's management fee is about 1.49 percent. I believe that the large index funds have done well because they have been over-weighted in large-company growth stocks. A recent Merrill Lynch study concurs: "The S&P 500 Index has indeed taken on more sector concen-tration in the last few years" (*Financial Planning*, February 2001, p. 24). As incredible as it may seem, in any heated auction market (*all stock exchanges are auction markets*) buyers will often pay $150 for a $100 bill. There is no doubt that this kind of exuberance infects investors from time to time, even the index fund buyers, creating more demand for a few large companies. As markets broaden we will find active managers beating the index funds. Even so, in the last ten years active management of concen-trated funds (those with fifty or fewer stocks) have outperformed their indices, but with greater volatility than the indices. But remember, we can reduce volatility with asset allocation. All of these factors argue for active management.

The efficient market hypothesis (EMH) works in academia for devel-oping market theory, but behavioral finance has shown that EMH does not work in reality, at least not as consistently as the college professors claim it does. Therefore, many active managers who do not think in lockstep with the S&P 500 index stocks (or other indices) can and do outperform the index when the hot air is gone from the large-cap growth sector balloon (which makes up a significant portion of the index). In a poor large-cap growth stock cycle the indexers will suffer, trying to exit through the same door only to be crushed in its narrow opening.

All in all, what I believe most retirees want is not to beat an index, but to meet an income and growth objective, to feel secure that their needs will be met for years to come. That is, they want to have a person understand their hopes and fears, and assist them in managing their personal money. Recently my wife and I put our house up for sale. The realtors who went through it were impressed that although it was moderate in size the builder had "thought of everything." The builder was my dad, and because he had a keen sense of what people cared about in a house, it became easy to sell. An investment policy should be developed so well that you should walk away from it saying, "We thought of everything. We worked with someone who cared about us."

When written down, your goals and objectives take the form of an investment policy statement (IPS). When you consider comanaging your retirement, one professional you should hire is a person who will help you write this statement, but it still must take your personal input for it to be called your own. The following example is similar to my own IPS that is attached to my last will and testament. It is one way my wife will know how I would recommend our retirement money to be managed if I die or become incapacitated.

Investment Policy Statement

Your Name

Introduction

The purpose of this document is to make clear the objectives, goals, and guidelines for the portfolio to be put under management through a strategic asset allocation program. It should serve to communicate my wishes to my investment consultants and outline a meaningful set of guidelines that are specific enough to allow for efficient management of my 401(k) funds.

The assets in this portfolio will be used to fund my retirement beginning January 1 of next year. Currently, the value of the portfolio to be managed is approximately $500,000, which can be invested with a thirty- to forty-year time horizon.

Investment Objectives and Goals

Given the nature of these funds, their time horizon, and their use to fund retirement, the primary objective of the portfolio is to preserve principal and earn a moderate amount of current income.

As such, the securities in the portfolio will include mutual funds (or separately managed accounts) that will be invested in common stocks, bonds, and cash equivalents.

Target Asset Mix

Asset class	Minimum weight	Target weight	Maximum weight
Equities	45 percent	50 percent	65 percent
Fixed income	30 percent	45 percent	60 percent
Cash and equivalents	0 percent	5 percent	15 percent

The program will measure performance quarterly versus appropriate indices for each asset class. My goal is to maintain the following overall portfolio balance:

35 percent large-cap funds included in the S&P 500
10 percent mid-cap funds measured by the S&P mid-cap index
 5 percent small-cap funds similar to those held by the Russell 2000 index
25 percent intermediate government bonds together with corporate bonds
20 percent corporate bonds measured by Lehman Brothers Intermediate
    Government/Corporate Bond Index
 5 percent money market fund

As well, included in my portfolio objectives is to outperform inflation by at least a 3 percent real return per year, given my risk tolerance level. My downside risk tolerance for the total portfolio should be limited to no more than 15 percent in one calendar year. I am seeking conservative growth of capital.

Investment Guidelines

Investments should be made consistent with the quality deemed appropriate in a fiduciary relationship and to which a prudent investor would adhere. All assets must have readily ascertainable market value and be easily marketable.

Limitations and Constraints

The portfolio should be diversified to the extent a prudent investor might propose and to avoid any undue exposure to any segment of the economy or any industry segment. No more than 60 percent of the portfolio will be invested in any single asset class. At least four asset classes will be used in my asset allocation model.

Equity investments made by mutual fund managers are to be chosen from the New York Stock Exchange, the regional and international exchanges, or the national over-the-counter market. Funds must have at least a three-year track record to be included and have a consistent style.

Cash reserves should be invested in interest-bearing securities or in an appropriate money market fund.

Account Review Practices

The investment program will provide for a quarterly review of the performance results of the portfolio, including comparisons to the predefined investment goals. In addition, the firm will provide the following:

• Written confirmation of each transaction
• Monthly statements detailing portfolio positions, withdrawals, additions, and any other activity

- Monitoring of fund managers for consistent style discipline and manager turnover
- Rebalancing of the asset classes within 30 percent of preset limits anually

It is expected that each mutual fund manager will invest their respective portfolio in a manner consistent with their stated investment style and discipline. Together we will review the portfolio in the context of the herein stated investment objectives, goals, and each fund's investment style.

Acknowledgment

Having reviewed this statement, I believe it accurately reflects my investment goals and objectives for my retirement portfolio in the program. Should any changes in my objectives occur, I will notify [company name] and my investment consultant, and we will redefine the goals of the portfolio.

The signature below affirms the contents of this statement.

Client signature _____

Date _____

The beauty of the IPS is that it answers the questions, What happens if I become mentally incapacitated or die? What happens if my FA retires? Simple. The IPS is your personal statement of how you managed your money, and thus can be handed over to another person or FA along with your investment portfolio. Certainly minor changes can be made to fit a new advisor's preferences, but the power of the IPS is that it transcends time, place, and people. Oversight of the portfolio's performance standards and guidelines cannot be made much clearer than this. No financial consultant can say, "I do not understand what you are trying to do."

Concluding Remarks Regarding an IPS

Once we begin to see that risk and return are not coincidences, the development of a prudent portfolio is possible. We then look to optimize the portfolio and determine how to create the least risky asset mix to reach the desired goal. Next, we set up an investment program that will both choose the investments and monitor them. If you do not have a formal investment policy statement like the one above, I would suggest getting one written.

Some advisors summarize in a letter what I have written in the above IPS. You may even find advisors who list many investments services in a brochure but fail to create a formal IPS. I believe a written Investment Policy Statement is like a driver's manual: it gives you a better way to see what you are getting for your money and how to fix it if it needs repair.

Jeffery Rattiner, CFP, writes to financial advisors, "An IPS is a detailed work program of sound long-term investing, tailored specifically for the individual clients by establishing various parameters that will serve as a decision-making guide. . . . This will protect their portfolios from ad hoc revisions that threaten the long-term policy you and your clients have established" (*Financial Planning*, February 2001, p. 119).

Going back to William's investment statement, I believe we could have done better for him if we mixed in at least a 25 percent equity ownership to make his retirement plan less volatile and more productive. Since he could accept some downside risk over the next fifteen years, the stock portion could have helped him grow his principal and income. If he had looked at our model for a conservative domestic account, which would have restricted his ownership of securities as to exclude international stocks, he would have created a more stable portfolio. If his income goals were set too high for his portfolio expectation, I would have told him so. And this is the dilemma in which investors always find themselves: that to meet long-term goals one gives up safety for return, current comfort for future comfort. One advisor tells his retirees: "There is an old person who must be taken care of, and that old person is going to be you."

Balancing Your Expectations

In his book *Asset Allocation*, Roger Gibson writes, "Very often, however, client goals are more ambitious than can realistically be achieved. . . . Human desires tend to exceed the resources available to fund them" (p. 96). Mr. Gibson continues, "Sound investment objectives are built upon realistic capital market expectations and reflect the limitations of the client's available income and resources." The consultant and planners should be very concerned about not setting the client up for failure by taking too little or too much risk. Too little and one is subject to inflation risk, known as *time-horizon risk*; too much and one is subject to market risk—uncertainty of returns. Matthew Peterson, an advisor with CMS Financial Services of Rockville, Maryland, states that "Clients often mistake their own risk tolerance, and usually overstate it." He uses a Monte Carlo analysis to show various possible returns and the probability of getting those returns, with the aim of getting clients to the appropriate risk level. Many retirees find, as years go on, that they have made major investments in the wrong asset classes because they have misjudged their ability to measure risk. *You cannot make up for many years of lost opportunity or bad advice.*

In the planning of a long-lasting portfolio, one must be aware of all economic scenarios. Mark Twain said, "History may not repeat itself, but it often rhymes." The consultant helps you to understand that your portfolio need not be the one that will yield the highest returns in any one year, but one that can make it through the storms of uncertainty that plague the investor and the markets.

A final step is to back-test the portfolio over different economic periods when the economy was poor as well as when it was roaring. The database to do so is available, but usually is purchased only by professionals. They can take different economic cycles and test an asset allocation program to see how well the total portfolio would have performed in the past. Learning how an asset allocation behaves in different market conditions helps to create a more stable, long-term portfolio. The stock market is both volatile and unpredictable, much like the weather where I live in upstate New York. In one day, we can see forty-degree swings in temperature, with a summery day turning into a snowstorm. Here one truly learns a lesson in building all-weather portfolios. A major mistake for retirees is not to create this type of investment plan. The investment policy should be written so that you can keep calm in your hammock during the rolling of the seas, never to make a change in course under duress.

If a client like William becomes concerned about leaving a legacy to his only child, he may in time want to be more aggressive. That is, he may change the portfolio's goals and thus the investment strategy, asset allocation, risk factor, target rate of return, and so on. His investment mix changes only if his investment policy changes. If the account is a nonqualified account with no tax shelter, tax considerations regarding investments become a major issue when picking or changing investments. Revising an investment policy is not to be taken lightly, because you will be either increasing your short-term risk exposure or decreasing your return expectations. If you moved money into technology stocks without thinking through the risk exposure, for example, you made a major policy error, and if you made the change in 2000, you paid a steep price.

13

How to Pay for Financial Management Advice

"A hard beginning maketh a good ending."

—JOHN HEYWOOD

With the severe declines in the markets in 2000, 2001, and 2002, all fees and annual expenses will come under heavier scrutiny by the investor. How long will people pay fees during a period of declining values? No one knows. For the benefit of the client, every FA should be concerned about the internal expense of any portfolio he manages, because he is being paid to keep costs down. If an advisor can save you money, he can make more for you, and that is part of his duty. If two funds or money managers have similar returns and investment styles, and one has lower management cost, then that cost factor should be taken into consideration.

High expense is the reason many advisors I know have discouraged clients from investing retirement money into variable annuities. Many of us can manage money with fewer total fees and less expense than the average annuity charges. On the other hand, money that is not coming from 401(k) or 403(b) plans—that is, nonqualified money—can be invested into an annuity to gain the tax-sheltered advantage. Money in savings bonds, stocks, and regular bank accounts is nonqualified money. Since the tax bite can decrease returns, checking out the annuity offerings is a good idea.

The public is confused about what charges and fees are associated with investing. The fees and commissions vary, but I will list a few types here so that you are aware of them.

- *Management fees* pay for the transactions of stocks or bonds and the research it takes to pick the winners. These fees are usually deducted from your account value *before you see your return*. You can find them in the prospectus under "Fund Expense" or "Expense Summary." The fees range from .25 percent to 2.5 percent.

- *12b-1 fees* must be added to management fees for some funds. These can range between .2 percent and 1 percent. If you purchase B share or C share funds with no initial front-end load, the internal fees can range between 1 percent and 2 percent. These are fees usually paid back to the brokerage firm annually for selling you the fund. Some firms reimburse you these fees if you are a fee-only client. Here the fee pays for the commission paid the broker who sold you the fund. Confusing? Sure is. Some of the no-load funds do not charge 12b-1 fees.

- *Other expenses* can increase fees another .5 percent on A share funds, even if you paid an up-front sales charge.

- *Maximum sales charge* is the percentage charged on A shares up front as a percentage of the offering price of the fund. This can range from 4.5 percent to 6 percent of the initial investment. B shares have no initial sales charge, but usually have higher 12b-1 fees and back-end sales charges that decline over time, known as contingent deferred sales charges. C shares have these as well. All are spelled out in the prospectus, but they are not easily deciphered.

I was once a mutual fund A share guy—when that was all that we had to sell—then a B share guy, and now and then a C share commissioned salesperson. The advantage with A shares is that putting enough money into them can reduce the sales charge significantly. The problem is that if the fund is not working for you and you want to move money out, you will be charged again if you move to another A share family of funds. Many advisors buy these shares, thinking the fund will be the best thing forever, and forget about monitoring it. Not good! Remember that with A shares, advisors are getting paid by the mutual fund company when the load fund is purchased. We know funds drift from style, lose management teams, and underperform their peers. Because the fund company paid the advisor when you bought it, the FA tends to hold these funds longer than may be good for your portfolio, and may fret, as I did, about charging another commission to move you into another fund family. You can see that the back-end load of B share funds can cause the same anxiety in some advisors. The C share mutual funds over the long term have higher annual expenses versus a fee-only program that allows for continuous management. That arrangement means the FA can buy no-load and load funds at no commission, charge a fee, and still save you on management expenses annually over the C share fund. Because you are paying the FA on a fee-only basis to buy or sell funds, he or she is free to hire or fire the fund at no added cost to you and with no time constraint. With a fee-only basis, the advisor is removed from the commission dilemma that he or she faces in managing money. It may cost more on a fee-only basis, but the unbiased objectivity unlocks that talent of the advisor. If the advisor does not live up to what your relationship promised (given time), you can sell all and move to another company without bleeding all those front-end or back-end charges.

If you own a variable annuity within a rollover account and you are happy with it, I am not going to encourage you to change without serious thought about the back-end sales charges you may incur to remove the funds. (It is the back-end sales charge, CDSC, that turns me off from buying an annuity to begin with.) If you have had great returns, then again you need to see what services your FA offers while you continue to own these securities. When attempting to evaluate the investments you now own, do not get upset with your lack of knowledge; we all continue to learn. William Arthur Ward's advice becomes the following investment proverb.

Investment Proverb 22

There are three mistakes to avoid: Remorse
over yesterday's failures, anxiety over
today's problems, and worry over
tomorrow's uncertainties.

If we can live by these bits of wisdom, we will forever avoid MSSS—the monthly statement shock syndrome. We will have a peaceful portfolio, in spite of what occurs in the marketplace.

Fees Associated with IRA, 403(b), 401(k), and Variable Annuities

If you are working for a not-for-profit employer, such as a school district, you may want to check your qualified TSA (or TDA) contract. These 403(b) plans are often set up with payments into an insurance variable annuity (VA). Little has been said about these contracts, but I find that as you approach retirement you can investigate the rollover of these to a rollover IRA that is not a variable annuity contract. There will not be any taxes due so long as the funds go from variable or fixed annuity to rollover IRA at a brokerage firm, mutual fund, or bank. Earlier I outlined the value of taking this approach: possible lower annual fees, flexibility in moving it later, and the availability of more investment choices. Although these annuity contracts have a guaranteed death benefit, you have to decide whether the fees you pay annually are not better spent on management of your account. Most likely, the fee known as the *M&E ratio* is higher than asset management fees charged by fee-only advisors. The annual fees are often higher if there is a monetary up-front bonus for signing on and possibly more restrictive back-end charges.

Bob Veres, who has written articles for the *Journal of Financial Planning* (and now is an editor at Morningstar), has said that the M&E ratio (usually 1.1 percent up to 1.5 percent of the assets in an annuity) is much too high for the benefit received. Although a few new annuity companies offer less expensive internal fees—Vanguard and T. Rowe Price come to mind—still the M&E fees are not going to pay for one-on-one retirement planning and investment management services, unless advisors tack on an additional management fee. In New York state (it may be different in other states) the benefit is that you are insuring the loss of value of your initial investment (less withdrawals) upon death and not before. But after a few years, shouldn't your account (adding your withdrawals) be above water? And if so, then what good is the entire insurance premium you are paying? The insurance companies set this fee, and I believe they are making an annual income that more than offsets the risk of the guarantee they offer. *No matter what your age, you pay the same fee!* A fifty-five-year-old has less chance of dying than a seventy-year-old, yet pays the same annual expense.

By rolling money into a managed account you will not have the death benefit offered in a VA, but look at the savings. On a $500,000 rollover of a TSA, which has a low 1.2 percent M&E ratio, you can save as much as $6,000 annually. With that savings you can hire a professional investment management consultant who has access to thousands of funds or individual money managers who can set up a personal investment policy with you.

Even if you are still working as a teacher, for example, if you are over fifty-nine and a half you can transfer your TSA to a rollover *without* closing your existing 403(b) account if the plan allows for in-service distributions. Later, when you retire, you can transfer the remaining funds. There may be a surrender charge for making the transfer out, and you can request the cost from your insurance company with a phone call. You can then weigh this cost (the disadvantage) against the advantages of making the move. I have done several of these transfers, and what people like most is the increase in personal attention given their account, as well as the fee savings. If you are ill, you may want to keep the annuity because of the death benefit. The insurance industry has made good arguments for the value of a variable annuity, but when I talk to advisors, few own annuities, and none own them for rollover IRA or 401(k) plans.

Comparing Internal Expenses

Some ask, "Isn't the insurance M&E risk expense worth it if I can get a guaranteed death benefit?" A good question to ask your advisor and for us to consider. Let's compare the cost of the annuity insurance expense to a standard term insurance policy. Suppose you place $500,000 in an annuity and leave the funds in the account for ten years. The worst ten-year period the S&P 500 index has done in the past fifty years had a break-even return. For example, if we keep the principal flat for ten years (if that were to grow, your expenses would be even higher), what would the insurance expense be? Assuming you are one of the following ages, you are insurable, and you are given a flat-premium term-life policy, Table 13.1 shows your insurance cost versus your annual annuity fee.

The premiums for an insurable woman would be slightly less. After the tenth year the insurance premiums would be higher than the M&E ratio, but by then your account should be higher than the original investment. Do you want to buy insurance in an annuity, or is it better that the money work for you in a different way?

Table 13.1   Term Insurance Cost Versus Rolling Over $500,000 into an Annuity and Paying a Fee of 1.2 percent

Your age	Ten-year term insurance annual premium	M&E costs of a variable annuity internal fee
Male 50	$1,080	$6,000
Male 55	$1,415	$6,000
Male 60	$2,435	$6,000

Since most people do not make calculations of the fees they are being charged, and because the markets have been good (and the charges have been paid for by good markets) people have not bothered to look too closely at internal VA expenses. When the markets begin to deliver less return, these fees will come into question. Moreover, if you buy insurance outside your nonannuity retirement plan, and you die while carrying the $500,000 policy, your heirs will end up with the insurance face amount and the rollover account. Annuity companies charge different internal fees, having various features that guarantee your investment less your withdrawals. The question is, Do you need these guarantees that you are paying for?

Let's suppose you removed no funds from your retirement account, and one of three scenarios occurred. If you had a 50 percent appreciation in your account, no appreciation, or 50 percent depreciation in your original $500,000 retirement funds and you owned a $500,000 insurance policy, here are the results if you started at age sixty and died in five years. This calculation is then compared to a rollover variable annuity with internal expenses paying for the guaranteed death benefit. The three scenarios are detailed in Table 13.2.

In each case the participant in a rollover IRA had a larger estate (and money to pay income taxes) from the rollover plus insurance versus the variable annuity investment. On top of that, the insurance is income tax free to the survivor, and the internal cost of the annuity would be higher than the premiums on the $500,000 insurance policy!

You might wonder, Why are there are no financial advisors I have met who have bought an annuity with their own rollover or IRA money? Because most know the negatives, as summarized here:

- Limited number of investment choices, although they have been getting better

Table 13.2   Sixty-Year-Old Male with $500,000 Term-Life Insurance Policy
Death of Participant After Five Years with a $500,000 Retirement Account

	Scenario 1: 50 percent appreciation	Scenario 2: No appreciation	Scenario 3: 50 percent depreciation
Insurance payoff	$500,000	$500,000	$500,000
Portfolio payoff	$750,000	$500,000	$250,000
Total payoff	$1,250,000	$1,000,000	$750,000
Versus			
Annuity payoff	$750,000	$500,000	$500,000

- Back-end deferred sales charges, which cost you if you want an early out
- Higher overall annual fees that are nonnegotiable
- Paying for insurance on something that need not be insured, because it is meant to grow in value and pay you while you are living, not when you are dying
- Most annuities pay advisors' commission up front (you cannot expect a high level of services from the advisor year after year when you have already paid him or her)

Shop for Yourself

The arguments for the movement to a fee-only asset management account are powerful. In the financial services industry there is now a boom in the number of financial advisors, but you must shop around. An advisor who makes you feel very comfortable is probably telling you what you want to hear. Your best advisors can be honest and a bit uncomforting. People provide an ever-widening range of services today. They extend from financial advisors who sell a product (with little follow-up), to the FAs who offer many services for a commission or fee, to FAs who have the kind of investment management skills demanded by major endowment funds and pension plans. The latter financial advisors can help you develop a personal investment policy, keep costs down, make investment recommendations tailored to your time horizon, and purchase and monitor those investments.

You have the right firm if the investment process takes the following steps:

1. *Listen*—Has the firm allowed you to speak about your goals and to ask questions?
2. *Analyze*—Did the firm analyze your risk tolerance and short- and long-term objectives?
3. *Calculate expectation*—Does the firm offer projections of investment returns?
4. *Back-test*—Has the portfolio design taken into consideration performance in past market conditions?
5. *Monitor*—How will the firm oversee the investment performance of each manager?
6. *Review*—How often are the portfolio's performance and goals reviewed with you?

Conclusion

Ironies especially entertain me, and they abound in this business. For example, in the year 2000, Vanguard 500 Index Fund had become the single largest mutual fund in America. Add to it the other 128 S&P 500 index funds, and you have a total of $267 billion dollars. That equals 7.7 percent of all money invested in mutual funds in 2000, according to Morningstar. Add that to the other retirement money invested in S&P 500 indexing, and you have the single largest investment held by retirement plans in that year. While these S&P 500 index funds began 2000 at the pinnacle of their success, they ended 2000 with the worst performance since these funds opened! The index itself had not faltered so poorly since 1974. The irony is that success in business is often the penultimate red flag. When every analyst following Qualcomm in December 1999 placed a buy recommendation on the stock, the share price was doomed. It is not surprising that when panics occur in the markets, as in the October 1987 crash, so do the best buys. When people call to buy a stock from me, I first ask whether it is at its high—and it usually is. Isn't that ironic? In an article entitled "Detective Stories," *Barron's* asked money manager Michael Margolis of Avalon Research, "I thought the average person could stay competitive by clicking Yahoo!" Margolis answered: "The chances are slim-to-none that they can compete with the pros. The fact is, it takes my firm a lot of payroll and a lot of work to really get a [stock] story surrounded to where you have a high level of confidence. That's nothing you can research in two seconds" (*Barron's*, March 26, 2001, p. 31).

In the decades to come, new millennium retirees will need to know *with confidence* that good stewardship will be exercised over their retirement funds, and that their advisors care enough to put the retirees' interests before their own. Without a professional discipline and lots of time, the individual investor is at a serious investment disadvantage. A person with a retirement fund will need to produce a steady, long-term income without running out of money and without undue risk. To do so, she must take action and not wait until time wears away investment opportunity. One of my favorite Italian proverbs is "Between saying and doing, many a pair of shoes is worn out." From my experience, financial professionals prevent retirees from procrastinating, helping them to create and execute a sound investment policy that complements their lifestyle. Chances are that those things the behavioral finance people talk about—greed and fear—will be all but forgotten.

Investment Proverb 23

Happy retirees have a keen sense not for choosing the right financial investments, but for choosing the right financial advisors.

Endowment fund managers have been successful at producing a growing income stream lasting decades; with modern investment techniques and a trusted advisor, so can you. There is no excuse for not evaluating your goals and your retirement plan and convening a meeting with an advisor to discuss an income for life.

Evaluating Your Relationship with a Financial Advisor

"Haste, haste has no blessing."
—SWAHILI PROVERB

Although there are different opinions on what makes for top-notch investment advice for retirees, I believe that you will not be dissatisfied by what I consider important. Whether you have a financial advisor or not, you want to familiarize yourself with the following questions. They are a summary of the book's theme: how to comanage your retirement money like a CFO, because CFOs know the questions they want answered. Keep in mind that your FA will be the most important member of your financial team. Answer the following question by circling the appropriate number on the scale (1 is lowest, 5 is highest) or "yes" or "no" ("yes" being 5, "no" being 0).

1. How satisfied are you with the time and attention your FA gave to you? Did he or she perform an initial comprehensive review of your financial affairs, including important insurance issues, and help you understand or write your personal investment policy before making any investment or asset allocation decision?

   1 2 3 4 5

2. How would you rate your FA's listening skills? Does he or she understand your risk tolerance, desire for consistent returns, and ultimate goals for your investment account?

   1 2 3 4 5

3. How do you rate your FA's due diligence efforts to find and choose the correct money managers or mutual funds to meet your asset allocation?

   1 2 3 4 5

4. How satisfied are you with the explanation your FA gave regarding how his or her fee is structured?

   1 2 3 4 5

5. How comfortable are you with your FA's response to questions regarding how the firm will monitor all recommendations—including mutual funds, money managers, and/or individual securities—and make any necessary changes?

   1 2 3 4 5

6. What is your satisfaction quotient regarding ease of access by phone to your FA (or the person in charge of your overall plan) at any time?

   1 2 3 4 5

7. Are a review session of your account and a discussion of your goals done at least once per year, and do they answer all your questions and contain those factors that create a strong working relationship?

   Yes No

8. How highly do you value the financial wisdom, experience, credentials, and code of ethics of the person who is handling your account?

   1 2 3 4 5

9. After following up with and grilling the advisor's references, how do you feel these people would rate the overall service they received from the FA?

   1 2 3 4 5

10. When including your advisor on your team, what level of confidence do you have in his or her professionalism, expertise, and willingness to work with other advisors (attorney or accountant, for example)?

    1 2 3 4 5

If you have not contacted an FA, these questions will bring you closer to learning how to evaluate a relationship with a professional you may work with for a long time, possibly for the rest of your life. Taking the time to learn about investment services and the people who provide them will pay off in nightly dividends. Bob Veres, publisher of the trade newsletter *Insider Information*, writes, "Unlike medicine, financial planning is too young to have rules about what makes for a good practice."

From reading this book, you now understand the value of professional advice and the many factors that make up the investment process. You must rate the relationship with your FA and the services he or she offers. From the questions we just covered, I would put trust in those FAs and firms that score 40 or above. If your firm ranks between 35 and 39, you may want to see where the firm can improve its services to you. If the score is below 35, you may want to interview other FAs to see whether they can offer you a more comprehensive service geared toward the needs of a retiree. If the score is 45 or more, then you can refer the person (or firm) to your best friend's mother. When working with an FA, be honest and expect honesty in return. The management of a large sum of your money is the responsibility of both of you. Do not be afraid of the truth, even if it may not be what you want to hear.

You may feel overwhelmed by the information presented in this book regarding the complexities involved in the long-term management of retirement assets. You may be retiring early, with your life expectancy thirty to sixty years longer than you first assumed. You say that your retirement plan is in good shape, but you ask yourself, Do I have enough or how much do I need? Without seeming pessimistic, you know you may encounter during those golden years another one or two recessions, natural and human-made catastrophes, or even a cold blast of hyperinflation. You believe Social Security will be there, but it will not go as far as your dad's check did. Your monthly pension, after taxes, still could leave you shy—if you have a pension at all. You want to have a lifestyle that is fulfilling and enjoyable, but you are not sure how much you can comfortably spend today, so as not to be a ward of the state tomorrow. Retirement could become more stressful than having a job! You want your spouse (or children) to have some or all of you retirement nest egg, but you are not certain if your estate will be blown to pieces by taxes.

Even if you have a financial plan, you may now wonder: are the return projections based on average return assumptions too optimistic and no longer valid? You have come to realize these issues are as vast as any glacier, yet your life is not moving at a glacial pace. You know you are ultimately responsible for the task ahead, but to whom do you go for assistance? Who will help you man your seaworthy ship, the one that will carry you through crashing waves on the journey to safe harbors? Someday you will want to recline like a tired sailor into your favorite hammock, but to whom will you hand over the wheel? In the end, either you walk blindly into the dilemma you face or you make tough decisions now and find consolation in knowing you are on the right financial course. If you go through the process taken by the endowment fund CFO to investigate and establish investment guidelines, to create a timeless stream of income, you will build the peaceful portfolio that is right for you. My hope is that this book will guide you to develop a relationship with a person (or firm) that has the expertise to be your comanager, coach, or friend, possibly for a lifetime.

Appendix

How Does the Tax Relief Act of 2001 Help Those Age Fifty and Over Create New Savings Opportunities?

*"Mr. Burns, what do your doctors say about
smoking cigars and drinking wine at your age?"*

"Oh, they're all dead."

—GEORGE BURNS, AT AGE NINETY-TWO

Anticipating a need for more retirement savings, on June 7, 2001, President George W. Bush signed into law the Economic Growth and Tax Relief Reconciliation Act of 2001 (EGTRRA). Among the more important aspects of this act are the changes made to raise contribution limits of employer-sponsored retirement plans and IRAs. Some say it is the most important act to increase retirement savings in over thirty years. EGTRRA also implements changes that allow people age fifty and over to make additional "catch-up" contributions. Get it while you can. All new contribution limits end beginning in 2011, when this aspect of the act expires. Furthermore, beginning in 2002, for those in the middle and lower income brackets, this act provides a temporary *tax credit* for contributions made by taxpayers to IRAs or qualified plans. Be sure to check with your accountant to see whether your contributions qualify for a tax credit in 2002 and thereafter.

If you have no retirement plan, then you may contribute to an IRA or Roth IRA at higher levels than you were allowed before 2002. If you have a retirement plan, then you must check to see whether your income level disqualifies you from participating in a traditional or Roth IRA. You must have *earned* income—wages, salary, and so on—to contribute to these plans. Tables A.1 and A.2 show how much you can defer beginning in 2002.

Table A.1   Traditional IRA and Roth Contribution Limits

Year	New contribution limits	Add catch-up for age 50 and older
2002	$3,000	$500
2003	$3,000	$500
2004	$3,000	$500
2005	$4,000	$500
2006	$4,000	$1,000
2007	$4,000	$1,000
2008	$5,000	$1,000
2009	$5,000 plus inflation	$1,000
2010	$5,000 plus inflation	$1,000

Table A.2   401(k), 457, and 403(b) (TSA) Salary Deferral Limits

Year	New contribution limits	Add catch-up for age 50 and older
2002	$11,000	$1,000
2003	$12,000	$2,000
2004	$13,000	$3,000
2005	$14,000	$4,000
2006	$15,000	$5,000
2007*	$15,000	$5,000
2008	$15,000	$5,000
2009	$15,000	$5,000
2010	$15,000	$5,000

From 2007 to 2010 the contribution limits and catch-up numbers can be higher if government indexes the limits to inflation.

Table A.3   Simple IRA Plans

Year	Contribution limits	Catch-up contributions
2002	$7,000	$500
2003	$8,000	$1,000
2004	$9,000	$1,500
2005*	$10,000	$2,500
2006	$10,000	$2,500
2007	$10,000	$2,500
2008	$10,000	$2,500
2009	$10,000	$2,500
2010	$10,000	$2,500

* From 2005 to 2010 the contribution limits and catch-up numbers can be higher if government indexes the limits to inflation.

For example, Bill turns fifty in 2002. By contributing to a 401(k) plan in 2002, he may defer $11,000 plus $1,000 for a total of $12,000. During 2003, the new law allows Bill to contribute $14,000 to his defined contribution plan. If Bill did not have any retirement plan, then he may contribute up to $3,500 to an IRA or Roth in 2003. Employers of small companies can set up simple IRAs. Their deferral limitations are listed in Table A.3.

The new act increased the income limits for other retirement plans as well as employer-sponsored defined-benefit pensions. By allowing higher income limits, employees with larger incomes (over $170,000) will be able to contribute more dollars toward retirement. Check with your accountant to see how the laws affect your personal finances. When applying the new rules to your personal situation, you must check with your employer to see whether the plan documents allow for changes.

Retirees were once limited in their ability to transfer retirement funds to other plans. For example, 401(k) plans could not accept 403(b) money. New rules known as *portability rules* now allow employees to move eligible distributions from government (457) plans, TSAs, and 401(k)s to any of these plans, or they can be rolled over to an IRA without a tax consequence. With ease, the investor can consolidate all retirement plans into one plan. Before 2002, a spouse inheriting a retirement plan could only roll over retirement funds to a rollover IRA. Now a spouse can roll over money from a deceased spouse's retirement plan to his or her own qualified plan. You must check your plan documents to be sure they are updated for the law changes. I have never met a retiree who said, "I'm sorry I saved too much," but I have met some who said, "I wish I had saved more."

Glossary

"The word crisis, *when written in Chinese, is composed of two characters. One represents danger; the other represents opportunity."*

—John F. Kennedy

Words tend to change in meaning over time, and slang goes out of fashion like Internet companies. Some words may mean different things to different people. In trying to understand financial concepts, the words are quite important, and the context in which they are used must be understood.

AIMR standards Reporting of investment results can be (and have been) fudged. The Association for Investment Management Research (AIMR) has set standards for money managers that, if complied with, allow for more accurate and consistent reporting. With reliable information, investment management analysts or consultants can calculate periodic returns and risk-adjusted returns. They then can compare these returns to other managers in the same peer group and to benchmarks. You must have at least a five-year track record to meet fully audited standards, but you can begin to comply by those standards with three years of track record.

Alpha Measure of a manager's contribution to portfolio return, compared to a passive market index portfolio, adjusted for risk and based on beta, or systematic risk of the market. "Alpha is generated if a money-manager's returns are equivalent to an appropriate benchmark, if the risk taken is less than the benchmark" (Ben Warwick, *Searching for Alpha*, John Wiley & Sons, 2000, p. 15). Alpha helps to determine whether returns are coming from brains versus luck.

Asset allocation plan (or strategic asset allocation) The process of determining the amounts of money to be invested in given percentages into different asset classes within one portfolio. The strategy must be flexible and not exclude the possibility that additional asset classes may appear. In investments, change is inevitable.

Asset classes Best described by saying stocks are grouped by size of the companies into large, medium, and small, and into foreign and domestic. Bonds are grouped usually by length of maturity and kind, such as short-term, intermediate, and long-term, foreign and domestic, and tax free and taxable. Thus, an asset class broadly defines an investment category. By identifying a security's asset class we can more easily compare and evaluate it against other securities that share similar characteristics. Asset classification is not for people who are purists, unless they buy only index funds. A mid-cap fund manager may buy some large capitalized stocks, or may lean the other way and blend in small companies. So, too, with large-cap fund managers taking small positions in mid-cap stocks. Academic evidence strongly suggests that the vast majority of a fund's performance is due to its asset allocation, so buy those funds that are true to the asset class in which they claim to be investing.

Back-test Your portfolio model (or investment style) can be tested over different market conditions to see how well it would have performed in those times. Because the market is cyclical, past performance of various asset classes can show us how a portfolio could have behaved. Although some asset classes are new and have little history, by making assumptions that are reasonable and back-testing these assumptions, one can see better into the future. Thousands of different variables affect investment return. Rather than planning blindly, back-testing helps one become aware that a portfolio can take thousands of different paths.

Behavioral finance The new academic studies that examine the rational as well as the irrational behavior of investors. Rather than looking at the underlying investment values of the securities in the marketplace, the studies seek to find the effects that events, emotions, and volatility have on security prices in general. Educators believe that if one can improve investor behavior, one can increase investors' returns. Scientists at MIT and elsewhere have recently found that the basis of human reasoning is our ability to feel. The investor is a feeling, thinking being—whether good or bad—and it takes a good amount of experience and training to become proficient at investing.

Carve-out rule This allows retirees to draw money from a retirement account without penalty before they are fifty-nine and a half, but only if they have reached fifty-five years old. It is used only if you are retiring and your employer is willing to pay you a sum of money before you roll funds into a rollover IRA. Once money is in a rollover IRA, the carve-out rule cannot be used. You may want to carve out enough to meet your needs for a few years until you reach fifty-nine and a half.

Comprehensive financial review (or plan) A review of all aspects of a client's financial picture. Included in this, yet going beyond it, is the reading of retirement benefits, wills, insurance policies, disability income policies, and a search for any other risk exposure. Also included are analyses of cash flow, personal balance sheets, income tax strategies, and retirement and estate planning goals. The advisor may help you allocate assets and make investment suggestions. This service can be performed on a fee basis or on a retainer basis. Some advisors do it for a fee, but waive the fee if you execute commissioned transactions through them.

Correlation This describes how asset classes move in time with each other. When two assets move up or down in perfect lockstep, then you have perfect positive correlation. For diversification purposes you do not want perfect positive correlation. Imperfect correlation is what reduces the risk of owning two or more assets. When one asset is not performing, another may be moving ahead, much like a good player pulls his team along to victory. *Covariance* is the term given to how asset classes move relative to one another. Mathematical challenges do appear if asset classes' covariance changes over time, necessitating ongoing analysis.

Designated beneficiary The primary beneficiary or beneficiaries (PB) named to inherit your retirement account, as opposed to the secondary beneficiaries, also known as *contingent beneficiaries*. There could be more than one PB named, and any PB can disclaim money to another primary or contingent beneficiary after the IRA owner's death, allowing for greater flexibility, in general, than what 401(k) plans offer. The designated beneficiary has to be named in the plan document but does not have to be determined until December 31 of the year following the IRA owner's death.

Disability waiver People suffering from a verifiable disability can remove money from a qualified retirement account without penalty for early withdrawal.

Due diligence The process of investigation to determine the capability of the money manager. The returns of a money manager or an investment company, the method used to invest, and any fraudulent activity that may have occurred may be examined. Due diligence does not end with the investment, but continues afterward, making sure that the firm sticks to its objectives and investment policy.

Fiduciary person Someone who assumes the responsibility to manage money and property of another. A trustee is a fiduciary.

Financial planner An advisor who can view the entire financial picture of a client and make recommendations so as to better the client's financial strategy. The following are just a few questions to discuss with financial planners: What services do they offer? How do they charge for services? What are their credentials? How do they keep up with changes in regulations, economics, and legislation? What is their experience and background? What associations or institutes do they belong to, and are they still in good standing? Check out their references and interview at least three firms to find the right fit for you. There are almost sixty designations in the financial industry, and only a handful are discussed in the book. Remember that these titles are a good starting point, but the ability to pass a test does not always transfer into the ability to work with real people, nor does it guarantee the planner has a heads-up view on current planning matters.

Future return expectation A return is assigned to each asset class prior to owning the investment. It is a lucky guess! Actually, trained analysts create assumptions regarding the potential long-term returns for a specific asset class or stock. Their objective return expectations keep all of us from getting too enthusiastic or too depressed about markets. You want sound judgments regarding expected returns. Although these assumptions can change slightly from year to year, they are necessary in forming the efficient portfolio you want to own.

Gap years Those years between the time when you retire and the time you begin to collect Social Security. For some it could be ten years or more, and filling those years with income will put many portfolios under the stress of withdrawing more than should be taken. For many, a part-time job to bridge the gap years will be an important source of income.

Income in respect of a decedent (IRD) This is income received by a beneficiary of a retirement account after a person dies. It is taxable at the income tax level of the receiver. If the heir can defer taking part of these funds or stretch out payments over a long period, then taxes can be saved.

Investment decision The decision to own an individual stock or bond. I have not seen any clients on their own make consistently good investment decisions over a long period of time. They buy what is hot only to sell when it is cold; often they buy on little research, making an investment decision based on something heard on TV or from a friend. Lots of research and a little timing go into a good investment decision.

Investment management consultant An advisor who specializes in the development and implementation of an investment strategy that meets your personal investment objectives. He or she may help you write an investment policy statement and develop with you a strategic asset allocation plan and find investments that meet the demands of the plan.

Investment management decision The choice of how much to invest in stocks, bonds, and cash equivalents over a long period of time. This process is not well understood, because we often do not see the entire picture from the perspective of these three categories. People can vastly improve their returns by sticking to an allotted percentage in each asset class, rather than timing the market, trying to go from cash to stocks to cash again. Academic studies have shown that the investment management decision is as important as which stock you should own.

Investment policy The client who comes in and says, "Just make me lots of money," does not have an investment policy. A personal investment policy must reflect many facets of the individual. Risk tolerance, investment expectations, time horizon, past experiences, performance monitoring, and more go into developing an investment policy.

Investment policy statement (IPS) A formal written document that outlines the client's personal investment policy (PIP). These terms refer to the client's clear understanding of his or her investment objectives, goals, risk tolerance, expectations of returns, investment limitations and constraints, portfolio monitoring and rebalancing guidelines, and the performance review procedures. An IPS is signed by the investor for each money manager hired, so that the management firm knows the investor assents to the manager's investment style and discipline. An IPS is written to cover the entire portfolio if different mutual funds or managers are hired. Every retiree with an investment policy statement has taken the time to complete a process that delivers a great deal of confidence regarding how money is to be managed.

Investment process The time spent investigating how to invest retirement funds. Usually this process begins with reading good books, and then, with the help of an experienced financial advisor, developing a method to reach your personal objectives.

Joint life expectancy The life expectancy of two people given by actuaries and used in the calculation on the payout from retirement plans. It is not how long two people will actually live. These life expectancies can be found on a table provided by your advisor.

Large-cap growth An asset category or class of stock. Large companies, usually with a capitalization above $20 billion, are considered large-cap stocks. When a fund or money manager buys only from this group, he or she is known as a large-cap manager. This is where we get the large-cap growth style designation. *Cap* is short for *capitalization*, which is calculated by multiplying the corporation's number of outstanding shares times its price per share. S&P 500 is a large-cap index that is used as a measure of the value changes in large companies.

Life expectancy If you think you are going to live as long as they say you will, you will know when to spend your last buck. Right! The life expectancy here is an actuarial number given a large population. Many people will live beyond that number, and it is meant to reduce your retirement plan to zero at some finite time.

Life settlement transaction The transaction that is made between the owner of a life insurance policy and a firm willing to pay the owner for assigning the face value payoff over to the new firm. An owner can also borrow money from a company using the death benefit as the collateral.

Long-term care Health care services given in a nursing home, at home, and at some assisted living arrangements. People who suffer from chronic illness or old age may need daily assistance with some or all of these activities of living: bathing, dressing, eating, toilet use, transferring, and so on. According to Health Insurance of America, there are 1.6 million people over sixty-five in nursing homes. As well, there are 13 million people receiving home health care, of which 40 percent are between the ages of eighteen and sixty-four.

Modern portfolio theory (MPT) A theory heavily subscribed to by endowment funds, which says that you must consider the risk of an investment portfolio as well as its expected return. It also informs us that proper diversification can by itself reduce the risk of owning assets, because investments do not move in synch with each other. So in theory, although you own risky investments, when mixed with low-risk investments the combination reduces total volatility. Because these different asset classes do not move in synch, more consistent returns can be produced. A high degree of computer technology is used in developing balanced portfolios using MPT. The introduction of MPT has led to many valuable MPT statistics—standard deviation, alpha, beta, R-squared—that assist in the development of portfolios and comparing returns. Harry Markowitz wrote his thesis on portfolio selection in 1951 (later to be known as modern portfolio theory), which earned him the Nobel Prize in economics in 1990. The theory works with past investment data; therefore, its shortfall is predicting future performance.

Money management This term is used by professionals to refer to the skill of researching and then buying and selling securities—stocks, bonds, or cash equivalents—for oneself and others in order to produce investment returns. All mutual funds hire people with money-management talent, and so do pension funds and endowment funds.

Monitoring The final stage after implementing an investment strategy is to monitor the investments and the managers. Portfolio manipulation, style drift, management changes, consistent philosophy, and portfolio overlap of securities are some of the factors monitored.

Net unrealized appreciation (NUA) The difference between the cost of stock and the sale price of a stock at the time it was received. The stock in this case must qualify as a distribution of company stock received from a distribution of a 401(k) plan or ESOP. If you receive such stock, check with a financial advisor or accountant regarding the tax implication of holding the shares or selling them. If the shares are rolled over into a rollover IRA you will lose the NUA advantage.

Nominal returns The return on an investment that does not subtract the effects of inflation.

Pension maximization A term used to describe an insurance strategy of getting more annuity income without losing a death benefit. One would take an annuity on one's life alone and with extra income purchase an insurance policy for heirs to receive. A financial advisor can make the calculations to see if this strategy can apply to your circumstances. First, you must be insurable, and second, you may need to buy term insurance to make it affordable. Permanent insurance is more costly, but longer lasting.

Performance review Each investment and asset class contributes something to your portfolio. Although the total portfolio performance must be reviewed at least annually, each member of the investment team— each money manager and/or mutual fund within the portfolio—must also be examined. It is good to see how well they are doing against benchmarks or their competition—their peers.

Personal investment policy (PIP) A long-term strategy formulated by analyzing specific investment objectives and constraints. The policy must reflect the risk tolerance and income and growth needs of the client and establish guidelines to keep track of the investment strategy that is taken.

Range of returns This is the potential outer limit of the returns expected from various asset classes or the entire portfolio. If the range of return is two standard deviations on either side of the average return, then there is a 95 percent chance that your return will fall within that range. So if the average return is 10 percent and the standard deviation is 15 percent, there is a 95 percent chance that the return you will get will be in the range between negative 5 percent and 25 percent. This analysis helps one to better predict the long-term variability of returns within the portfolio.

Real return (or real rate of returns) What you get after you deduct the inflation rate (the CPI) from the return you received on your investment is called the real return. (In 1974, doing this made grown men and women cry.) The actual return is that return you get without subtracting the inflation rate.

Rebalancing This is not an Olympic sport, but it does take guts. It is an important ongoing activity where one sells those asset classes that have become overweighted (performed well) in the portfolio and reallocates the funds to others that have become underweighted (performed less). This process will keep the percentages invested in each asset class close to the targeted weights specified at the beginning of the strategy. By doing this you capture upside, while getting the portfolio back to a risk level that is appropriate for the account.

Reduced lifetime benefit A retirement benefit that not only pays you an annuity income for life, but pays your spouse a life income.

Registered investment advisor (RIA) A firm or person who offers investment advice. The principal of the firm has passed an exam in securities law and now is registered to buy and sell securities for clients. Such a person or firm may not have any investment expertise or track record. If one is looking at independent firms and not member firms of the NYSE, a retiree must interview several RIAs to find the one with the required expertise. An investment management consultant works to uncover RIAs who can best meet the high standards required to manage your money. Most investment counselors are RIAs and must file forms ADV Part I and Part II with the SEC. ADV Part II is sent out to prospective clients interested in knowing more about the RIA. Be sure to ask for it. Before hiring an RIA, due diligence must be done. Banks are exempt from registration. Most brokerage firms are registered investment advisors and can lead you to qualified investment advisors, mutual funds, and money managers, or manage the money themselves. There are about 20,000 RIAs. Most of them work as independent consultants and are not employed by major brokerage firms.

Required beginning date (RBD) The year after you turn seventy and a half is the year you must begin taking a minimum distribution from a qualified retirement plan. If you wait until that year you will need to take two distributions. Normally people take out their first distribution the year they turn seventy and a half so they are not forced into a double payment in one year.

Required minimum distribution (RMD) IRS code demands that you withdraw a minimum distribution amount at the required beginning date from your retirement plan. If you do not withdraw the proper amount, then you will be heavily penalized. At seventy and a half it is good to check with your financial advisor regarding this matter. As of January 2001, the new regulations have, in general, lowered the RMD and have made the calculations easier.

Risk factor The variability of an investment return, also known as the *standard deviation*. Because the markets change, the risk factor changes over time. Although no one claims to know for certain the future variability, it does give us a factor to be used in putting together an efficient portfolio. It also helps us to calculate how much of a percentage may be placed into each asset class and how a portfolio may behave.

Risk premium The return on an investment that exceeds the riskless return, which is usually pegged at the three-month treasury bill rate.

Risk tolerance How much of a decline in value of your portfolio can you stomach in any one-month or eighteen-month period? Your risk tolerance is the stress that your portfolio's swings can give you. Some people who are retired have no risk tolerance. Maybe a good advisor can show you how to accept more risk for a good reason.

Rolling period The time period used to find the average return number. For example, January 1, 1980, to December 31, 1989, is a ten-year period. To examine the rolling ten-year returns from January 1, 1980, to January 1, 2000 (twenty years), begin by getting the average return from January 1, 1980, to January 1, 1990, which is the first ten-year period. Next, moving up one year, find the average return from January 1, 1981, to January 1, 1991—the second ten-year period. The third period runs from January 1, 1982, to January 1, 1992, and so on. Because you roll forward one year to get the next ten-year stretch, it is called a ten-year rolling period from one starting date, in this case January 1, 1980, to the end date, January 1, 2000. If you get the average returns for each ten-year period until you reach the period January 1, 1989, to December 31, 1999, you will have returns from twelve ten-year rolling periods.

Rollover IRA This is an individual retirement account set up to receive distributions from any qualified retirement account, such as a 401(k), 457, 403(b), 401(a) pension, or cash balance plans. The Retirement Equity Act of 1984 (REA) gives certain rights to spouses of certain retirement plan participants. REA requires spousal consent in order to withdraw a lump sum payment of cash benefit from any pension plan. And it requires spousal consent if death benefits are to be paid to anyone other than the spouse.

Separate account (or a segregated account or individually managed account) An investment account whereby you can see the investments purchased and sold by the money manager that you have hired. Unlike a mutual fund, where you pool your money with other investors and own a share of the fund that owns shares of stocks or bonds, in a separate (or segregated) account you have a direct ownership in the security in your account. You have more tax control over the securities, but usually less diversification than you would have in a mutual fund. Because most separate (or segregated) accounts have minimums from $100,000 up to $1,000,000, you would need substantial wealth before your advisor could recommend several managers in order to get your account diversified.

Spousal rollover The 401(k) or rollover plan that is left upon death of the owner to the spouse can be rolled over to the surviving spouse's own rollover. The spouse then can begin a new payout schedule and name new beneficiaries. The children do not have this option of rolling over the inherited retirement funds, but if they are named as heirs, they can retitle the account and take payments. Only a spouse has the right to roll over assets.

Standard deviation See *risk factor*.

Stretch-out I do not mean to put people on the torture rack, although it could be painful not to use the stretch-out provisions allowed by the IRS code to take the minimum payments from a rollover IRA. Payments to children who are heirs of a rollover IRA should be made over their life expectancy, thus keeping as much money in a tax-deferred account and paying taxes on withdrawals at the lowest tax rate possible.

Style The investment method used to produce returns. Usually the money manager or mutual fund determines the style. For example, growth-style managers are not going to buy a lot of stocks that pay high dividends, such as a utility company. They purchase firms they think will grow sales and earnings faster than most other firms. Value-style managers may not buy an Internet company that does not meet cash flow requirements used in their stock-picking method. Value managers are looking for companies with strong balance sheets, but whose underlying value is not reflected in the stock's price. There are some whose style is to go "anywhere," a blended style. A style is an investment philosophy.

Substantially equal periodic payments (SEPP) (or rule 72t) To take money out of a retirement plan before age fifty-nine and a half, a retiree would need to calculate an annual payout based on life expectancy. Once the payout begins, it must continue until five years pass by or until the person reaches fifty-nine and a half, whichever comes later. There are several methods to make the calculation, and you may want a financial advisor to assist you. Doing it correctly allows you an income before fifty-nine and a half without triggering a 10 percent IRS penalty.

Survivor income After the death of one spouse, the living spouse may find he or she needs more income. A financial planner will help determine where this additional income will come from and what income could be lost if one spouse dies. Often some Social Security income is lost, but there may be pension fund income also.

Target rate of return In the building of an efficient portfolio we need to combine many asset classes, each with a long-term expected rate of return. The combination of these assets yields a target rate of return; there is a 50 percent chance of exceeding it and a 50 percent chance of falling short of it. The target return gives us some framework by which to set an income stream for the retiree.

Time horizon Time horizon is an estimation of how long the money under management needs to last before you outlast it. A sixty-year-old should be planning on a time horizon of at least thirty years; I usually add another decade for advances in medicine.

Variable annuity (VA) An insurance company annuity contract in which you are offered securities and at least one fixed-income account. You allocate your premiums paid to investment units, which change in value as the performance of the underlying investments (such as stock funds, bond funds, and/or money market funds) change *minus* the contract expenses. Agents of insurance firms sell VAs, and they are paid a commission for placing money in them. There are a few no-load annuities, but to receive investment advice on these the advisor may charge a fee. In contrast, a fixed annuity contract issue by an insurance company gives you a guaranteed interest rate for a fixed period, and then pays you a fixed rate of return when you need the income. An immediate annuity contract is issued when income is paid out immediately after you pay the premium, and, generally, the principal is no longer accessible.

Resources

I encourage you to check out the readings and organizations listed here to supplement what you've learned in this book.

Books and Newsletters

Arnott, Robert D., and Frank J. Fabozzi. *Active Asset Allocation.* Probus, 1992.

Bernstein, William. *The Intelligent Asset Allocator.* McGraw-Hill, 2000.

Bodie, Zvi, Alex Kane, and Alan J. Marcus. *Essentials of Investments.* Irwin, 1994.

Ellis, Charles D. *Investment Policy—How to Win the Loser's Game.* Dow Jones Irwin, 1985.

Ferguson, Karen, and Kate Blackwell. *The Pension Book: What You Need to Know to Prepare for Retirement.* Arcade Publishing, 1995.

Gibson, Roger C. *Asset Allocation: Balancing Financial Risk* (3rd Edition). McGraw-Hill, 1999.

Ibbotson Associates, Inc. *Stocks, Bond, Bills, and Inflation (SBBI) 2002 Yearbook.* A series of books that are published annually.

Jaffe, Charles A. *The Right Way to Hire Financial Help.* MIT Press, 1998.

Owen, James. *The Prudent Investor.* Probus, 1990.

Picker, Barry. *Barry Picker's Guide to Retirement Distribution Planning.* Self-published, 2001. (800) 809-0015 or www.bpicker cpa.com.

Slott, Ed. *Ed Slott's IRA Newsletter.* Self-published annually. (800) 663-1340 or www.irahelp.com.

Trone, Donald B., William R. Allbright, and Philip R. Taylor. *The Management of Investment Decisions.* Irwin, 1995.

Organizations

American College of Trust and Estate Counsel
www.actec.org

American Institute of Certified Public Accountants
(888) 777-7077
www.aicpa.org
www.cpapfs.org

American Savings Education Council
www.asec.org
For information on 100 financial and retirement planning calculators.

Association for Investment Management and Research
(800) 247-8132
www.aimr.org
info@aimr.org
Investor's Right to Know: Selecting Investment Advisors (free booklet).

Economic Policy Institute
www.epinet.org
For economic statistics, opinions, and a useful unemployment insurance calculator.

Financial Planning Association
(800) 322-4237
www.fpanet.org
membership@fpanet.org

Institute of Business & Finance
www.icfs.com
icfc@icfs.com

Internal Revenue Service Online
www.irs.gov
Tax information on retirement plans and answers to frequently asked questions.

International Association of Registered Financial Consultants
(800) 532-9060
www.iarfc.org
director@iarfc.org

Investment Counsel Association of America
(202) 293-4222
www.icaa.org
icaa@icaa.org

Investment Management Consultants Association
(303) 770-3377
www.imca.org
publications@imca.org

Life and Health Insurance Foundation for Education
www.life-line.org
For information on life, health, and disability insurance.

MSN Retirement Planner Online
www.money.msn.com
Find retirement income calculators and retirement planning articles.

National Academy of Elder Law Attorneys
(520) 881-4005
www.naela.org
Questions and Answers When Looking for an Elder Law Attorney (free booklet).

National Association of Estate Planners & Councils
(866) 226-2224
www.naepc.org

National Association of Insurance and Financial Advisors
(703) 770-8100
www.naifa.org

National Association of Personal Financial Advisors
(800) 366-2732
www.napfa.org
info@napfa.org

National Association of Philanthropic Planners
(800) 342-6215
www.napp.net

National Bureau of Economic Research
(617) 868-3900
www.nber.org

Pension Rights Center
(202) 296-3776
www.pensionrights.org

SIA Investor
www.siainvestor.com
Securities Industry Association online educational resource, including
    retirement calculators and a dictionary of terms.

Social Security Online
(800) 772-1213
TTY: (800) 325-0778
www.ssa.gov
Information on Social Security and Medicare, and a wealth of
    information on retirement planning, including calculators.

Society of Certified Senior Advisors
(800) 653-1785
www.society-csa.com

Society of Financial Service Professionals
(610) 526-2500
www.financialpro.org
custserv@financialpro.org
Taking the Mystery out of Financial Planning (free booklet).

U.S. Department of Labor
(800) 487-2365
www.dol.gov
For information on worker's rights, wages, benefits, Medicare, and
COBRA.

Index